SHED SIDE

ON MERSEYSIDE

In memory of my parents, Ruby and Ted, who could never understand the lure of those 'smoky, dirty engine sheds' but who, nevertheless, had the grace to allow me to pursue my interests.

SHED SIDE
ON MERSEYSIDE

KENN PEARCE

SUTTON PUBLISHING

First published in 1997 by
Sutton Publishing Limited · Phoenix Mill
Thrupp · Stroud · Gloucestershire · GL5 2BU

British Library Cataloguing in Publication Data
A catalogue record for this book is available from the British Library

ISBN 0-7509-1369-X

Jacket pictures: Front: Birkenhead's 42942 waits at Liverpool Exchange station to take a special to Goole, September 1966 (photograph Paul Finn). Back: 'Jubilee' No. 45726 Vindictive storms past another engine on the climb to Edge Hill station, 6 June 1959 (photograph R.M. Casserley).

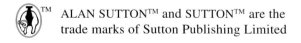

ALAN SUTTON™ and SUTTON™ are the
trade marks of Sutton Publishing Limited

Typeset in 11/13 pt Bembo.
Typesetting and origination by
Sutton Publishing Limited.
Printed in Great Britain by
Butler & Tanner, Frome, Somerset.

CONTENTS

ACKNOWLEDGEMENTS

This book would not have been possible without the assistance, generosity and encouragement of a large number of people, most of whom have assisted from a considerable distance. This assistance has been particularly appreciated given the difficulties experienced when researching a subject from the other side of the world.

Contributors have been generous and patient in loaning photographs, transparencies and documents to some unknown fellow half a world away – someone who had simply appealed for help via local newspapers or railway journals. I hope their faith in this project has been rewarded.

Particularly noteworthy were the efforts of former railwaymen – some in their seventies or eighties – who have corresponded with me. In some cases they have diligently written out in longhand page after page of replies to my questions and details of their experiences. To the former railwaymen – irrespective of your contribution – I say thank you. **This book is dedicated to you**.

Mention must also be made of the group of railway enthusiasts, again none of whom I have had the pleasure of meeting personally, who have gone out of their way to photocopy, loan or supply material for this book. Whenever the momentum for the project began to falter they would invariably come through with further interesting information or details of another useful contact. I always looked forward to the postman's deliveries!

Finally, thanks also go to my uncomplaining wife, Michelle, who has gradually seen parts of our home succumb to more piles of 'railway stuff for the Merseyside book'.

Thanks are extended to the following people and organizations:

The Engine Shed Society and John Jarvis and Phil Mackie. Also, John D'Arcy, Rob Bartlett, John Beadles, Murray Billett, Jim Blackburn, Jack Buckley, Ken Carson, R.M. Casserley, John Corkill (for his foresight in the 1960s in recording on film and in notes the changes occurring around him), Doug Crisp, J. Davenport, Maurice Dickenson (for reading part of the draft), Gerald Drought, Charles Ebsworth (who regularly sent his air-mail replies), Ken Fairey, Paul Finn, Mrs Irene Firmin, John Gahan (who with John Corkill checked the Edge Hill text), Duncan Gomersall, M. Greenham, Peter Hands, Charles Hibbert, Roger Jermy, Bert Kelley, Tom Lockwood, Steve McNicol (with his old ABC 'Combines'), Chris Magner, Frank Mangan, Frank Mason, Michael Mensing, Jack Mitchinson, R. Nevin, Raymond Nixon, Jim Oatway, Dot and Jim Patterson, Jim Peden, Leonard Pentin, Richard Picton, Nick Pigott,

Mick Pope, Thomas Prior, Steve Raymond, Stan Rimmer, Phil Rosenberg, Joseph Ross, Anthony Rowland, Allan Sommerfield, D.R. Steggles from Devon Library Services, Bill Stubbs, G.A.J. Terry, Melvin Thorley (for his enthusiasm), John Tolson, Bill Tomlinson, Bill Walker (who remarkably saved his 1960 diary notes), Martin Walker of Liverpool Central Libraries, Dennis Williams (for giving me his recollections even during illness) and Stephen Wolstenholme.

I hope I haven't overlooked anyone but if so, my sincere apologies.

Short trip working was part and parcel of regular rostered work at many depots, including those on Merseyside. Here, grimy 'Black 5' No. 45346 heads an Up empties freight a quarter of a mile south of the site of Sefton Park station on 19 September 1961. Sefton Park station, situated on the Lime Street to Crewe line, was opened by the LNWR in June 1892. It stood beside Smithdown Road near Garmoyle Road. The station was closed on 2 May 1960.

Michael Mensing

INTRODUCTION

If anyone can be held responsible for my affection for the steam motive power depots of Merseyside, it has to be Kenny Caddock. Kenny was a schoolmate larrikin who could have doubled for a youthful George Formby (that buck-toothed, thickly accented Lancashire comedian of many postwar black and white movies). Kenny was interested in steam locomotives, and, on discovering a kindred spirit who had recently moved back to the 'city' after a time in nearby Widnes, proceeded to show me around a few localities that had dozens of them!

Our first joint foray to Edge Hill – Liverpool's premier engine shed – in 1963 left an indelible impression on my mind as I watched dozens of grimy workhorses being prepared for their next turn of duty. Edge Hill sheds spanned nineteen lanes and retained extensive repair and administrative facilities. Also embedded in my memory are the oil-soaked floors, sulphurous smells and the cacophonous din of safety valves lifting. Following that first visit to Edge Hill further forays always filled us with a great sense of anticipation, a feeling which was heightened by the fact that, usually, the visits were unauthorized.

And what sights greeted the visitor, to mingle with the smells and sounds? Maybe a 'Patriot' or 'Royal Scot', perhaps a visiting 'Britannia' Pacific from Crewe or Carlisle, or even a B1 from the Eastern Region, or the return home of one of Edge Hill's maroon-liveried 'Duchess' Pacifics?

However, as important as Edge Hill was, it was only one of as many as seven steam sheds that provided motive power to the stations and extensive goods yards of Liverpool and Birkenhead in the early 1960s. Soon I and other 'train-spotting' schoolmates summoned enough courage to venture to other haunts of steam such as Speke, Aintree, Bank Hall and Birkenhead. Little did we realize how brief a period we had left to savour steam on Merseyside and, indeed, British Railways.

Aintree was always associated with the clanking of 'Austerities', invariably in appallingly grimy or rusty condition, Bank Hall with its proud quartet of 'Jubilees' working Scottish expresses and defiantly holding off diesel intruders, and Birkenhead with its huge allocation of Standard 9Fs. So big was this shed's allocation of these freight locomotives that on a Sunday afternoon the surrounding district was bathed in a thick smoky pall as engines were prepared for another week's work on Shotton Steelworks' trains.

These, then, were the Merseyside steam depots viewed from the perspective of one railway enthusiast. Understandably, it was not the perception of the men who had to work at these places, or even those residents who had the misfortune to live nearby.

A view of the 'old' shed at Edge Hill in August 1958, and one that perfectly evokes the atmosphere of a large steam shed in the late 1950s. This summertime view includes, on the far left, Stanier 2–6–4T No. 42583, and behind it an ex-LNWR G1 (probably No. 49137) with 'Jinty' tank No. 47490 in the rear. On the right-hand side of the view can be seen Stanier 'Crab' No. 42954 and another 'Jinty', No. 47656.

J.A. Peden

Work at these sheds was hard and dirty toil. By the 1960s modernization of the railways was in its final phase. That meant minimal resources were available for upgrading old facilities (some of which dated back to the nineteenth century) at places like Edge Hill, Bank Hall and Aintree. These facilities would be made redundant when the modernization of British Rail was complete, and so were considered expendable.

Steam was on its way out and modernization with all its supposed reliability and comforts beckoned to railwaymen (who had suffered disgraceful working conditions over many years) like the sirens who tempted sailors in ancient times. Little wonder then that crews grew testy when forced, by circumstance, to climb back into the cab of a steam locomotive after the vanguard of modernization – the first generation of mainline diesels – proved far less reliable than claimed. When the fires were dropped finally on the last

Birkenhead shed, as many enthusiasts remember it, 18 February 1967. By the mid-1960s row upon row of Standard 9Fs were a common sight. In this view a numberplate-less No. 92160 awaits its next turn of duty, No. 92045 is behind.

J.M. Tolson

steam engines to be based on Merseyside, in May 1968, there were few railwaymen to mourn their passing. Similarly, few housewives living near these smoky facilities would have shed a tear at steam's demise. At least they could look forward to a far cleaner atmosphere come washday!

Now the sheds, like most of the engines they once housed, have gone forever. Only at derelict Aintree could the ghosts of footplate characters such as 'Headlamp Harry' or 'Dusty Rhodes' once be imagined on a windswept winter's night, the apparitions maybe clanging a shovel in the cab of a wheezing 'Jinty' tank, or watering a ghostly Stanier 'Crab'. But the imagery is brief and nothing more than a trick of the light. The graffitists scrawled their reality over surviving walls at Aintree.. The tracks which once led into the loco shed have, like the engines they had guided, long since gone, and in February 1996 the shed structure was levelled.

The marble memorial plaque which, for many years, hung in the lobby at Edge Hill shed, honouring 8A Driver Joseph Ball and Fireman Cormack Higgins. The pair were in charge of the 1315 hrs Liverpool–Euston express on 20 May 1937 when a collapsed smokebox deflector plate in their 'Princess' class engine cause a blowback that turned their footplate into a furnace. The incident occurred as the crew were nearing the end of their journey – at Primrose Hill tunnel on the approach to Euston. Ball and Higgins stayed at their controls, however, and brought the train safely to a stand outside the tunnel. Unfortunately the crewmen were so extensively burnt that they both died in hospital. Following the closure of Edge Hill's diesel servicing depot the plaque was moved to platform 1 at Liverpool Lime Street station where it is now on display.

John Corkill

Merseyside has lost much of its industrial and maritime prominence during the past thirty years. The port no longer carries the volume of traffic it once did, in terms of either shipping or rail goods, and with that loss has gone much of Merseyside's railway heritage and soul. However, some of the memories, stories and images are recaptured for posterity in the following pages.

Kenn Pearce
Adelaide
South Australia

THE SEVEN SHEDS OF MERSEYSIDE

Although it may be hard to imagine today, in January 1950 a total of 404 steam locomotives were allocated to the seven motive power depots that serviced Liverpool and Birkenhead. The locomotives were required to handle the huge volumes of goods and passenger trains travelling into and out of the Merseyside area, besides working the extensive goods yards around Liverpool and Birkenhead. Merseyside's undisputed premier shed at this time was Edge Hill, where 112 locomotives were permanently allocated − ranging from the former London Midland & Scottish Railway's 'Princess Royal' class Pacifics (for London expresses) down to a pair of ex-Lancashire & Yorkshire 2F 0−6−0 saddle tanks, for humble yard shunting.

With the introduction of the first British Railways' standard class locomotives still some months away, most engines allocated to the seven Merseyside sheds were of ex-LMS, L&Y Railway or ex-London and North Western heritage. At Birkenhead, forty ex-GWR locomotives − including six 'Grange' class 4−6−0s and nine class 2021 0−6−0 tank engines − shared the stalls with some fifty ex-LMS engines. In Liverpool, at Brunswick shed, and within sight of ships plying the River Mersey, the railway enthusiast could see ex-LNER J11 and J10 0−6−0s and N5 0−6−2Ts sharing oilcans with Stanier 'Black 5s' and ex-LMS 4−4−0s. At Walton shed, ex-LNER, and in particular ex-Great Central types were predominant.

By 1955 the total number of steam engines permanently allocated to Merseyside sheds had only fallen marginally to 375. Edge Hill shed by now boasted some 116 permanently based engines, while over the Mersey, at Birkenhead, there were seventy-six locomotives allocated, of which four were 'Granges' and five 43XX class Moguls.

The introduction, in 1951, of the British Railways' standard classes had resulted in Bank Hall shed receiving, by 1955, five of the Class 2 2−6−0s and two of the Class 2 2−6−2Ts constructed under the modernization program. However, Edge Hill remained Merseyside's 'top shed' and its stud of express passenger locomotives reflected the city's importance as a commercial centre. Thirteen 'Patriot', six 'Jubilee', ten 'Royal Scot', a 'Duchess' and five 'Princess Royal' Pacifics were on hand to head the city's most important passenger trains.

Four years later, during the early stages of dieselization, Merseyside steam allocations totalled 345 locomotives. Edge Hill, surprisingly, had received a further boost in its allotments and now could boast some 123 engines − seven of which were 'Princess' Pacifics. These engines became virtually synonymous with Liverpool−London expresses in the pre-electrification period. At the same time the shed boasted twenty-four 'Black 5s' and twenty-three ex-LNWR and ex-LMS 7F 0−8−0s.

By 1959 Birkenhead had lost its permanent allocation of ex-GWR engines, although these types would continue to work into the Mersey port for some time. Ex-LNER

One of Parker's N5 class 0–6–2 tanks originally built for the Manchester, Sheffield and Lincolnshire Railway in the last years of the nineteenth century. During most of the 1950s four locos of this class were usually based at Walton-on-the-Hill, one of them being this example, No. 69298, captured on shed on 16 February 1958. By 21 May 1955 this engine and three others of this class, Nos 69265, 69344 and 69356, were based at Walton.

J.A. Peden

types were still in evidence at Walton-on-the-Hill shed, where a solitary J10 0–6–0 was also shedded beside three N5s.

By late August 1961 signs of the modernization of the Liverpool–Crewe main line were becoming apparent with the removal of the last remaining main line semaphore signals on the Crewe line, and the commissioning of a power signal-box at Edge Hill. By the end of that year allocations of steam engines to Merseyside were still relatively high, although mass withdrawals and shed closures would soon indicate the beginning of steam's decline in the area.

As at 4 November 1961, a total of 239 steam locomotives were allocated to Merseyside's six surviving sheds (Brunswick had closed in September). Edge Hill still maintained 101 locomotives including five Pacifics, five 'Royal Scots', ten 'Patriots' and a sole 'Jubilee' 4–6–0. At the same time it also retained its link with its London and North Western heritage by maintaining eighteen ex-North-Western 7F 0–8–0s on its roster.

Liverpool's other 'passenger' shed, Bank Hall, had (with the exception of Walton-on-the-Hill) Merseyside's smallest allocation with only thirty-two engines. However, among its roster were three 'Jubilees', *Mars, Dauntless* and *Glorious* and some of British Railways'

At the 'new' end of Edge Hill shed on 29 September 1957, 'Jubilee' No. 45623 *Palestine* rests in light steam. The 'Jubilees' had strong ties with Liverpool's premier shed – nine of the class were based there in 1950 and eleven by late 1959. The dieselization and electrification of the early 1960s resulted in a decline in the number of the class present at the shed, so much so that by November 1961 only No. 45578 *United Provinces* was allocated to Edge Hill. However, 8A might have rued the demise of its 'Jubilees' a couple of years later, especially – as Bill Walker recounts later in the book – when 'Black 5s' were sometimes substituted for unavailable 6P and 7P engines. This engine was finally withdrawn from Newton Heath shed, Manchester, in July 1964.

J.A. Peden

smallest engines, Pug tanks Nos 51206/32/53, which worked the nearby docklands. These three, together with No. 51246, were by the end of the year placed in storage after the introduction of diesel shunters made them redundant. Also at this shed were ex-LMS Kitson 0–4–0ST, Nos 47001 and 47002.

At Aintree, the sole surviving ex-LYR dock shunter, No. 51537, still found limited employment in the local shunting yards when the depot's small diesel shunter was under repair.

The closure of Brunswick shed (27F) on 11 September 1961 resulted in the transfer of most of its engines to Trafford Park or Speke Junction shed. However, the remnants of Brunswick depot still remained in 1994, with one full shed wall still erect.

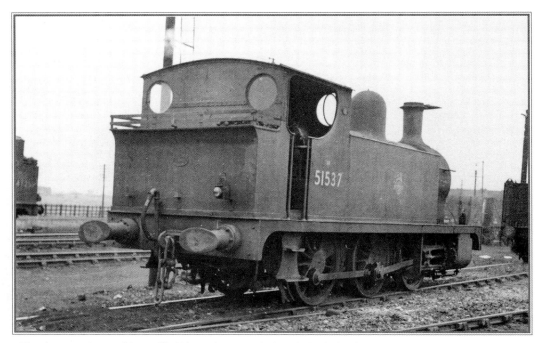

The three survivors of Aspinall's (Class 24) 0–6–0 dock tanks built for the LYR from 1897 were all based at Aintree by 1954: Nos 51535, 51537 and 51544. They saw much useful work in the nearby sidings. One of them, No. 51537, was destined to be the last in traffic and was not withdrawn from traffic until 1961. It is seen here at Aintree shed in the late 1950s.

Len Pentin

In the summer of 1961 Edge Hill's remaining 'Princess' Pacific No. 46208 *Princess Helena Victoria* was returned to duty after a period in storage. Later in the year the engine would be returned to storage as were other survivors of the class at Carlisle Kingmoor, Carnforth, Willesden and Rugby. Four of the more unlucky members of the class (Nos 46204/10/11/12 and among them former Edge Hill engines) were withdrawn in the period ending 7 October 1961.

At Birkenhead shed, still under the jurisdiction of Chester and coded 6C, forty-nine steam engines were allocated, made up predominantly of ex-LMS tanks for the Chester section of the Paddington passenger service, together with Hughes-Fowler and Stanier 'Crab' 2–6–0s. Its largest engines were Stanier 'Black 8s' and 'Austerity' 2–8–0s.

Just fourteen locos were based at Walton-on-the-Hill depot by the end of 1961. The allocation included nine Fowler 4F 0–6–0s. This shed closed in December 1963.

By May 1964 the situation on Merseyside had altered further. Only 217 engines were allocated to the five surviving sheds: Edge Hill, Speke Junction, Birkenhead, Bank Hall and Aintree. Although Edge Hill remained 'Top Shed' its primacy was now under challenge from across the Mersey where Birkenhead depot retained fifty-four engines.

Included in Birkenhead's allocation were ten Standard '9F's, the first representatives of

The turntable at Edge Hill shed was behind the 'coal hole' and immediately beside the 1-in-27 incline (seen behind the engine in this view) which was the main entrance and exit off shed. Here 'Black 5' No. 45187 is turned ready for its next turn of duty on 28 March 1968. The shed was little more than a month away from closure to steam engines. Engine No. 45187 briefly survived Edge Hill's demise to be one of the engines transferred to Patricroft (Manchester) depot. However, it was condemned within a month of its reallocation.

Ken Fairey

what would become a major allocation of this type to the shed. Bank Hall shed still retained two 'Jubilees', No. 45627 *Sierra Leone* and stalwart No. 45698 *Mars*, for use on the Scottish services from Exchange station. At Speke Junction two 'Jubilees' (No. 45663 *Jervis* and No. 45664 *Nelson*) were also allocated briefly for working Ford car trains – a type of engine not previously based at this shed. Two of only five named Stanier 'Black 5s' were also based on Merseyside with No. 45156 *Ayrshire Yeomanry* being allocated to Edge Hill, and No. 45154 *Lanarkshire Yeomanry* to Aintree (and later Speke Junction). Edge Hill, of course, still had on its books two of the 'Duchess' class Pacifics (*City of Edinburgh* and *City of Lancaster*) and the pair would survive in traffic until late 1964, when together with other survivors from the class they were condemned.

By November 1966 mass condemnings of British Railways' steam locomotive fleet resulted in only slightly more than 200 engines remaining on Merseyside, and only four sheds – Edge Hill, Speke, Birkenhead and Aintree – still in use. By now Birkenhead shed had by far the largest allocation of engines – seventy-two in all, including fifty-six Standard 9F engines which were chiefly utilized on the Shotton Steelworks' trains and other heavy freights in the area. Surprisingly, Hughes-Fowler 'Crab' 2–6–0s and Stanier/Fairburn tank engines survived on passenger trains to Chester until early 1967. Speke Junction, another freight shed, was next in importance in terms of sheer numbers of steam retained: fifty-three locomotives, twenty-three of them being Stanier 'Black 5s'. Edge Hill could now muster only forty-seven engines from just three classes: twenty-nine were Stanier 'Black 5s', fifteen Stanier 8Fs and three 'Jinty' tanks.

Barely eighteen months later the last steam allocations would be eradicated from Merseyside sheds with the closure of Edge Hill and Speke Junction depots in May 1968, and so would end the district's long association with the steam locomotive – an association that stretched back 138 years.

8A EDGE HILL

There was always a great sense of anticipation when visiting Edge Hill motive power depot. As you walked through the small pedestrian tunnel leading from Tiverton Street, and out over the lines skirting the nineteen-covered-track shed (being careful not to attract the attention of the shedmaster in his office facing the tunnel) it was just a quick dash to an entrance between a stores building and water storage towers. You were then 'on shed'.

And oh what sights, sounds and smells would greet you – whether enthusiast or railwayman! The air was usually heavy with that unforgettable mix of sulphurous smoke, hot oil and steam. Dim outlines of engines could just be discerned in the swathe of smoke and steam; metal tools clanged on oil-caked floors; and the ribald joking of a group of long-haired engine cleaners (and even maybe a playfully thrown lump of coal) would rent the air. Sometimes in the centre of the shed an English Electric Type 4 (Class 40) diesel would be parked, its engines throbbing away on idle. But always there was the incessant hiss of steam being raised, the clang of a shovel feeding a firebox, safety valves lifting unexpectedly with a deafening roar, or the gurgling of water as draincocks emptied the contents of a boiler into the ash pits.

The first locomotive shed at Edge Hill was established practically at the dawn of the railway steam age in England. In 1830 the Liverpool & Manchester Railway built an engine house near Chatsworth Cutting. The Grand Junction Railway then built an engine shed near the L&M Railway shed in 1834. A second shed of three tracks was built at Edge Hill by the GJR in 1839 and this allowed its first shed to be used for repair work. Within months of erecting its new shed, the GJR decided to move its works facilities to Crewe, allowing the Edge Hill facilities to be used by the L&M Railway.

With the GJR's surrender of the Edge Hill site there was then plenty of room for the expansion of shed facilities in the area. But it was not until 1864 that the London and North Western Railway (which had absorbed the GJR and L&M Railway in 1846) built the Edge Hill engine depot that was to become so familiar to steam enthusiasts this century. While under LNWR ownership, Edge Hill was given the shed code number 26. Although it had no sub-sheds of its own, it was still considered important enough within the railway to command its own District Locomotive Superintendent.

Edge Hill depot was considerably enlarged in 1902 to become two sheds, set adjacently, totalling twenty tracks – nineteen of them covered. Six of the covered tracks were straight through stalls. Offices were provided on the Tiverton Street-facing side of the shed, sheerlegs were located on lane No. 15 and a wheel drop in lane No. 6. (The shed roads were numbered upwards from the northern side.) Initially a pair of 42 foot turntables serviced engines' needs at the shed, as well as a large standard LNWR coal stage with tank. The turntables and coal stage were separated from the shed by an embankment which carried tracks across the shed yard.

The 'coal hole' at Edge Hill was the term used by both railwaymen and enthusiasts for the area occupied by the mechanical coaling stage and ash disposal unit. Here, 'Britannia' Pacific No. 70010 *Owen Glendower* receives attention on 28 May 1966. The coaling stage at Edge Hill was built by the LNWR in 1915. Wagons were hoisted up a gradient by capstan and rope and discharged their coal into one of three 40 ton capacity bunkers beneath. After releasing their loads, the wagons rolled, by gravity, to an empties siding.

John Corkill

In 1915 a concrete mechanical coaling stage was built on the site of the former coaling facilities. (At about this time too, the most northerly of the shed's two turntables was replaced with a 60 foot diameter unit.) The coaling stage was serviced by wagons which were propelled along a ramp, after which the coal was emptied directly into bunkers beneath. The coal supplies were divided into three sections holding different grades. The best grade was retained for express passenger engines working from the shed, while the other grades were retained for goods, shunting and local passenger engines. A smokeless coal grade was also retained for engines working the Waterloo and Wapping tunnels.

Coal supply at the depot was from several sources. According to Charles Ebsworth, a former driver at Edge Hill, most main line coal at the depot was 'Barnsley Seam' and, later, 'Newilhouse Seam' from Barnborough Colliery, South Yorkshire, on the Dearne Valley line. The 'blind' or smokeless coal was supplied from Bedwas Deep Pit near Newport in South Wales.

Edge Hill was substantially rebuilt and modernized by the London Midland and Scottish Railway, which took control in 1923; after this there came a gradual influx of what had previously been thought of as 'foreign' engine types. In 1934 new ash handling machinery was installed beside the shed's 42 foot turntable and the coaling stage, and four years later the older section of the depot was largely rebuilt to incorporate a new 'single pitch' LMS-style roof. Water softening facilities were also provided in the yard between the 'old' and 'new' sheds. The outbreak of war delayed completion of the replacement of the roof in the newer shed – referred to by railwaymen as 'The Camp' – until 1949. Re-roofing costs at Edge Hill were put at £27,036 in 1947.

Plans for the demolition of large sections of Edge Hill shed were drawn up as early as 1959. However, the shed remained unaltered until 1966, when a portion of the older shed was demolished to allow the construction of a small diesel servicing depot in the locomotive yard. The remainder of the steam shed survived until shortly after the end of steam on British railways in 1968.

Edge Hill was closed to steam from 6 May 1968, and the final closure of the depot – as a diesel inspection facility – occurred on 6 June 1983, when responsibility for these duties was transferred to Allerton traction depot.

Since 1968 Edge Hill depot has been demolished and the entire site levelled; in January 1991 work began on transforming the former engine shed site into an industrial park. In 1992 the site was linked to the nearby Wavertree Technology Park by means of a road bridge across the Liverpool–Manchester main line. Edge Hill's new role as an industrial annexe of Wavertree Technology Park has been slow to develop, with just one tenant there in late 1996.

In the period immediately following the Second World War to the end of the steam age, Edge Hill had strong ties with some of steam's most illustrious locomotive types.

The 'Turbomotive' 'Princess' Pacific, No. 6202, was a frequent resident at Edge Hill before its eventual rebuild to a conventional Pacific and then its untimely destruction in the Harrow disaster of 1952. Similarly the final 'Claughton' class 4–6–0 from L&NWR days, No. 6004, which survived its classmates by eight years, was shedded at Edge Hill during its last years under British Railways' ownership.

Charles Ebsworth, who worked at Edge Hill from 1936 until the shed's closure to steam in 1968, remembers the final 'Claughton' in traffic:

> No. 6004 was limited mostly to local freight work to Mold Junction, Crewe, (Stockport) Edgeley or Warrington, on an out-and-back job which left 8A and returned with the same set of men.
>
> If you had 6004 on a job that you worked so far and rostered for relief, you would find the relief (crew) would refuse to take charge and argue they were 'not signed for this class'.
>
> The local control office would often say, 'fresh engine and hook 6004 off and go home light, she's no use to us'.

The 'Claughton' was a strong locomotive, Mr Ebsworth recalls. However, with its tender carrying only 3,000 gallons of water you had to be very careful with her. Also, there was the open uncomfortable footplate which was unpopular with modern crews. 'The open footplate could be deadly in winter,' he said. 'In snow or rain there was no protection when the engine was stationary, same as the "Super Ds".'

Also surviving at Edge Hill were the ex-LNWR 'Cauliflowers', another class of engine that Mr Ebsworth remembers from his early years at the depot. They would do the work but with the usual LNWR conditions: no comfort or weather protection for the crew.

They were a dead loss compared to the modern types which were more available.

We used to get one in the early days off Wigan Springs Branch shed on the 6.15 a.m. tranships to Ince Moss, Wigan, pick up odd wagons at Huyton, Huyton Quarry, Rainhill, St Helens Junction, Earlestown, Newton-le-Willows and Golborne yards and warehouses, running with five to twelve wagons between sites.

Then it would be on shed at Springs Branch and then home on a passenger – stand up all day.

In the 1950s engines of the 'Royal Scot' and 'Princess' classes predominated at 8A. In 1950 there were thirteen 'Royal Scots' allocated to Edge Hill. By 1958 six 'Princess' Pacifics – half the class – were shedded at the depot. However, it was not until the end of 1960 – just four years before the demise of the Stanier Pacifics – that Edge Hill became the regular home for some of the 'Duchess' Pacifics. ('Duchess' Pacifics were briefly allocated to Edge Hill during the 1950s – generally for a month or so at a time – and these included Nos 46226, 46228, 46236, 46251 and 46254.) In September 1960 No. 46233 *Duchess of Sutherland* was drafted to the shed and in April of the following year it was joined by No. 46229 *Duchess of Hamilton*, No. 46241 *City of Edinburgh* and No. 46243 *City of Lancaster*. Although the 'Duchess' Pacifics were moved to Merseyside ostensibly to replace the 'Princess' Pacifics, one of the latter, No. 46208 *Princess Helena Victoria*, remained at Edge Hill right up to withdrawal in October 1962.

THE MEN OF EDGE HILL: THE LATE 1930S, THE WAR YEARS AND THE 1950S

Mr Jack Mitchinson came to Edge Hill in the late 1950s from Warrington Dallam, and in 1958 took up what was then the new appointment of shedmaster at 8A. As shedmaster, Mr Mitchinson was responsible for the day-to-day running of the depot. Originally, on the London Midland, the responsibility for the running of an 'A' shed was in the hands of the Assistant District Motive Power Superintendent. Mr Mitchinson occupied the shedmaster's position at Edge Hill for two years before being promoted to ADMPS.

As ADMPS, Mr Mitchinson would assist his superior, and stand in for him as chairman at any of the Local Departmental Committees at any of the depots in the district. The LDCs were made up of three elected members of the footplate grades and one elected member of the shed grades, and usually the shedmaster, his chief clerk and a running foreman on the management side. They were held periodically with an agreed agenda to discuss, and to sort out, any problems. On one occasion Mr Mitchinson, as ADMPS also had to fill in as DMPS at Chester, while that shed's head was away.

When Mr Mitchinson arrived at Edge Hill there were about 200 drivers, 50 passed firemen, 150 firemen and 100 cleaners, including passed cleaners working at the depot. Artisan staff included fitters (including two leading fitters who ran the running shed's

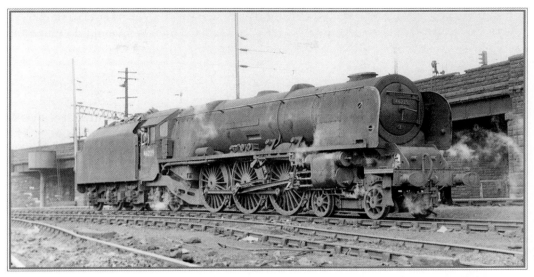

A somewhat grimy 'Duchess' Pacific No. 46229 *Duchess of Hamilton* backs away from Edge Hill depot on 24 September 1961. At this time the locomotive had been based at 8A for just five months, being one of three Pacifics drafted to the shed in April 1961. The engine would remain at Edge Hill until February 1964 when it was withdrawn from service and, thankfully, retained for preservation by Billy Butlin. *Duchess of Hamilton* eventually had the distinction of being the last engine of its class to leave the remains of the steam depot when it was serviced there before working a special train to Manchester in 1980.

Ken Fairey

repairs), fitters' mates, turners, coppersmiths, etc., numbering some 200 people in all. These artisans were supervised by one regular day foreman fitter and two shift foremen. Shed 'staff', comprising washers-out, tube cleaners, coal men, ash-fillers, knocker-uppers and others, numbered some 150 people. All were supervised by three shift chargehand cleaners.

Mr Mitchinson recalls the running down, and arranging for scrapping, of steam being dealt with – at first – by the Divisional Motive Power Superintendents at Crewe, Derby and Manchester, and later by the Chief Mechanical and Electrical Engineer. Staff at local shed level did not have any say in the decisions.

Another former Edge Hill man who worked at the depot for many years, including the period which saw the demise of steam, was Stan Rimmer, who joined Edge Hill's cleaning staff on 3 December 1934, when the depot was still part of the LMS. 'There were no specific promotions on the railway first,' he said. 'A firing instructor would give you a show around an engine on how to shovel coal on a fire, and how to work an injector. All of the information was picked up by watching.'

In January 1935 Mr Rimmer and two other cleaners were sent to Heaton Mersey (Stockport) shed:

Our weekly pay was £1 10s, or £1.50 in today's decimal coinage. I had to pay £1 a week for lodging, so there was not much spare cash to come home at weekends.

Before we left Edge Hill we were to make out a transfer as a cleaner or we would have had to stay at Heaton Mersey. Needless to say I did and was back at Edge Hill a couple of weeks later.

Cleaning shifts in those days were eight and a half hours a day with a half shift on Saturday, adding up to forty-eight hours a week.

It wasn't long before Mr Rimmer was moved from the shunt links and the local goods links to the 'extra' link which had no booked work. He recalls there being about fifty drivers and fifty firemen, some of whom started their week on Sundays and some on Mondays. He recalls:

> You were given a large piece of paper and on it would be the date and the prepared time to work on it. You then went home and waited for the knocker-uppers – there were three on each shift. You never knew who the driver would be until you booked on. There were some good drivers and some bad.

Joseph R. Ross was another ex-footplateman who joined the railways before the Second World War and did not retire until 1980. He started work in January 1938 with the then LMS at Speke Junction, working first as a 'call boy' or 'knocker-upper', rousing railwaymen for work, and received the princely sum of £1 10s a week.

In October 1940, when he was seventeen years of age, Mr Ross was 'passed out' to fire steam engines, although he was not allowed out on the main line until his eighteenth birthday. However, because of staff shortages this was quietly overlooked and in November 1940 he got to do his first main line job. Two months later Mr Ross was transferred to Edge Hill (8A) shed as a fireman, and at first endured some hostility from firemen there because he was senior to many of them. However, after a few months he found that 'they turned out to be a great crowd'.

Of the shifts and hours worked in wartime, Mr Ross say 'you'd have gone pale' if they were recounted. For £4 1s he worked a seven-day week. Shifts were usually eight hours in length. After he'd gone off shift he would have to stay in, in order to make sure he didn't miss a messenger from the shed, carrying his paperwork for the next shift. 'If I went out and they came I would lose a night's pay. It was bed and work – no play,' he recalls.

Mr Ross was still living with his parents at Vineyard Street, just a 'stone's throw from Speke Junction'. His father, who also worked for the railways, was employed at the local depot and eventually went on to record fifty years on the footplate. While Mr Ross senior had only a short walk to work after receiving a message from the shed, his son faced a 'five mile bike ride day or night in all kinds of weather'.

Joseph Ross's two favourite engines of the 1940s and 1950s were 'Jubilee' 4–6–0s (in LMS days known as 5XPs), No. 5724 *Warspite* and No. 5726 *Vindictive*. Both were very good for firing 'but like all LMS engines, eaters of coal,' he said.

Speaking of some of his fellow railwaymen, Mr Ross said there were some he 'wouldn't trust with a pram. And the good drivers you could count on one hand; if you got one of them it was worth going to work. It was a treat to fire for them. For the others, it was back-breaking work.'

The deep cuttings leading into Lime Street station were where the enthusiast and interested rail travellers could witness the evocative atmosphere and brute power of steam. In this view, taken on 6 June 1959, 'Jubilee' No. 45726 *Vindictive* works an express passenger train hard on the climb to Edge Hill station, while another engine, almost hidden by steam, follows on an adjacent line. Former Edge Hill footplateman Joseph Ross rated *Vindictive* one of his favourite 'Jubilees'.

R.M. Casserley

Out of fifty-three firemen in the 'extra' link at Edge Hill shed, nine would work the 'top link' turns to London, working out of either Edge Hill or Lime Street. Mr Ross remembers one back-breaking job for firemen was the 0900 hrs. Lime Street–Leeds, hauling twelve carriages (400 tons) and rostered usually for a Stanier 'Black 5'. The train was timed to take 130 minutes to reach Leeds, with six intermediate stops. For the return trip, Mr Ross said a 'hooker' or pilot (the latter term was only used by LNER men) was provided from Leeds to Manchester. 'But home to Liverpool you were on your own and often had no coal by the time you reached Lime Street and had to be dragged up to Edge Hill sheds by another loco,' he recalls.

During the war years Mr Ross remembers that all of the Lime Street–London jobs were handled by straight-boilered 'Royal Scots'. It was only after the war that the 'Lizzies' ('Princess') and 'Duchess' Pacifics assumed a greater role. He remembers all of the London passenger workings out of Lime Street as being heavy, 'usually seventeen carriages on or 600 tons'.

The 'Scots', in their original condition, Mr Ross remembers as 'rough'. They rolled, besides being heavy on both coal and water. However, the first 'Scot' to be rebuilt with a taper boiler, No. 6170 *British Legion*, was considered a vast improvement.

One of the engines sometimes assigned to working the London run, until its rebuilding and untimely destruction in the Harrow disaster of 1952, was the

'Turbomotive' No. 6202. Mr Ross remembers this engine, in its original form, as one hated by all firemen. 'When you fired it you knew you'd done a day's work working either way, Euston or Lime Street. You were swept out [no coal in the tender] and had to be dragged back to the sheds, either Camden or Edge Hill.'

On the goods side, another train often worked by Mr Ross was the 5.40 p.m. 'London Meat'. This was a fifty-van train loaded with meat which was 'timed to the minute' and made its first stop at Willesden. The usual roster for this job was either a 'Baby Scot' (Patriot), a 'Black 5' or a 'Jubilee'.

Yet another goods turn worked was the 0250 hrs Edge Hill to Carnforth train over the former Lancashire and Yorkshire Railway route:

That was a heavy train, and your engine was always a 'Super D' [ex-LMS 0–8–0] with a double cab.

You booked off at Carnforth private lodge, you slept and booked on at 7.45 p.m. and worked a 9.50 p.m. Carnforth–Crewe with a 'Black 5'. Your loading was fifty-nine vans mixed, putting off and picking up at Lancaster.

We got relieved at Springs Branch (Wigan) around 11 a.m. the next morning, you finished up at Edge Hill with twelve hours on and buggered!

Mr Ross admits that despite the many hardships endured, he would still work on the railways if he had his time over again. But if he had known what Edge Hill would hold, he might have preferred to stay at Speke Junction.

Edge Hill was rough, the men were hard and you could count on one hand the good drivers. One driver I fired for was guaranteed to slip on a dry rail. The reversing gear – he didn't know what it was for. He didn't know that if he pulled it back it was easy for the fireman.

On a 'Royal Scot' they had a long firebox and a 6 foot tall man could stand up inside. It would take me half an hour to fill it up with coal until I couldn't get any more in. Then I was ready to back up on the train, Euston or Lime Street.

Seventeen on, 600 tons; with a good driver I'd have a good trip. With the other clown I would never have the long-handled shovel out of my hand. His motto was arrive before time and to hell with the fireman, or hang him up at Crewe and ask for another one. That's something they never did to me.

I found that if you had the gauge right on the mark or blowing off he'd kill you. I used to keep it just under the mark so he'd have to work it accordingly.

For all that I wouldn't have missed it; it was my life and all those idiots I fired for are now all driving in the sky.

Typical of the many railwaymen who spent their whole life's work at one shed or railway location is Charles Ebsworth, who started work as a cleaner at Edge Hill on 6 April 1936. He did not leave 8A until the closure of the shed to steam in May 1968, when he was relocated to Lime Street station.

Mr Ebsworth became a 'passed cleaner' eligible to undertake firing duties in 1938, progressing to a 'passed fireman' (able to drive locomotives) in 1950. With the slow influx of diesels in the late 1950s, he became a junior diesel instructor in late 1959 with the arrival at Edge Hill of the brand-new English Electric Type 4 (later Class 40) D215. He continued instructing crews in handling diesels until his retirement, aged sixty-four, in November 1981.

Mr Ebsworth recalls that when he started at the shed in 1936 there were two foreman cleaners there. One of them, Old Ben, was an ex-First World War soldier who had a wooden leg and referred to everyone as 'Cock'. At the end of his first week at work, Mr Ebsworth was told to come in at midnight. Usually, cleaners worked regular day shifts until passed out for firing, then they rotated on six shifts: midnight, 6 a.m., 9 a.m., 1 p.m., 4 p.m. or 8 p.m. start. The men not yet passed were assigned regular days. However, Old Ben had picked four cleaners to start work on nights and this was specially to clean the 'Turbomotive' Pacific No. 6202. (The other foreman cleaner at Edge Hill at this time was a man Mr Ebsworth remembers only as 'Jemmie', who had only one arm and was feared by all the cleaners.)

In the 1930s the Running Shift Foreman were usually ex-Edge Hill drivers who had been promoted when the 'all line' vacancy and promotion conditions started. When Mr Ebsworth began at Edge Hill most of the RSFs had come from Wigan Springs Branch shed and were referred to by Edge Hill staff as Wigan 'so-and-so's, such as 'Wigan Dick'.

One such man who caused much controversy at the time was a chap nicknamed 'Wyatt Earp', a young man who sported a moustache, a rarity for a young man in those days. The word around the shed was that 'Wyatt Earp' had only got the RSF job because his father was a loco inspector at Camden. His appointment coincided with the introduction of smokeless zones and 'Earp' was disparagingly referred to as the 'son of a smokejack'. He was disliked by some crews, described as an efficiency merchant, diligently checking crews' booking-on times and so on.

Recalling his earlier years of service, it was a humble ex-L&YR saddle tank, and the lowly task of shed and locomotive coal wagon shunt duties, that provided Mr Ebsworth with his first task as a fireman:

My first main line trip as a fireman was as a passenger to Speke Junction shed, where I prepared a loco then travelled light engine to Garston Dock banana sidings. We then worked special banana steam-heated vans from Garston Docks to Camden Yard, London, as far as Crewe Basford Hall sidings.

Of the era when he first began at Edge Hill, Mr Ebsworth remembers the shed hosting 'Princess' Pacifics Nos 6200 to 6202, 'Royal Scots' Nos 6140 to 6144 and 6158 to 6164, and 'Jubilees' Nos 5580, 5613, 5670 and 5671. The 'Lizzies' were used on the Euston expresses and the 'Scots' and 'Jubilees' on Leeds, Birmingham and Carlisle services.

The war years, 1939 to 1945, he considers ruined the railways. Railwaymen were not called up to serve in the armed forces because it was a reserved occupation, and there was little low morale: 'But the worst aspects during the war years were the air raids,' Mr Ebsworth said.

Another of Edge Hill's favourite engines of past years to survive into preservation is the celebrated Stanier Pacific No. 46201 *Princess Elizabeth*, although by the time this photograph was taken on 2 July 1962 the engine was based at Carlisle Kingmoor shed. This was the last summer in traffic for the Pacific under British Railways' ownership, and it was withdrawn at the end of the year.

John Corkill

On the dock jobs you could be stuck in tunnels or in the open at signals for five or six hours, or long hours spent in sidings or on permissive block slow lines behind, say, five trains in front waiting.

Then there was sorting at, say, Warrington, Crewe, Nuneaton or Edgeley; the railway system was choked with war department traffic.

Other frustrations that engine crews faced during the dark years of the war included the exceedingly poor coal, 'a 50/50 mix of slack and smokebox char'. 'There was also a lot of complaint about the continuous afternoon and night work but it was accepted because the money was good,' Mr Ebsworth said.

Mr Ebsworth also recalls some unpleasant experiences of life on the footplate during the war, and nominates 'boneshaker Stanier 5s, long hours and irregular shifts' as the main culprits:

Locos [during the war] got run down; the Stanier Class 5s, for example, had very bad wear in the horn blocks, severe knocking in the axleboxes, cracked frames, rivets loose – boneshakers.

The long hours were also unappealing – thirty-six hours was one of my longest spells, coming home working a freight ex-Carlisle.

As an 'extra fireman' I booked on at 2300 hrs on twenty-six Sundays out of thirty for the 0100 hrs 'Special Meat' goods to Willesden. We usually got to Rugby and were relieved after twelve hours on duty.

FITTERS' TALES: MAINTAINING THE LOCOS

As an 'A' depot, of course, Edge Hill was able to undertake very heavy repairs on steam as it had a fully fitted machine shop with a blacksmith's section, a white-metalling section and planing machine for crossheads and axleboxes. It also possessed small lathes for doing work on rod bushes, large lathes for carrying out work on axleboxes and eccentrics. There was also a coppersmith's hearth, a water press for rod bushes and, around 1958, a vertical drilling and boring machine was installed. However, this investment in modernization was atypical. Most of the shed's other machinery was quite old, although nevertheless capable of considerable accuracy.

Edge Hill also had its own wheel drop and wheel lathe, enabling all mileage examinations to be carried out, not only on its own engines but also on those from Warrington Dallam, Brunswick, Speke Junction, Widnes, Northwich and Sutton Oak (St Helens). Former Edge Hill fitter Maurice Dickenson was at the depot from 1947 to 1968. He recalls that, interestingly, the wheel drop was also used for changing engines on diesel railcars for about two years until Allerton (new) depot opened in 1961. The final drives on railcars were also changed outside 'The Camp' using the shed's steam crane, which lifted the railcar at one end enabling its bogie to be removed and the final drive to be changed.

Among some of the more unusual locomotives to find their way to Edge Hill for servicing were ex-LNER types such as the J39 0–6–0s and the occasional O4 class 2–8–0, which visited the depot from Brunswick shed in Liverpool's dockland when that depot's sheerlegs were out of action. There were also occasions when the J10 class 0–6–0s from Brunswick would come in for repairs. Ex-LNER B1s would also be serviced at Edge Hill after bringing in trains to Riverside station, including troop trains, or after hauling freights into Merseyside.

Some jobs were beyond Edge Hill's facilities, and these included cracked frames (although these could initially be handled by the shed until the damage got out of hand), some firebox repairs such as wasted seams, besides rough riding of engines and axlebox and driving wheel wear.

In late 1957, or early 1958, one of the Ivatt 'Duchess' Pacifics provided a first for Edge Hill when No. 46256 *Sir William A. Stanier F.R.S.* had its trailing 'Delta' truck removed on Edge Hill's wheel drop, which was sent on to Crewe Works for attention.

Maintenance staff at Edge Hill, such as John Corkill, who joined the shed in the mid-1950s, usually found the Stanier types, the 'Black 5s' and 'Black 8s', the easiest to work on. But not so the ex-LMS 'Super Ds' which were very solidly built. Mr Corkill remembers:

Everything about these locomotives was heavy. A job that cropped up now and again on them was the renewal of the inside back cylinder cover joints. This job meant the complete removal of the inside motion – everything.

Stanier 8Fs were highly useful engines, called on for a variety of tasks, including providing power for the Edge Hill breakdown train when it was required. Here No. 48249 heads 8A's 30 ton lift, Ransome Rapier crane No. RS 1069 past the Manchester end of the depot with the grid iron marshalling yard in the background. This crane, which came new to Edge Hill shed in 1942, was cut up in 1966 after a mishap when it went over a bridge. The crane was replaced for a short time by Bank Hall's 35 ton Craven lift No. RS 1017 which John Corkill recalls as 'a nice little crane', dating from 1912. RS 1017 was eventually replaced by another Ransome Rapier 30 ton lift, No. RS 1070. Edge Hill's breakdown train was usually made up of the crane, a riding and mess van, a tool van containing packing and other materials, and the 'German van' containing heavy hydraulic jacks controlled by a central console. The equipment was referred to as MFD gear.

John Corkill

Another nasty job on the Super Ds was the renewal of broken studs on the footplate spring safety bracket. After saying this, however, it was music to the ears to stand at the top end of the shed – by the Manchester line – and listen and watch one of these locomotives slog its way up to the top of the 'Grid Iron' from the docks with a very heavy train.

Charles Ebsworth also remembers the ex-London & North Western types with considerable distaste:

The ex-LNW classes required a lot of running repairs between duties. Worst were the 0–8–2 and 0–8–4 tank locomotives. The securing bolts from side tanks to frames always leaked and the sanders became waterlogged. Brakes [also] required adjusting every trip.

The Wapping and Waterloo tunnel trips, also Alexandra and Canada dock trips, were flat-out jobs and engines were hammered.

By the early 1960s the last vestiges of LNWR motive power at Edge Hill survived in the form of the 0–8–0 7Fs. This fine view of No. 49126 at Edge Hill was taken on 29 September 1957. Although he found 'everything on the engines heavy to work on', 8A fitter John Corkill said the sound of these engines working hard on a freight was music to the ears. Two years after this photograph was taken there were still twenty-three engines of this class based at Edge Hill. All of the 8A-based 7Fs were withdrawn by the end of 1962 (with one or two survivors transferred to Crewe South or Bescot). One engine, No. 49375, evaded the scrap merchant for two years, hidden away in the 'old shed' until at least late 1964.

J.A. Peden

Edge Hill at the time of Nationalization was still a major stronghold of ex-LNWR and derivative types, including eight of the survivors of a 1923 design of 0–8–4T heavy shunting locomotives. No. 7956 is seen at its home depot, Edge Hill, in 1946. Although this engine survived to become part of British Railways' stock, it was not among the three survivors based at Edge Hill two years later. Charles Ebsworth recalls these tank engines as among the worst of the ex-LNWR types he had to work on, 'the securing bolts from side tanks to frames always leaked and the sanders became waterlogged. Brakes . . . required adjusting every trip'.

John Rowlands

In contrast, Edge Hill's 'Jinty' tanks were considered good and reliable machines and were quite popular with engine crews. They would fuss about with empty stock at Lime Street, Downhill or Edge Hill carriage sidings, or at the nearby Grid Iron. One of them, No. 47406, spent much time at Stanley on the Bootle branch near Lister Drive. By the mid-1960s it could also be found on the shed shunt.

These tank engines generally only returned to the depot in the early hours of the morning. Repairs would then be carried out. Typical complaints from crews might include brakes requiring adjustment, sanders not working, or maybe a check on a report of big ends knocking. John Corkill commented:

After a report from the driver about this, one would set the engine, dive underneath and slack the big end cotter. Then set screws off, climb up over the crank axle and thump the cotter down.

Sunny day at Edge Hill as 8A 'Jinty' No. 47357 simmers outside 'The Camp'. This engine (a personal favourite of mine, remembered for its amber-painted cabside numbers and numberplate) was withdrawn from Edge Hill on the last day of 1966. Luckily it eventually found its way to Woodhams scrapyard at Barry, South Wales, from where it was rescued in 1970. It has been in traffic at the Midland Railway since June 1973.

John Corkill

I had a nice 7-pound hammer for this job. When one was satisfied with the cotter tightness, the set screws would be re-tightened and the job would be done.

I would say the Jinties were well liked by everyone who had anything to do with them. In fact, the Class 08 diesel shunter which worked down at Lime Street [until early 1993] was often known as 'The Tanky'.

Edge Hill never had a long-standing allocation of 'Britannia' class engines, although No. 70015 *Apollo* was based there for a short time in 1952, and Nos 70031 *Byron* and 70032 *Tennyson* were there for spells in February and March 1953. Maurice Dickenson remembers that *Apollo* 'disgraced' itself while based on Merseyside when it failed at Lime Street prior to working a 1610 hrs to London, when a rear driving wheel moved on the axle. The fault was reportedly caused by the axle being hollow and modifications were subsequently made to eradicate the trouble in the 'Britannias'.

'Britannia' Pacific No. 70048 *The Territorial Army 1908–1958* about to leave Edge Hill shed on 5 April 1963 to take out a train. By the mid-1960s 'Britannias' were frequent visitors to 8A, often working the 1950 hrs 'Carlisle freight'. They also bridged the gap on several occasions in the 1960s to haul London expresses as far as Cheshire when electric overhead wires were severed by accidents. No. 70048 was withdrawn from traffic in May 1967, from Carlisle Kingmoor.

John Corkill

Bill Walker, who until recently was in charge of locomotive operations at Western Australia's Mount Newman Mining Company, was, in 1959, a fitter at Chester motive power depot when an opportunity arose to spend a year at a major depot learning various aspects of depot operations and administration. The Locomotive Improver's course was seen as a training ground for future shed foremen. Bill explained:

One of the reasons (ironically) why I went to Edge Hill MPD was to get diesel experience. When I was with Bill Backhouse, Edge Hill's mechanical foreman, he showed me how important preventative maintenance was in keeping locomotives in good order.

I recall . . . that the 8P Pacifics at Edge Hill were shopped into Crewe Works more frequently than at other depots because of wear on the horn checks and axleboxes. This was said to be because of Edge Hill drivers' practice of driving with a short cut off on the reverser.

Busy scene at Edge Hill on 2 June 1957 as Mold Junction 'Austerity' No. 90606 simmers on shed in company with one of 8A's 'Jinty' tanks and a 'Super D'. Although quite common on Edge Hill until the early 1960s, Merseyside Austerities were chiefly based at Aintree shed until the mid-1960 when they were transferred away to the Eastern and North Eastern Regions. Brunswick (in the early 1950s) and Birkenhead (the late 1950s) also had small allocations of these engines. This engine, in fact, was drafted to Birkenhead in June 1960 and spent more than two years based there, going to Sutton Oak (St Helens) in September 1962. The engine survived in traffic on the North Eastern Region until February 1966.

Duncan Gomersall

Bill Walker found that Edge Hill – apart from being geographically distant from its self-named railway station, and a devil of a place to get an engine into ('I have seen the shed on three different sides before we got into it') – supported a different railway allegiance to that which he experienced at Chester.

At Chester the fitters always talked about the company, that is the London & North Western Railway company . . . they regarded themselves as railway company men. The ex–Great Western shed was down the road and the men that worked there, worked for the Great Western company. I don't recall that feeling at Edge Hill among the fitters although it was apparent among the drivers.

One recurring memory for many of the men who worked at sheds such as Edge Hill was of the dirt and grime. Even thirty-five years removed from Edge Hill, Bill Walker can still recall that aspect:

Working in the smokeboxes of engines was very dirty and very hard work. One common job we had was to take out the blast pipe, which was done by cutting off the corroded nuts. Rocker grates were another difficult job.

A Working Life at Edge Hill

Charles Ebsworth considers that the worst period of working at Edge Hill was the four years he spent in and out of the No. 5 passenger link:

In ten weeks' work we had five early morning turns taking the 0550 hrs to 0730 hrs early passenger turns to Manchester, Wigan, Crewe, Birkenhead, Chester and other destinations. All these five turns booked on at 0300 hrs to 0400 hrs and you had to prepare locomotives, i.e. 47480 or 42588, prior to preparing your own loco and going off shed.

In the ten weeks' work on the link we prepared seventy-nine locos in addition to our own – it was known as the preparing or fatting link. On the local jobs you worked one never stopped, fill tanks, hook on, run around, hold points, fill tanks, hook on.

As it was a 'passed fireman's' link, one prayed to be brought off for driving. The preparing work was hard on the fireman, he had to carry, the length of the shed, sometimes six or seven buckets of sand, fill lamps, get shovels and tools from the stores, make up fire and oil, climb underneath motion and bogies for the driver.

I was with one driver transferred to Edge Hill from Aintree who couldn't get to 8A for the booking on time as his first bus was 0530 hrs, so the fireman had to do the driver's oiling as well as his own work.

I must have walked miles each week, up and down the shed, to and from the stores or sand furnace, before going off shed. The diesel multiple units got rid of this preparation but at a cost to promotion, no fireman links came into being, that's why I took the instructor's job [on diesels].

But compared to other sheds, Mr Ebsworth rated Edge Hill no worse than other depots: 'The worst fault was a shortage of day work – some depots were a lot better than 8A with less afternoon and night work.'

By 1950, and now qualified to drive engines, Mr Ebsworth found his initial rosters involved disposing of engines on the shed. This was basically going through the gamut of servicing locomotives: to take them to the coal stage, to water them, to turn them, to clean the firebox, ashpan, smokebox, to stable the engine, or simply to shunt those engines under repair or undergoing boiler washouts. Other tasks involved running light engines between loco sheds or control relief of crews who had worked excessively long hours. Mr Ebsworth remembers:

Our top jobs were Liverpool–Euston and my first was the 2300 hrs (start) one Sunday night to work the 0030 hrs sleeper to Euston. The train had stops at Edge Hill, Runcorn, Crewe, Stafford, Tamworth, Nuneaton, Rugby, Northampton, Bletchley, Watford and Willesden.

Edge Hill's No. 46119 *Lancashire Fusilier*, photographed here on 24 September 1961, was the last 'Royal Scot' to be based at the shed. This engine was involved in a tragic collision with 'Crab' No. 42885 while hauling the 'Irish Mail' at Penmaenmawr in North Wales on 27 August 1950. Five passengers aboard the mail train and a sleeping car attendant were killed and thirty-five other passengers were injured.

Ken Fairey

We had 'Royal Scot' No. 46119 *Lancashire Fusilier* fresh off Crewe Works after the Irish Mail crash at Penmaenmawr, on the North Wales line on 27 August 1950. It was not a free steamer.

After lodging at Camden, our return working was the 1805 hrs 'Merseyside Express'. Our booked loco, No. 46203 *Princess Margaret Rose*, had failed with a split injector steam pipe and so we had No. 46247 *City of Liverpool* back – my first 'Duchess'.

Great care was required with these engines stopping at dead-end platforms as the boiler length combined with right-hand bends prevented sighting of the buffer stops until the last seconds.

Later I was 'knocked' to book on at 0645 hrs to assist the 0815 hrs Lime Street to Camden men. Their loco had failed as usual with a split steam pipe – the 0815 hrs was a Class 7P job. So they had Stanier '5' No. 45005 of Edge Hill and I had No. 45039, nearly new out of Crewe, rebuilt with manganese steel axlebox frame liners, so no knock. It was a good trip.

We made loads of driving turns, and cash, with this bout of failures the 'Princesses' had become prone to – we called it hooking on to London and back.

Mr Ebsworth worked on through the 1950s and following his progress to junior diesel instructor his steam driving turns became fewer. Of the legacy of pre-grouping designs that survived at Edge Hill by the 1950s, Mr Ebsworth said:

The ex-LNWR classes at Edge Hill required a lot of running repairs between duties. My only long-term work on ex-LNWR types was on the 0–8–0 'Super Ds' and the 0–8–4 trips tanks. Both were a dead loss, no proper seats, awkward to fire and no weather protection, although later some 'Super Ds' were fitted with tender cabs for tender-first working.

The tunnel and dock shunt locos used blind [smokeless] coal and had to be coaled from 'loco coal' wagons in the shed by hand.

Edge Hill men worked passenger turns to a wide range of destinations including Shrewsbury, Chester, Llandudno, Preston, Wigan, Manchester Exchange and local passenger services to places such as St Helens.

Freight turns took crews away to many of these destinations as well as Carnforth, Belle Vue (Manchester), Stockport, Burton-on-Trent, Nottingham, Sheffield, Bolton, Buxton, Stoke, Rugby and Camden. Mr Ebsworth explained that, 'loadings freight-wise were always full in earlier years and then started to decline from 1965. A full load would be forty-nine wagons and a brakevan.'

There were few workings at Edge Hill that could be described as 'unusual'. However, the most eagerly sought 'extra work' was the 'Yank boat trains' between Euston and Liverpool Riverside station. Mr Ebsworth again:

Prior to 1950 all Down trains required two or three ex-LNWR 0–6–2 Coal Tanks between Edge Hill station and Riverside owing to weight restrictions over the dock gates road bridge just before Riverside station. These dock gates were renewed, along with the tracks on top, in 1950 and from then the train engine – up to [the power of] a 'Royal Scot' – had to work the full roster, that is empty coaching stock Edge Hill Downhill sidings–Riverside–Euston–Camden loco or vice versa.

Many railwaymen have expressed differing views on the merits of the express Pacifics built by the LMS. In the main, most had nothing but praise for the 'Duchess' Pacifics, although opinion varied on the 'Lizzies' or 'Princess' engines. Mr Ebsworth's view is that:

The 'Duchesses' were the best locos; to prepare it was mostly grease. With four cylinders in line there was no mainframe whip or flexing. They were also better tune maintained.

The 'Princesses' suffered frame whip, that is with the inside cylinders driving the leading axle, and the outside cylinders driving the middle axle, outside cylinders flexed and the securing bolts were prone to drop out.

There were also cracked frames, and excess side-to-side flexing in the cab by the firebox. The boiler was only secured to the frames at the front on the smokebox saddle. The rear of the firebox was anchored in slides to allow for expansion.

Another of the ex-LNWR types which survived at Edge Hill to early Nationalization was the Webb Coal Tank. No. 6917, seen here at Edge Hill in 1947, together with No. 6900, saw some use on Riverside trains until bridge strengthening enabled larger classes to negotiate the line. By 1950 the five survivors of this class were all based away from Liverpool, concentrated at Bangor or Monument Lane.

John Rowlands

The steam pipes from the footplate manifold to the live exhaust steam injectors mounted behind the footplate used to split or break at floor level with the side to side oscillation.

On the first two 'Princesses', Nos 6200 and 6201, the valve gear had oiling corks with very poor access for inside valve gear. It was deadly, many men put on an old boiler suit over their overalls just to oil underneath. On engine Nos 6203 to 6212 most of the motion was grease – a shed staff job – but both classes of Pacific had poor water capacity.

If any sets of water troughs were out one had to be careful as to where the water columns were. Invariably, at station stops it was put the bag in and top up.

Camden [shed] was noted for putting 'run-downers' on 'local' work. In Camden's opinion Liverpool and Manchester jobs were classed as local work despite the fact that Liverpool and Manchester trains had more coaches to haul than the Scotch jobs.

For many years the mere mention of Edge Hill shed was synonymous with 'Princess' Pacifics and 'Royal Scots'. The 'Princesses' or 'Lizzies', as they were more often referred to by Liverpool crews, monopolized the Euston expresses, while the 'Scots' reigned

Although the 'Duchess' Pacifics had a final flurry at Edge Hill during the early 1960s it was Stanier's 'Princess' class engines which had the historic links with Merseyside. By 1959 there were seven of these Pacifics based at Edge Hill, including the now preserved No. 46203 *Princess Margaret Rose* and this engine, No. 46211 *Queen Maud*, photographed on a grey 15 February 1961 before leaving the shed to work the 1725 hrs 'Red Rose' express to London Euston. Behind *Queen Maud* is a 'Crab' Mogul, a type of engine uncommon at Edge Hill until the early 1960s when the last of the ex-LNWR 0–8–0s based at 8A were withdrawn.

John Corkill

supreme on services to destinations such as Leeds, Carlisle and Birmingham. With the onset of electrification of the main line to Crewe the 'Scots' began to be drafted away from Edge Hill from the early 1960s, with the last Merseyside 'Scot' (No. 46119) not leaving Edge Hill until after its withdrawal in November 1963.

Even after that, and with declining numbers in traffic, Edge Hill was still visited by surviving members of the 'Scot' class (by then based at Carlisle Kingmoor) during the summer of 1965.

While critical of some of these engines' defects, Charles Ebsworth is quite definite about which members of the 'Scots', and the similarly proportioned rebuilt 'Patriots', crews preferred to handle:

Our favourites at Edge Hill were No. 46124 (London Scottish) and (rebuilt 'Patriot') No. 45527 (Southport). The Preston men loved us to bring No. 45527 on the ex-Lime Street 12.45 a.m. Glasgow mails and passenger, which we worked to Preston for 2.16 a.m. departure. The Preston men who worked forward to Glasgow said that

Although the last of Edge Hill's 'Royal Scots' had been withdrawn by the end of 1963, these engines continued to visit the shed virtually right up to the end of their operational existence. When this photograph was taken of No. 46115 *Scots Guardsman* in light steam at Edge Hill on 4 June 1965, only one other 'Scot' remained in service, No. 46140. Both would be withdrawn by the end of that year. I was delighted by *Scots Guardsman* during the summer of 1965 when it was rostered on the 1950 hrs 'Carlisle freight' from Edge Hill – a turn usually booked for a 'Britannia', Standard 9F or the ubiquitous Stanier 'Black 5s'.

John Corkil

'Patriot' or better known as 'Baby Scot' No. 45533 *Lord Rathmore* raises steam at Edge Hill on 24 September 1961. *Lord Rathmore* was a long-time regular at 8A, based there from at least 1 January 1948 right through to its withdrawal (with three other 'Baby Scots' at the shed) on 6 October 1962.

Ken Fairey

No. 45527 was the only one to keep time between Shap and Carlisle, and between Beattock and Carstairs, running downhill with the regulator shut.

We worked the 4.55 a.m. ex-Preston (12.10 a.m. ex-Glasgow) home to Lime Street and although the coal was out of reach of the shovel, and had to be picked down from the back between firings, the small 'Scotch' slack burned in the tubes and one had a stream of sparks from the chimney from Preston to Coppul, and from Springs Branch to Bryn, and St Helens to Thatto Heath.

But the engine would blow off against the injector boiler feed. The straight-boilered 'Royal Scots' often had to have a prolonged blow up before leaving Preston, Wigan and St Helens. The idea was to get the boiler full and 250 lb/sq. inch steam up before tackling the banks. The Preston men often arrived late with an empty boiler and 150 lb/sq. inch steam. With 6 foot 9 inch driving wheels the skilful driver had to coax them up to speed gradually.

Even if time was lost between Lime Street and Edge Hill, on a Carlisle train it could be regained. However, if a heavy-handed driver was driving and tried to thrash the loco into speed – a few slips and one's firebed had gone up the chimney.

We've gone on an all-stations with twelve carriages on from Lime Street to Llandudno and burned 6 tons of coal, then coaled the 'Scot' up out of a wagon at Llandudno and worked the same twelve [carriages] all-stations to Crewe and burned another 5 tons. On relief at Crewe, for Euston, the Crewe relief would say, 'Christ mate, where's the coal. We haven't enough for Euston.'

It was okay if one could stand up to the punishment.

It is Mr Ebsworth's opinion, and that of many footplatemen, that both the original 'Royal Scots' and 'Baby Scots' (or 'Patriots') were adequate for their tasks but tended to get run down easily because of flawed Derby design features. Small axlebox dimensions led to face and hornblock wear, and the original Midland-type springs and hangers soon lost 'tune'. He recalls that:

In latter days both classes had their blast pipes 'nibbed' at the top in order to split the blast and increase steaming, and unfortunately increase coal consumption too. With longer trains, steam heating was increased from 50 lb/sq. inch to 60 lb then 70 lb and this was all a drain on the boiler; adding the water and continuous blow-down didn't help either.

The right-hand exhaust steam-powered injectors always gave trouble on the 'Baby Scots'; the earlier type, two-wheeled supply injectors on the 'Royal Scots' were more reliable.

However, the main weakness was the Derby-type smokebox base and the difficulty in making the main steam exit joints airtight. These exited through holes in the base of the smokebox; a pad of cement around these pipes was a seal of sorts but red-hot smokebox cinders used to cause cracks, resulting in air leakage, smokebox vacuum and poor steaming.

The re-boiling of both classes was a big improvement, particularly the 'Baby Scots', which got a new Stanier cab.

The 'Royal Scots' quickly became rough riders with severe fore and aft oscillation. This was cured, after much experimentation, with driving springs with different spring and numbers of spring leaves. The fitting of Ferrodo pads to the front bogie side bolsters also assisted. 'Scots' Nos. 46132 and 46142 were both used for driving spring trials, which led to improvements in riding characteristics.

Mr Ebsworth was also critical of the Midland-designed cab on the 'Scots' because the back half was unbolted to enable the works' cranes access to lifting lugs in the rear frame cross beam. Out on the road, the whole roof would vibrate up and down and shake the cab side panels to which were fixed the crew's seats. 'The above joint would spring, and rain ran down your neck if you were sitting down,' he said. 'Both classes in their rebuilt form steamed okay.'

On the question of whether he had any favourite work when working at Edge Hill Mr Ebsworth had this to say:

There was no favourite work for me, speaking personally; to most outsiders our job was looked at through rose-coloured spectacles.

If you went out on Saturday or Sunday nights at weekends or holidays you nearly always still had to rise at 3 a.m., ride a pushbike to work for 4 a.m. on, or some other unearthly hour.

In railcar days the 0909 hrs ex-Lime Street to Newcastle looked wonderful. But it was 5.15 a.m. on duty, which meant getting up at 4.15 a.m. We protested at 8A many times. Number 3 goods link in twelve weeks' work had ten weeks of p.m. work between 1 p.m. and 11.45 p.m. You never saw your children for weeks.

Trouble was there was always a hard core of individuals who would work any hours anytime – a lot of single men with no home life. That's why I took to and finished up as an instructor on diesels as it was day work and every Saturday was a rest day off – I always thought of the family first.

When speaking about Standard classes, Charles Ebsworth clearly was not enamoured with the 'Britannia' Pacifics:

Their fault, as built, was that the cab was part of, and secured to and expanded with, the boiler – the result was draught and dirt in the cab. There was a forward facing gap under the cab floor which finished about 6 inches from off the tender front allowing an unrestricted rush of air to come through. If one watered the coal the drips running out off the shovel plate were blown all over the cab – there were no fall plates between the engine and tender.

Very soon the first 'Brits' went back into Crewe Works for modifications and a roll of thick rubber was fitted to the back of the footplate floor girder and the same on the front of the tender, level with the cab. These were a lot better but they soon got covered in small coal which jammed between the rubbing faces of the rubber rolls and cut the ¾ inch rubber which required frequent renewal.

The last batch of 'Brits' (Nos 70045–54) had an altered design of tender, a cab floor with normal fall plates at the rear which rested on a ledge on the tender front – plus a

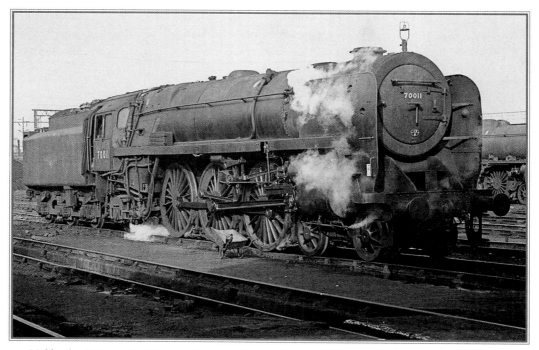

Unlike the 'Princess' Pacifics, the 'Britannias' were often a sad sight in their declining years. Here, on 14 September 1965, No. 70011 *Hotspur* of Carlisle Upperby shed awaits its next roster – nameless and numberless, and turned out in the unlined green livery applied to many of the class in their final years.

John Corkill

coal pusher. However, when first tried at Edge Hill the coal was out of reach by Stafford – it wouldn't trim forward. It caused complaints resulting in loco inspectors riding in the cab – they finished up the rest of the trip using the coal pick in the tender to bring coal forward for the fireman.

The 'Brit' only lasted a couple of months at 8A – we got our 'Royal Scots' back!

PAGES FROM A LOCO IMPROVER'S NOTEBOOK

Bill Walker spent several months in 1960 based at the Merseyside depots of Edge Hill and Speke on a Motive Power Improver on Probation course. The courses were developed to broaden selected staff's experience of all aspects of the operation of a motive power depot and, as such, they helped train prospective locomotive shedmasters.

Fortunately, during this training course, Bill Walker was required to keep a diary of his daily observations and experiences. Today, more than thirty-five years later, the diary entries provide a fascinating insight into the day-to-day operations of a large steam shed during a period of transition, and of the attitudes and tensions evident among the various railway staff grades during that time. I am greatly indebted to Bill Walker for saving such an historically important diary.

In 1961 Bill Walker was appointed to his first shed – Oxenholme – and so began a career progress that would eventually take him to Western Australia, and management of a private railway's locomotive department. The following entries are, unless otherwise indicated, exactly as recorded by Mr Walker during May to August 1960.

9 May 1960:
Shunting with a humpy in Down Hill Sidings. Monotonous. [Mr Walker comments that a 'humpy' was better known as a 'Jinty' tank. In Chester shed (where he had come from) we always called them 'Humpies' and I was surprised when I later learned that some people referred to them as 'Jinties'. Some Edge Hill staff recall a 'humpy' being better known as an ex-LNWR 'Special' tank.]

10 May 1960:
On a humpy at Lime Street station, more interesting. They have small signals for shunting engines called dummies. They also have limit of shunt boards just outside the station.

11 May 1960:
On a class 8 (Stanier 8F) at Park Sidings and Grid (Iron). Also had a run out to Wapping Sidings at Edge Hill station. We were supposed to get the engine ready, but due to shortage of engines we had to re-man one. This engine had been re-manned several times and was low on water and coal. The coal it had on was poor quality.

[undated] May 1960:
On a 'Super D'. Started off in Park Sidings, took a train to Canada Dock along Bootle Sidings and then went to Alexandra Dock and worked a banana train back to the Grid. Finished back at Park Sidings. Began to see how some of the other departments' work fits in with everyone else.

17 May 1960:
On a 'Super D' (No. 49394) again, went to St Helens. Saw how railway wastes money. Atomic shelter obsolete. ['I was told a story that a railway control room was built in an atomic shelter and was then made obsolete. We passed it at Huyton Quarry.']

18 May 1960:
On a 'Super D' again, went to Lea Green colliery [beyond Rainhill] to work a coal train back. Also did some shunting up there. Saw the old Rainhill station and Crown Street tunnel and old station there, skew bridge and value of novelty.

19 May 1960:
On a 'Super D' (No. 49404) again, went through Waterloo Tunnel twice; gradient of 1 in 57. You have to keep the sanders working and keep flat out because of the smoke, should you slip. It is nearly 2 and a half miles.

The ex-LNWR Bowen-Cooke 'Super D' eight-wheelers were a feature of Edge Hill shed right up to the early 1960s. Their solid chunky features meant they presented some real hard graft for fitting staff who had to carry out maintenance work upon them. However, the deafening bark of their exhaust – two loud beats, followed by two soft beats – working up the slope from Edge Hill, with anything up to fifty wagons in tow, was quite a performance to fitting staff such as John Corkill. No. 49394 was among those engines which were rebuilt from 1936 with Belpaire boilers. It awaits its next turn of duty outside the 'old' shed on 5 April 1959. Behind the engine's smokebox door can be seen the two-level girder railway bridge that carried traffic from Wapping Dock, and the lower level bridge – double track – that ran down to Olive Mount, under the circle line bridge and Rathbone Road bridge. Engine No. 49394 was withdrawn from traffic at Edge Hill to the period ending 6 November 1962.

Ken Fairey

24 May 1960:
On the 0115 hrs to Saltney (Chester). More drivers around at night. Saw all the activities in the goods yards. [On this trip Mr Walker and his crew ended up at Mold Junction shed where he had once worked as an apprentice, so there was much talk with his old friends. Among the news he had to tell was that he had just attended an engagement party at Dingle, a Liverpool suburb, at which the soon to be celebrated Gerry and the Pacemakers pop group performed.]

25 May 1960:
On the 0125 hrs to Edgeley (Stockport). Very slow journey. Got relieved fairly quickly and the Running Shed Foreman asked the driver to work one back but he refused, saying that he had done this previously, being promised a through road, but then a

local man was allowed to get in front of him, and he was late getting back. We travelled back by passenger (train) to Manchester.

2 June 1960:
On the 2030 hrs Camden (London) with Dave Roberts and Jack Hart. It took us 6½ hours to get there. Arrived at 0300 hrs, had a meal and went to bed for 0400 hrs. The road [railway track] runs alongside the barracks. ['I was given room No. 1 at the barracks. I thought "that's nice", but it was the worst room, very noisy.']

We went down double-headed ('Black 5s'), you get coal dust off the front engine. ['I remember I got coal dust in my eye and could not sleep because of the pain. When I got up I went to the shed for someone to get the coal out of my eye.']

We went via Northampton. Came back double-headed and due to the number of excursions it took us 9 hours to get back. The other engine was a Manchester engine, we split up at Stafford.

He took 10 and we took 29 (we went faster without him). We picked up some at Crewe South Goods Yard. We had to tell the Manchester men we were coming with them and then the shed staff turned us off in the wrong order, and we had to shunt in the yard to get right. The barracks was not very good.

Lime Street before the wires intruded. 'Duchess' Pacific No. 46231 *Duchess of Atholl* of Polmadie shed, Glasgow, waits to get the right-away with an express on 20 September 1959. Within three years, sights such as this would become the exception rather than the rule. Lime Street was opened by the LNWR in 1879, replacing an earlier terminus that had been completed on 15 August 1836.

H.C. Casserley

Saturday 4 June 1960:
On the 1330 hrs to Chester, a medium fast passenger train.

7 June 1960:
On the 1005 hrs Birmingham. Fast passenger, relieved at Crewe then we relieved other men and brought their engine on to Crewe South for turning and water. Back to Edge Hill with 57 wagons = 63 wagons. The engine was a 'Crab' and it was a struggle and took a good while to get back.

8 June 1960:
On the 0720 hrs to Manchester. Local passenger to Manchester took 2 hours. Left the engine on Patricroft shed (45438). A very slow job going but worked a flyer back.

9 June 1960:
On the 0350 hrs to Carlisle. Locomotive No. 48464. No hurry to get away, a slow journey and relieved at Carnforth and went back to Lancaster to get a passenger train to Carlisle. When we got to Carlisle we saw the men who had relieved us, they had already booked off. Carlisle barracks was good. Booked on at 0110 hrs. Saw the difficulties of the fireman coming up Shap; the water going down at the same time as the steam, it was mainly due to poor coal.

11 June 1960:
On railcar. Two trips to Wigan and two to St Helens. You just have sufficient time to walk from one end [of the railcar] to the other and then start off again. The driver has to be relieved after the two Wigan trips to get his meal time. They used to do one trip to Wigan.

13 June 1960:
On the 0905 hrs to Crewe and return by passenger.

14 June 1960:
On the 0730 hrs to Stafford. Got off at Crewe and returned by passenger.

15 June 1960:
[On the] 0900 hrs to Leeds with Dave Roberts and Stan Rimmer. Very fast (No. 45521 *Rhyl*). Came back coupled (double headed) with a Manchester crew. Late start and lost time between Leeds and Huddersfield and we had to start pushing him to get him moving. Got in on time.

Edge Hill 'Scots' like Nos 46119 and 46124 were also used on trains to Leeds, and recounting his first attempts at trying to fire a 'Scot' at high speed in 1960, former Motive Power Improver on Probation Bill Walker recalls his experience on the 9 a.m. Lime Street to Leeds Central.

After we left Earlestown the fireman asked if I would like to try firing the engine. I had fired engines previously, on slow trains, but this was a different proposition.

We were travelling down a slight incline at 75 mph. I steadied myself in the middle of the footplate, filled the shovel with coal, turned to face the fire. The engine lurched one way and I went the other way, the shovel hit the front of the firebox below the firehole, and the shock travelled up my arm and down my spine.

The shovel dropped from my numbed fingers and the crash as it hit the footplate was accompanied by laughter from the driver and fireman. I did successfully fire it later when our speed was slower. We arrived at Leeds Central on time. The fireman uncoupled the engine from the train and, leaving the driver to take care of the engine, he took me to the nearest public house for a well-earned drink.

16 June 1960:
See above, with Stan and Mac. ['I cannot remember Mac's full name. We had engine 45531 *Sir Frederick Harrison*, a "Patriot" class. From memory we had a very rough ride.']

17 June 1960:
Arrived 10 minutes early on the 1000 hrs Euston and returned on the 0815 hrs Lime Street. Camden barracks by shunting yard.

20 June 1960:
On Engineers' Train – ballast. ['Possibly with a "4F".'] This engine is hired out to the engineer and it does a lot of waiting about.

21 June 1960:
On 0900 hrs to Leeds.

22 June 1960:
On the 1700 hrs to Leeds, the fastest train out of Lime Street. Nine minutes to Huyton and 18 minutes to Earlestown. They work a very slow passenger train back.

23 June 1960:
Dave and Stan on the 0945 hrs parcels; an off-side door opened between Lime Street and Crewe. We had to hold up at Crewe while various people had a look at the door. Worked the 1645 hrs back (The Shamrock) with 46204 *Princess Louise*. Have a time to make any time up with a steam engine. ['I remember the return trip with No. 46204. Stan tried to get up to 100 mph. We got up to 90 mph before the signals went against us.']

27 June 1960:
On the 0913 hrs railcar to Wigan and 1026 hrs to Preston, and 1116 hrs to Wigan. The driver was on a diesel and he refused to let me on without a diesel pass. [Returned] on 1307 hrs Wigan to Lime Street and 1410 hrs to Wigan and back.

'Royal Scot' No. 46119 *Lancashire Fusilier* waiting to leave Lime Street station on a grey 19 September 1961 with the 1100 hrs to Newcastle. This 'Scot' was the last of its class to be based at Edge Hill, eventually being withdrawn from 8A at the end of November 1963 nearly a full year after No. 46124 *London Scottish* was transferred to Carlisle Kingmoor. Edge Hill 'Scots' like Nos 46119 and 46124 were also used on trains to Leeds.

Michael Mensing

Edge Hill's 'Black 5' No. 45312 threads through Rathbone Road coal yard, just east of 8A, on 16 November 1965. I have vivid memories of seeing this engine trundle through Edge Hill station with a train of empty coaching stock about a year before this photograph was taken. On that occasion the locomotive had recently been outshopped from Cowlairs Works, Glasgow, and was resplendent in fully-lined black livery at a time when such niceties were becoming rare.

John Corkill

28 June 1960:

On the 2200 hrs Euston with Bill Roberts, we arrived 20 minutes early. An extra driver had a notice about arriving early, approximately 45 minutes. The passengers arrived before their cars. We worked the 0745 hrs from Euston, it is the fastest train out of there 36 minutes (scheduled) to Watford 32 miles away from a standing start. [Mr Walker notes that at this time the schedule was slack because of electrification work underway at the Liverpool end of the service.]

30 June 1960:

On the 2300 hrs Euston with Camden men. Marked for a diesel (English Electric Type 4) but we had a steam engine. Worked the 0745 hrs back on a diesel (English Electric Type 4).

18 July 1960:

With the Outside Running Foreman:

Each engine coming on the shed is recorded. The Outside Running Foreman tells them what to do with it. A staff is kept available to dispose of and prepare engines and the work is given out by the Outside Running Foreman. He has to have a working knowledge of all the diagrams so that as each engine comes in he knows what job it goes back on and so can plan his work accordingly.

Home engines can be swapped about with arrangements made with the IRF. Foreign engines can not, without permission of control.

Due to shortage of engines some have to be remanned. In the case of extreme shortage of power, foreign engines can be used for short jobs provided they can get back to cover their own jobs.

Each engine is booked going off shed and the signal-box notified and the times recorded.

The office acts as a control point for the shed bank.

Nothing is allowed to move without the permission of the ORF. He has to be careful not to block anything in and this is sometimes difficult when he has engines approaching from several directions at once.

Engines usually come in down the back and go off the bottom end. A plan view of the shed is kept and as the engine comes on the shed it is marked on the plan and the position of it in the shed is seen at a glance.

The ORF also marks the board. The list of every job requiring an engine is kept and as the engines come on they are marked in this list.

25 July 1960:

Inside the Running Shift Foreman's office:
The biggest problem is finding men to work the jobs.

The shed is allowed a certain complement of men, this seems to take no account of men who will be absent and when the seasonal summer rush starts there are insufficient men. Every attempt is made to borrow men from other sheds but the same thing happens to them to a certain extent. The smaller the shed the less effect it has upon them.

If they have men available they are not always right over the road and require conductors [to show them the route]. More specials are run every day and no extra men allowed so therefore some of the freight trains are knocked off and the crews utilised.

Unfortunately, several moves have to be made to be able to use these men. Men are absent because of road learning, leave, leave in lieu, sickness and annual leave.

The list of specials which has previously been extracted from special notices and books etc. is checked over by the running shed foreman and a list made out for the outside foreman, and where the men and engines are supposed to come from.

A list is also made out for his own convenience so as to answer any queries from Lime Street.

One of the problems is getting the special notices in plenty of time. Other departments are supplied first. The RSF had to go to the control office to borrow some so that he could make out his Sunday list. The control have to know which engine is going on every job and if the men require relief.

They also have to arrange for the relief. A ticket is made out for each job with the

A fine study of Edge Hill's Stanier 8F (sometimes known as 'Consuls'), No. 48433. Edge Hill's allocation of these engines grew from a mere five at the shed in 1950 to eighteen by May 1964. Their increasing presence was determined by the demise of the ex-LNWR 0–8–0s, which had done most of the freight work before the 8Fs' arrival. This engine, photographed on 14 September 1965, was listed in John Corkill's work notes as 'awaiting shops' on 6 April 1968. However, three days later a decision was made to condemn the engine. It was among the contingent of engines awaiting despatch to the scrapyard on Edge Hill's final day of steam, 4 May 1968.

John Corkill

driver on it, engine and train he is working. He then makes out a yellow ticket for the relief driver and enters it in the book in red pencil. The guards' controller uses a blue ticket for the relief guard.

There is a layout of the local system on the wall. There are small holes on it on which tickets can be hung. It is very difficult to keep engines on their right diagram but every effort is made to do so. The controller allows foreign engines to be used for other jobs provided that they can be worked directly home from wherever they are going.

A number of men are allocated for the control but owing to present conditions these men are rarely ever available. During the day many men complain because they have been put off their own job but without doing this the job would stop.

On the afternoon turn:

One of the jobs is to fill in the boiler cards of where the engines have gone, and the mileage they have got, also the big engine book which has all the express passenger trains in. Also the late start book, in which the reasons for late starts are noted.

I also saw some of the difficulties of acting as foreman. The many arguments which he has to settle although he always has the right to pass a decision to the shedmaster.

The foreman's assistant takes care of the movements of the men, and he has to be very careful not to break any local or national (industrial) agreements between men and management.

They conveniently forget any in their favour but soon take up any against them.

On nights (midnight to 8 a.m.):

Tuesday 9 August 1960:

The analysis book is balanced on nights. In the usual position of no engines and men, then it might be found that 'foreign' men who should want a train have not arrived and so men will be required for this job.

In one of the ballast jobs in the morning, a diesel shunt was put on it and then found to be non-vacuum fitted. It seems all the 12000-class diesels are the same. A quick swap had to be made. This is an instance of how a small detail can be overlooked.

Wednesday 10 August 1960:

D9 and an EE (English Electric) 2,000 hp diesel were supposed to work a train from Euston but when they were coupled up to D9 they could not get her amps. She worked a later train up. But it goes a little deeper than this. It seems the driver of D9 did not want to fetch her at all. An extra driver complaining about his turn of duty because he could not follow it right through to the end of the week. The foreman's assistant said he could not because of some effect it will have the following week.

I had a job balancing the analysis book. You have to follow the job through the diagrams. This is a very difficult job because of the shortage of engines. Engines are not allowed to complete diagrams and it may be on a different diagram altogether.

It could take hours to fill this in correctly so a little fiddling is done. Specials are also supposed to be accounted for but they are conveniently forgotten!

I can see no use for it as some of the details are incorrect anyway. By trying to fill this in, the very difficult job of finding engines can be seen.

The large amount of engines which are foreign engines are kept here. When one of our engines does come back it is usually on an overdue washout and so is taken off the diagram it is on and then the RF (Running Foreman) has to provide another engine.

Class 5MTs are used in place of 6P and 7P, and 6P in place of 7P (engines). If this was not allowed the job would stop.

The load of the train usually has to be found out from control first. Occasionally it works the other way. A class 6P train might be overloaded and no 7P (engine) available (there never is). In this case two 5MTs would have to be put on it and another engine is wasted.

The huge cavern that was (and still is) Lime Street was an excellent place to observe steam, whether it was the rising anticipation of a departure, or an arrival, such as this relief train from Birmingham, headed by Aston-based 'Black 5' No. 45038, at 4.26 p.m. on Good Friday (31 March) 1961. Although steam had become increasingly rare at Lime Street by the mid-1960s, some Sunday services and certain late-night services would still fall to steam power.

Michael Mensing

We had a collision on the shed. One engine was taking water and was foul of another track. An engine coming on to the shed on another line ran into the tender of the engine which was foul. This engine had to be stopped and so another scramble to find another engine.

A driver put in a report about finding a guard in the middle of the four foot having apparently fallen out of his guard's van on the opposite track.

No engine was available for the 1100 hrs Lime Street to Euston due to D9 not coming up coupled, so it was arranged to put two class 5MTs on it. At 0720 hrs the 10.05 (Birmingham) New Street was stopped for a broken spring. It should have gone off to work an 0810 EC.

At 7.30 a.m. the 1000 hrs diesel, D234, was stopped with exhaust manifold, it had blown out. It had to be quickly arranged that two 5MTs would work the train because D234 would most probably not be ready for 11 a.m.

The two 5MTs were not available so two 5MTs had to be taken off other less essential work. Then the men had to be found for it. They had not been found for the 11 a.m. train.

During the night, a shift of six firemen was started. Care has to be taken to keep them in order because should there be a set back (there usually is in winter) they should have the same mate as they had before the move up. The seniority of the men can be told by their numbers. The lower the number the higher they are.

Thursday 11 August 1960:
Stan (the RSF) said he had a row with the chief clerk because he was working in the assistant's office and the CC made a comment on it. The RSF seems to get pushed around by everyone. He also had a row with the Mechanical Foreman.

He went over all the diagrams to see if some engine could work a job and he found it could not, so he had to use a diesel in the shed.

The Mechanical Foreman said it required a daily examination and he wanted to know why he was not told sooner. Stan had already done a lot of work in trying to find another engine. Early on he had a row with Ramsdale about who should rearrange the links. He said it was Rams' job. The Outside Foreman now had a row with Stan because he wanted Stan to do it, so he could take his place. The Outside Foreman then had two engines failed on him. This, combined with the other, resulted in making him ill and he had to go home early.

Friday 12 August 1960:
The men seem to have respect for Albert and he says this is due to getting a lot of them form '1s' when he first arrived. Also, he has an intimate knowledge of the national agreements and also how to interpret them.

He is called upon to settle many disagreements because he will make his decision and, because he is sure he is right, will stick by them.

Saturday 13 August 1960:
The Foreman's Assistant [position] is a very difficult job. This week they have a lot

A view of 'The Camp' end of Edge Hill depot looking towards Manchester. The sidings on the far right are Rathbone Road coal sidings and goods depot. In the distance one of 8A's 350 hp diesel shunters (probably D3019) pushes back a grimy Stanier 8F, which has either recently been lit, or has steam leaking from the firebox area. In the upper distance is the 'Grid Iron' sidings.

Charles Hibbert

of drivers away training on electrics, also diesel training and the holidays are still on.

At the moment they appear very quick tempered with the men. Part of this is most probably due to past experience but I think a lot of it is because of the difficulties of the job getting them down.

I think the same is said for the Foreman. Stan is always ready to align himself with the drivers and see their point of view but this unfortunately gets him in rows with the footplatemen when he tries to show them his point of view which they will not see.

These are in the minority if a detached but hard point of view is taken, the Foreman has less trouble for himself but usually gets himself disliked.

A larger amount of engines and men are required because of the extra specials run on a Saturday. An attempt was made earlier on in the week to get some of the sub sheds to take on some of the jobs. On some occasions they were able to. Why could they not have been allotted this work in the first place?

Most of the morning was taken up in doing manipulations of engines. Two passenger jobs came in with a class 8F and a 4P on. This meant they were two class 5s down. This meant 2s or 4s would have to go out and so whoever got these would have the same trouble again. But it had to be done to keep the job going.

This was probably a good job years ago but now it is just an existence or getting through your own shift. One night Stan and I went steam raising to try to get an engine out on time which had come late on the shed.

In the General Office:

Monday 15 August 1960:

With the CC. He usually answers any correspondence addressed to the DMPS and arranges a schedule of meetings for the DMPS. He examines all the various literature which comes in the mornings and decides who it is meant for.

A band of young enthusiasts watch closely as Edge Hill's No. 45376 trundles around the perimeter of the depot on 3 March 1968. At the bottom left corner of this view is the opening to the pedestrian tunnel that gave access to the shed from nearby Tiverton Street. Behind the young lads, in the distance, is the top of Edge Hill's unusual coaling stage, with a couple of wagons waiting to fill the plant's hoppers. In front of the coaling stage is the circular line which ran around the shed. No. 45376 was withdrawn from traffic at 8A to the period ending 20 April 1968.

Charles Hibbert

Tuesday 16 August 1960:

With Ray on the boiler cards. He gets a list of mileages of the various engines from the cost office, Crewe.

These mileages are taken from the driver's reports. He then enters these weekly mileages on the boiler cards adding them to obtain the number of miles run from the last mileage.

When they have gone 8000–8500 miles he sends out an advice note to the Mechanical Foreman's office. The mileage figures are up to three weeks behind and so the daily mileage put on by the RSF are added up to obtain a rough estimate up to date.

When the mileage exam has been finished a delay occurs until the correct mileage comes in. The mileage is then entered on the big card and checked against the mileage which is given between general exams.

I also saw how the driver's time is worked out. The main difficulty at the moment appears to be in deciding which rate applies to passed firemen. It cannot always be told from the driver's ticket.

Wednesday 17 August 1960:

Similar cards to the washout cards are kept for the railcar units for all the cars stationed under Edge Hill.

Each time a railcar is refuelled a note is made of its milometer reading. This is then entered on the white cards. Overall mileage and exams are also noted on these cards.

The reason for keeping this record is for filling in the large four-weekly form with details of mileage, oil and fuel used. But this is now sent to Allerton instead of Derby where the rest of the details are filled in and they send a master copy for the district into Derby.

At one time here they used to advise when the MUs were due for exams but they must do it on a daily basis now. A weekly return for gas, electricity and water used is sent to the various departments interested and this is done to make sure the railways are not overcharged. The canteen pays for the gas it uses out of its own fund.

INTO THE 1960S AT EDGE HILL

Stan Rimmer remembers the transition period from steam to diesel in the early to mid-1960s and the ruses that some railwaymen at Edge Hill would take part in to avoid working a steam engine. He said:

In one case we had a job to Camden, 8.45 p.m., which was well watched by firemen. In winter they would come up (around the back) to the shed diagram and see what engine was on the Camden turn. If it was a diesel they would come to work, but if it was steam they would go home and then ring the shed and book sick.

The foreman got to know about this and would mark a diesel up on the board. Then when it was about time for the fireman to book on, he would rub it off the board!

However, other ex-Edge Hill men explained that the new diesels were not readily accepted by some crews when they first arrived because of their 'closed in' cabs.

The exodus of steam filled Stan Rimmer with considerable regret: 'I didn't like the diesels because of the smell. I would sooner have had the smell of smoke and the gear oil and cylinder oil.'

Charles Ebsworth recalls his last steam turn, the 1835 hrs Edge Hill–Carlisle New Yard, which was routed through the Bootle branch to Aintree and Preston. For this turn, on a Friday night, 'Jubilee' No. 45670 *Howard of Effingham* was his rostered engine. For the return he was given a Sunday 0100 hrs departure – a fish van train to Wigan North Western – and assigned a 'Britannia' Pacific with an overfilled boiler.

We booked on at Kingmoor shed at 2315 hrs on the Saturday night. The loco was No. 70005 [*John Milton*], a 'Britannia'. It was off a boiler washout and the shed staff had overfilled the boiler.

The gauge glasses showed full and there was a good fire spread, but steam zero, only 40 pound (pressure) up at 'off shed' time. So we set off gingerly down Kingmoor bankhead to the turntable which was set 'wrong' for us.

We had to get the regulator well open to move at all. Once the excess water got past the regulator valve it expanded and steamed in the superheater elements. With 'shut' regulator and steam brake on we puffed towards the turntable well. There was no way of stopping No. 70005.

I quickly wound the reverser into 'back' and we slowed down and then started backwards towards the shed, brake still on.

I then got the cylinder cocks open, previously locked by hydraulic pressure, and finally stopped just outside the shed. After the fireman had set the turntable we had another go. We finally got turned and then went light engine to Carlisle yard tender first to pick up some of the train. [The journey eventually passed without incident.]

My fireman had swapped my regular booked mate for this one turn, as he had just been passed for driving and had 'signed' for the Carlisle road, so he drove from Carlisle station and I acted as fireman.

Of his eventual transition to working on diesels, Charles Ebsworth found that his early training when a young school-leaver found a use later in his railway career. He recalls:

On leaving school at fourteen I was offered a council job as laboratory assistant at Rathbone Road School – school hours at 10s a week until the age of sixteen.

I took this, and with the electrical knowledge and lecturing that was going on in the lab I learned all the basic DC knowledge. This electrical knowledge lay dormant until 1959 when the diesel instructor's job came up. Owning a motorcycle from 1937–9 gave me the basic knowledge about the internal combustion engine. So I took to the diesels like a duck to water.

Former Edge Hill footplatemen remember the condition of the 'Duchess' and (to a lesser extent) 'Princess' Pacifics based at Edge Hill by the early 1960s as being excellent,

Edge Hill's No. 46233 *Duchess of Sutherland* visits the 'coal hole' at the depot on 26 March 1963. This was the first of a quartet of 'Duchesses' to be drafted to 8A, arriving in September 1960. It was not withdrawn until February 1964 and, after an inspection by representatives of the Billy Butlin holiday camps, was selected for display at Butlin's Heads of Ayr facility. Eventually in the late 1970s, Butlins decided to divest itself of its quite stunning steam locomotive collection and the *Duchess of Sutherland* was acquired by the Bressingham Museum at Diss.

John Corkill

right up to their withdrawal. They had to be so for, although theoretically relegated to freight duties when diesels such as the English Electric Type 4s (Class 40) and Sulzers (Classes 44 and 45) were introduced, they often had to fill the breach when diesels, frequently, failed on passenger turns in the early transition period.

By the time the 'Duchess' Pacifics (Nos 46229/33/41/43) were allocated to Edge Hill, diesels were already making inroads into express rosters. However, steam still saw service on these duties. The Pacifics were also rostered to work fast freights to places such as Carlisle, and often the big engines were not sent back on a return diagram — Carlisle control would commandeer them for trains when diesels were not available. 'Princess' Pacifics would also get occasional flings on trains that had been, increasingly, diesel rosters. On 24 February 1962, for example, No. 46209 *Princess Beatrice* worked the 'Merseyside Express'.

During the summer of 1962 a passenger roster that gave the four Edge Hill 'Duchesses' a good run was the 0045 hrs train from Lime Street to Glasgow, then returning to Liverpool Exchange, arriving in early evening. The engine would then stay overnight at Bank Hall shed and work the following morning's 0943 hrs train to Glasgow, returning

Before the arrival of the 'Duchess' Pacifics at Edge Hill, the 'Princess' Pacifics ruled the roost, and in 1959 seven of the class were shedded at 8A, including No. 46200 *Princess Royal*, seen here on 5 April in that year. The engines dominated the London expresses until dieselization and electrification of the route in the early 1960s, and Bill Walker recalled earlier in the book one memorable trip with a 'Princess' when a signal check just foiled an attempt upon a 'ton' with one of the class. No. 46200, together with No. 46206, were the last engines of the class to be withdrawn in November 1962 with Carlisle Kingmoor being the final base for the class leader.

Ken Fairey

to Merseyside with an overnight train to Lime Street. On some occasions engines booked on this demanding diagram would be taken to work the 1010 hrs 'Merseyside Express' to London because of the absence of a diesel or electric.

Despite full electrification of the Liverpool–Crewe line from 18 June 1962, the following two months of that year saw numerous workings of 'Duchess' Pacifics and 'Royal Scots' on named trains in and out of Liverpool. These included No. 46248 *City of Leeds* on a Down 'Red Rose', No. 46243 *City of Lancaster*, No. 46253 *City of St Albans*, No. 46235 *City of Birmingham* and No. 46233 *Duchess of Sutherland* (all on Up 'Merseyside Express' trains), No. 46240 *City of Coventry* (on an Up 1350 hrs relief from Lime Street), besides 'Royal Scot' No. 46124 *London Scottish* on the Up 'Manxman', and No. 46116 *Irish Guardsman* on the 1100 hrs Liverpool–Newcastle working. The latter engine was also used on the 1100 hrs Liverpool–Newcastle on 23 July 1962, and the 1647 hrs balancing return.

Although during the winter of 1962 many passenger engines were placed in store at London Midland depots, with Edge Hill being no exception, steam was still in evidence on turns that had been previously surrendered to diesel. For example, 'Scot' No. 46144 *Honourable Artillery Company* was in charge of the 1500 hrs Liverpool–Newcastle express on 5 November 1962 after a 'Peak' diesel had failed at Liverpool. This same engine was in charge of the return 0945 hrs Newcastle–Liverpool working the following day.

By December 1962 all of Edge Hill's four Stanier Pacifics were in store at the shed, besides 'Baby Scot' No. 45531 *Sir Frederick Harrison* and 'Scot' No. 46110 *Grenadier Guardsman*. Also in store and condemned were the numerous ex-LNWR 0–8–0s which had been superseded by Hughes-Fowler 'Crabs', a class that was then relatively new to the shed. Despite this, on 14 and 15 December 'Scots' were again turned out to power the 1100 hrs Liverpool–Newcastle train with No. 46114 *Coldstream Guardsman* and No. 46168 *The Girl Guide* being in charge on respective dates. Meanwhile, at Lime Street 'Jinty' tanks continued to shunt the terminus, with one of the class, No. 47412, reportedly having been a regular there since 1956.

Extra train workings repeatedly brought the 'Duchesses' back to Edge Hill. Of note in late 1962 was the visit by class leader No. 46220 *Coronation*, which was selected to power the Queen's train to Merseyside on 14 December. The loco had run light engine from Edge Hill shed to Lowton Junction (at the northern tip of the Parkside triangle) for her trip into Lime Street. Sister engine, No. 46248 *City of Leeds*, was used to haul the Queen's return train from Liverpool to Watford.

Of the many unusual locomotives that would sometimes work into Liverpool, and find their way to Edge Hill depot, the most astonishing was the A3 Pacific No. 60045 *Lemberg*, which made it to Merseyside on Christmas Eve 1962, hauling the Newcastle–Liverpool express. A Sulzer Type 4 diesel had failed at Darlington, and because *Lemberg* was the southbound standby engine it was commandeered to take the train on to Leeds. At Leeds the engine that was to have taken the train on to Liverpool had been used on another job and the Edge Hill crew, on seeing the arrival of the 'foreigner', had to decide whether to take the A3 southwards. Edge Hill's driver, Mr Watson, seeing no prospect of a replacement, spoke to the Eastern Region driver in order to familiarize himself with the engine's controls and then decided to work through to Liverpool with the A3 Pacific.

Lemberg returned to its own territory on the 2235 hrs parcels to York on 26 December 1962 via Mossley Hill and Widnes Low Level, Warrington Arpley Low Level and Stockport, then as far as Leeds. On 27 December *Lemberg* was in charge of the 1025 hrs Leeds–Glasgow express via Settle.

Other more frequent 'foreigners' which found their way to Edge Hill from the Eastern and North Eastern Regions included 'B1' class 4–6–0s and occasionally 'K1' 2–6–0s. Among these visitors to Edge Hill were: No. 61255 on 3/1/63, No. 61110 on 22/12/64, 'K1' No. 62028 on 17/3/65, No. 61326 in June 1965, and No. 61306 on 19/7/66. The 'B1' class engines were often diagrammed into Liverpool on Healey Mills freights.

Among the smallest newcomers to Edge Hill in the early 1960s was ex-LMS 'Dock Tank' No. 47166, which was at the depot on 3 February 1963 after being transferred from the just-closed Bidston depot. It was subsequently employed on the shed shunt at 8A.

Lime Street in the 1950s and 1960s was always a good location to watch the trains come and go. Even during its quieter moments chances were a 'Jinty' tank would be fussing about the station. In this Good Friday (31 March) 1961, scene No. 47519 backs on to the empty stock from the 1010 hrs ex Euston watched by a small group of train-spotters.

Michael Mensing

On 14 December 1962 Queen Elizabeth II visited Merseyside and as befitted the occasion 'Duchess' Pacific No. 46220 *Coronation* was selected to power the train for part of its journey. The Royal Train is seen here passing Edge Hill shed.

John Corkill

Although essentially a diesel turn by May 1963, the 'Merseyside Express' from Lime Street to London Euston still occasionally reverted to steam power. For the Rugby League Cup Final on 11 May 1963, however, 'Black 5' No. 44897 arrived at Euston complete with that headboard fixed to its smokebox door. Five weeks earlier, on 3 April, a pair of 'Black 5s' were in charge of the 1500 hrs Liverpool–Newcastle train after a 'Peak' class diesel failed before the working. On the same day 'Jubilee' No. 45646 *Napier* was observed working a Newcastle–Liverpool train.

By 1963 the turns southwards 'beneath the wires' for Edge Hill's 'Duchesses' became rarer, so it was a matter of some comment when on 6 August 1963 a 'resplendent maroon-liveried No. 46243 *City of Lancaster*' arrived at Crewe with the Liverpool to Cardiff passenger train.

In early 1964 Edge Hill's 'Duchess' Pacifics also found unaccustomed work, rostered to power the 1900 hrs St Helens–Carlisle fast freight, a turn which previously had rarely seen this class so employed.

By late August 1965, 'Jubilee' No. 45633 *Aden*, which had been stored at Edge Hill for some time, was noted inside the southern end of the shed minus its tender. Meanwhile, classmate No. 45627 *Sierra Leone* of Bank Hall, which would become the last 'Jubilee' in service on the London Midland, worked the 1400 hrs Glasgow–Manchester passenger train on 21 August 1965.

Fowler's short wheelbase 2F tank engines were more popular at Birkenhead than Edge Hill shed. However, by 1961 one of the class, No. 47166, had been drafted to Edge Hill for shed shunting. It was eventually withdrawn to the period ending 18 May 1963.

Ken Fairey

Edge Hill's 'Duchess' Pacifics found a variety of work during their last months in traffic, including some tasks for which they were not designed. They were sometimes grimy and a little worse for wear, but they never suffered the indignity of running nameless while in traffic. Here maroon-liveried No. 46243 *City of Lancaster* prepares to back onto the 1900 hrs St Helens–Carlisle Upperby freight in August 1964. Regrettably, this engine missed out on being preserved – it was cut up at the nearby Wigan Wagon Works. The fact that the engine was without a tender (not an insurmountable obstacle by today's preservation rescues) and the size of the scrap price being asked, combined to dissuade one interested young doctor from securing its purchase from the scrap merchant.

Gerald Drought

'Britannia' Pacifics still found their way into Edge Hill regularly, right up to late 1967. Regular workings included freights to and from Carlisle and occasional outings on passenger turns usually between Liverpool and Crewe and return. However, on 5 June 1965 'Britannia' Pacific No. 70033 *Charles Dickens* found itself at the head of the 0945 hrs Liverpool Lime Street to Bournemouth West, and was recorded in the railway press of the time as having worked the train throughout.

The southern end of 8A's 'old' shed was used as a collection point for engines awaiting despatch to various scrapyards. Caprotti valve geared 'Black 5s' would share the lines with rusting 'Jinty' tanks or Stanier 8Fs – and the engines were often from depots subordinate to Edge Hill. In this view, taken on 29 December 1965, 'Jubilee' No. 45633 *Aden* of Warrington Dallam (nearest the camera) and classmate No. 45698 *Mars* of Bank Hall await their fate. *Aden* had been stored at 8A for about twelve months before it was eventually condemned, never returning to Dallam, while *Mars*, by contrast, had been a frequent (and much loved by some photographers) performer on Liverpool Exchange–Glasgow expresses during the summer of 1965. *Mars* had a long-running association with Bank Hall, having been based there from at least the late 1940s to its withdrawal – on the same date as *Aden* – 6 November 1965. It has again been paired with a Fowler tender, its Stanier tender no doubt being saved for a needy 'Black 5'.

John Corkill

On 18 April 1966 the Southport–London passenger services, which were a preserve of steam between Southport and Lime Street and usually in the hands of a Stanier '4' 2–6–4T, were axed. Typically the 1505 hrs Southport Chapel Street train would work to Lime Street, where the train would join the consist of the 1620 hrs to Euston. The Southport–London service reached Lime Street via Bootle Junction and Edge Hill No. 5 box. From 18 April this steam service was replaced by diesel multiple units connecting with the newly introduced electric services from Lime Street to the capital.

However, football fan 'specials' continued to see steam step into the breach on passenger duty. On 23 April 1966 seven Stanier 'Black 5s' were used to haul specials out of Liverpool to Bolton for an FA Cup football semi-final. Engines used for the trains were drawn from Edge Hill, Bank Hall and Speke depots and included Nos 44659, 44806, 45034, 45147, 45228 and 45412.

An example of how the railways wasted money in the final years of steam. On 2 June 1965 Warrington
Dallam's 'Jubilee' No. 45590 *Travancore* waits outside 'The Camp' at Edge Hill for repairs. The photographer
recalls that special authorization was obtained to carry out major boiler repairs on this locomotive. Edge
Hill's craftsmen did an excellent job on No. 45590, the engine returning to Dallam in pristine condition.
However, by December the engine was withdrawn from traffic, surplus to needs. The Stanier 8F raising
steam beside *Travancore* is No. 48462.

John Corkill

Early in May, because of a labour dispute at Allerton traction depot, a number of local
Liverpool passenger services to Manchester, St Helens and Wigan also reverted to steam
power after many years being multiple unit workings. One of the engines rostered for
uncustomary passenger workings was Ivatt '2' No. 41286 (from Sutton Oak) which
worked several Lime Street–Wigan North Western turns, among them the 1845 hrs, ex-
Wigan North Western.

On 1 July 1966 Edge Hill's named 'Black 5', No. 45156 *Ayrshire Yeomanry*, was on
similarly unusual duties when it worked the 0700 hrs Liverpool Lime Street–Manchester
Exchange, a working which for many years had been a diesel multiple unit turn.

Railway enthusiast specials also provided steam for extra duties, as on 22 October 1966
when former Festival of Britain Exhibition locomotive No. 70004 *William Shakespeare*

was used as power for the Liverpool University Public Transport Society's 'Wirral and Mersey' railtour.

By the end of 1966 the number of steam passenger workings rostered from Edge Hill shed was quite small and usually involved only such special workings. However, the 1100 hrs Liverpool–Newcastle express again reverted to steam on 27 December 1966 when Stanier 'Black 5' No. 44772 was in charge of the train as far as Leeds City. The turn was clearly a tall order for the engine, however, which left Manchester Exchange nearly 30 minutes late, and then had to be assisted at the rear as far as Miles Platting by Standard '5' No. 73045.

On 19 July 1967 one of the last three 'Jubilee' class 4–6–0s in traffic, No. 45697 *Achilles* of Leeds Holbeck shed, arrived at Crewe from Liverpool with a parcels train. On 22 August Edge Hill's wandering No. 45284 turned up on the 1400 hrs Manchester Central–Nottingham Midland train. The engine returned to Manchester on the 1645 hrs train, taking water at Derby. The 'Black 5' was reportedly the first steam engine to be seen at Nottingham Midland in more than twelve months.

By November 1967 the abolition of steam power on passenger trains was almost complete, with only a handful of regular steam turns surviving. One of the few rosters remaining included the Sundays 2338 hrs Lime Street–Leeds train, which was usually worked by a Patricroft-based 'Class 5'.

Patricroft's Standard 5MT No. 73067 awaits its next turn of duty at Edge Hill on 3 March 1968. In late 1967 (and possibly into early 1968) one of BR's final passenger turns still entrusted to steam was the 2338 hrs Liverpool Lime Street–Leeds train, which was booked for a Patricroft Standard 5MT. The makeshift numberplate and hand painted shed code on the smokebox door of No. 73067 atest to the activities of souvenir hunters in the final months of steam on BR. The engine was withdrawn later in the month.

Charles Hibbert

CONDITIONS ON SHED

John Corkill, who was a fitter at Edge Hill from the early 1960s right through to the end of steam there in May 1968, is very conscious of the primitive working conditions which he endured at the shed in comparison to facilities at modern depots such as Allerton.

Money for improvements had not been spent at Edge Hill for years by the 1960s, and I think that was true of most of the steam sheds. Considering the amount of activity going on at Edge Hill and surrounding railway operations there were very few complaints about noise or smoke levels from the public. The worst time for smoke was the early hours of Monday mornings, when the trip engines were being lit up in the running shed.

The atmosphere was quite intolerable and in my view totally unnecessary. For a modest sum I am sure air lines could have been installed around the running shed area, and some modifications done to the blower ring around the top of engines' blast pipes to accommodate an air line. With the air line coupled up to the locomotive and air line on, the smoke would be lifted clear of the working area.

Having said that, the atmosphere in the shed was equally intolerable when there were two or three English Electric Type 4 (Class 40) diesels running up. One's eyes would be quite sore and you would have to get out into the open air for relief. The air everywhere would be a thick blue haze, unlike the steam loco smoke which tended to hang around.

Yes, there was a lot that could have been improved upon. Smokebox cleaning, ashpan cleaning – better methods could have been adopted. I am sure if steam had been allowed to continue beyond 1968, these and other improvements would have had to have been made.

COUNTDOWN TO THE FINAL CURTAIN

John Corkill recorded the following work carried out on engines at Edge Hill during the final month of steam there.

The following is a key to abbreviations used: WOE – boiler washout and examination; P7, P3 – seven- to nine-week examination (P7) or three- to five-week examination (P3). These exams would entail changing gauge glasses, waterways to be rodded, injectors stripped and rebuilt, boiler blowdown examined; M2, M6, M8 – No. 2 mileage exam, No. 6 mileage exam, No. 8 mileage exam; SV – safety valves tested against a master gauge; TK – tank cleaning and internal exam of tank float and water sieve (usually carried out approximately half-yearly); BI – boiler inspector examinations; BM – boilermaker repairs; TC – top clack examination.

Saturday 6 April 1968:
44877   For P7 examination, top clack exam and repairs. Ready 11/4/68.
48433   Waiting shops.

Sunday and Monday 7 and 8 April 1968:
48752   For BM, WOE P3, M4 and BI. Ready 8/4/68.
48722   For WOE P7, four springs renewed on engine. Ready 11/4/68.
44777   For WOE P7 BI.

Tuesday 9 April 1968:
48433   Withdrawn from service.
45305   For WOE P3.

Wednesday 10 April 1968:
48308   For WOE P7.
45287   For WOE P7. Ready 16/4/68.
48206   From Speke Junction for tubes leaking. Ready 10/4/68.
44926   Tender being robbed for 48722. Ready 16/4/68.

Thursday 11 April 1968:
48308   Waiting shops.
48687   For WOE P7 SV, TC. Ready 16/4/68.

Friday and Saturday 12 and 13 April 1968:
48665   For WOE P3, TC. Ready 17/4/68.
44864   For tubes leaking.
48308   Withdrawn from traffic.

Sunday and Monday 14 and 15 April 1968:
44864   Also found to have defective piston valve, now awaiting a decision.

Tuesday 16 April 1968:
44926   Withdrawn from traffic.

Wednesday 17 April 1968:
44926, 48308 All motion from both cut up and loaded (into tenders).

Thursday 18 April 1968:
48293   For WOE P7, M8. Ready 19/4/68.
45187   For WOE P3, TK. Ready 19/4/68.
48692   For WOE P7. Ready 19/4/68.

Friday 19 April 1968:
48715   For WOE P7, M6. Ready 22/4/68.
44950   Safety valves changed. Ready 23/4/68.
45386   From Speke Junction, brick arch renewed.

Edge Hill shed in the dying months of steam. On 3 March 1968 Stanier 'Black 5s' Nos 45282 and 44864 await their next duty, both appearing to be a little the worse for wear. No. 44864 was a Speke Junction engine by 1960 but was transferred to Edge Hill in July 1963. It was a frequent performer on goods and special passenger trains out of Liverpool. The other engine, No. 45282, was a latecomer to Edge Hill, having only been based there three months when this view was captured on film. Both engines were withdrawn to the period ending 18 May 1968.

Charles Hibbert

Saturday 20 to Monday 22 April 1968:
As per 19/4/68.

Tuesday 23 April 1968:
48746   Failed at 0620 hrs – lead plugs. Ready late on 23/4/68.
45055   For WOE P7, element tubes leaking. Ready 26/4/68.

Wednesday 24 April 1968:
48529   For WOE P7.

Edge Hill's Stanier 8F No. 48746 awaits its next turn of duty outside 'The Camp' on 3 March 1968, while a footplateman makes his way to the office to book off. This engine is listed in John Corkill's shed notes as failing at 0620 hrs with lead plugs on 23 April 1968, although the engine was trafficable again later the same day. It was listed on 1 May 1968 in the shed repair schedule for a boiler washout and examination, plus a seven- to nine-week examination. The work was not carried out and the engine was transferred to Newton Heath (Manchester) shed upon Edge Hill's closure in May, where its serviceable life lasted barely a month.

Charles Hibbert

Thursday 25 April 1968:
48467   For WOE P3, SV. Ready 26/4/68.
48168   From Heaton Mersey, lead plugs leaking. Ready late on 25/4/68.

Friday 26 April 1968:
45231   For WOE P3. Ready 29/4/68.
48665   For WOE P7, BI. Ready 29/4/68.

Saturday 27 April 1968:
44713   Arrived on shed with the left leading tender axlebox hot.
         Home light engine to Lostock Hall (10D) at reduced speed.

Sunday and Monday 28 and 29 April 1968:
48614   Waiting shops.
48294   For WOE P7, SV, TC. Ready 30/4/68.

Tuesday 30 April 1968:
As per 29/4/68.

Wednesday 1 May 1968:
48374   For WOE P7, M2. Ready 2/5/68.
48746   For WOE P7 (not started).
45287   For tubes leaking, brick arch repairs.

Thursday 2 May 1968:
48614   Withdrawn from service.
48722   Large tube burst.

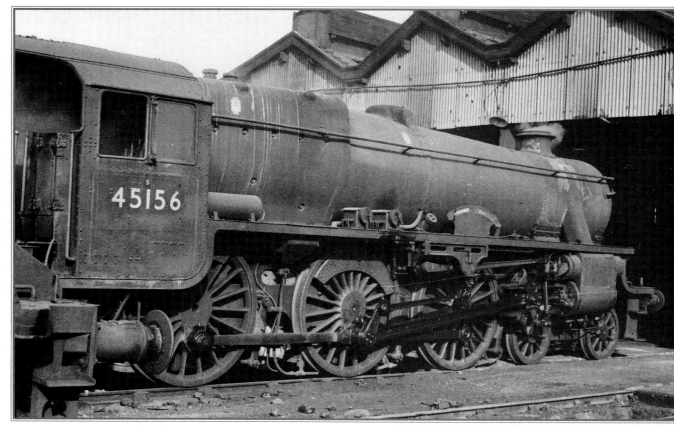

Edge Hill's celebrated sole 'namer' by early 1968 was 'Black 5' No. 45156 *Ayrshire Yeomanry*, which clearly had not long had its fire lit in this portrait, taken on 3 March 1968. This engine was withdrawn virtually at the end of British Railways' steam, succumbing on 10 August 1968. Following Edge Hill's closure in May 1968, the engine was transferred to Patricroft depot and when that depot shut, it was reallocated to Rose Grove shed. The unkempt condition of the engine was in contrast to its appearance in the final months, when it was frequently turned out in spotless condition.

Charles Hibbert

Friday 3 May 1968:
44867   Water gauge packing nuts blowing.

Saturday and Sunday 4 and 5 May 1968:
No repairs carried out.

THE END

On Saturday 4 May 1968, the last day of regular steam at Edge Hill, the following engines were recorded at the depot by John Corkill:

In working order: Nos 44777, 44877, 45156, 45231, 45284, 45287, 48045, 48056, 48168, 48293, 48374, 48467, 48529, 48665, 48692, 48715, 48741, 48752.

Also on shed but condemned: Nos 44711, 44864, 44926, 45376, 48012, 48308, 48433, 48614, 48722.

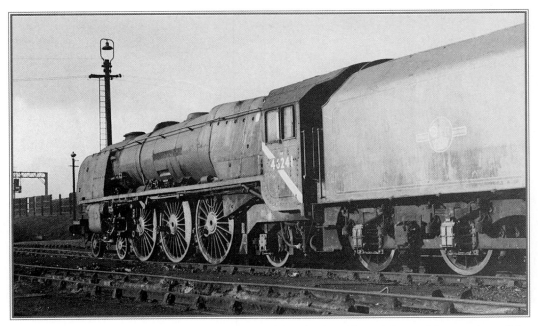

The summer of 1964 was the last for Stanier's renowned 'Duchess' Pacifics and the surviving members of the class were retired from service by the end of September. Edge Hill's remaining pair of 'Duchesses', Nos 46241/43 were shunted into the shelter of the 'old' shed, where their name and numberplates were removed and rods disconnected to make movement to the scrapyard less bothersome. On 27 November 1964 green-liveried No. 46241 *City of Edinburgh* awaits its final trip.

John Corkill

All serviceable engines left the depot the following day for surviving steam sheds including Lostock Hall and Patricroft, and Edge Hill was closed to steam from Monday 6 May 1968.

Among the survivors was 'Black 5', No. 45156 *Ayrshire Yeomanry*, which was reported to be in 'immaculate condition' acting as station pilot at Manchester Exchange during June 1968. This locomotive remained in traffic up to, and including 4 August 1968 – the final day of 'regular' standard gauge steam on British Railways – and, indeed, was earmarked for preservation by a local municipal authority. However, the preservation plans sadly fell through and one of Edge Hill's most popular 'Black 5s' was soon afterwards despatched to the scrapyard.

The final hurrah on Merseyside, of course, came just a week after No. 45156's last day in service with the infamous '21 guinea' special of 11 August 1968 over the Liverpool to Carlisle route. 'Black 5' No. 45110 was used to work the train from Lime Street to Manchester, from where 'Britannia' Pacific No. 70013, *Oliver Cromwell*, took over for the section to Carlisle.

Engine No. 45110 worked the return train from Manchester to Lime Street, after sister engines Nos 44781 and 44871 had brought in the train from Carlisle. By the time No. 45110 eased BR's final steam train into Lime Street's buffer stops, Edge Hill of course was an empty cavern – all of the condemned steam engines had been dragged to the scrapyards.

The very last Stanier Pacific to visit Edge Hill shed. In September 1980 Stanier 'Duchess' No. 46229 *Duchess of Hamilton* backs towards the shed to be serviced before heading the Liverpool–Manchester anniversary special. It was most fitting that one of Edge Hill's most illustrious allocations to have cheated the scrapper's torch should return 'home' after seventeen years' absence for one last time. In so doing the 'Duchess' almost certainly earned the distinction of being the last steam engine to be serviced at Edge Hill. What a shame an 8A shed code (instead of 5A Crewe North) could not have been affixed to the smokebox door of No. 46229 for that very special day!

Melvin Thorley

8C SPEKE JUNCTION

Together with Edge Hill, Speke Junction, which lay beside the Liverpool–Crewe main line, witnessed the final servicing of regular steam workings on Merseyside. Primarily a freight locomotive depot, it also retained in the 1960s a small allocation of passenger engines – following the closure of Brunswick shed, when it assumed responsibility for providing motive power for Manchester trains out of Liverpool Central High Level.

Speke was opened on 10 May 1886 by the London and North Western Railway. It had twelve covered tracks and at its height could accommodate nearly seventy engines. Situated in the triangle of the Allerton to Garston Docks and Ditton Junction lines, Speke's engines serviced the nearby yards, as well as long distance freight turns.

The depot was largely unchanged until after the Second World War, although office facilities were extended in 1923. By 1947 the LMS was still preparing layouts to include mechanical coaling facilities for the shed. Five years later, however, the work had only progressed as far as the sinking of trial bore holes to check the requirements for foundations.

Originally serviced by a traditional brick-built LNWR manual coaling stage with overhead water tower, Speke finally received its mechanical coaling plant and a new sand drying plant in 1955. Two years later diesel fuel tanks were installed for the increasing numbers of diesel shunters that were being drafted to the shed.

Speke was allocated the shed code number 35 under the LNWR and was often referred to as Garston shed by railwaymen. Such was its importance that it eventually became a district shed with nearby Widnes, allocated the code 35W, becoming a sub-shed. Speke was assigned the code 8C by the LMS and retained that designation until its closure on 6 May 1968. The shed was demolished a short time after closure and the entire site cleared.

I recall Speke as a depot that was a considerable distance out of town, closer to Widnes than Liverpool. Like most busy railway installations, the depot was not the place for youngsters to wander around unsupervised. However, during one illicit visit in 1965, a kindly railwayman, upon discovering our party of intruders loose in the shed, befriended us and provided an unofficial guided tour of the depot.

As well as showing us around the entire depot, our 'guide' provided us with yard rides in a couple of the diesel shunters which were based at the depot and finished off our visit with a good-natured sermon on the dangers of walking around busy steam sheds, before presenting us with surplus smokebox shed plates from the depot's stores. Such was the hospitality of one Speke railwayman!

A general view of Speke Junction shed just two months before it closed. To the left, distant, Stanier 'Black 5' No. 45349 leads a row of condemned classmates, and for some unknown reason has had a hole cut in its tender side.

Charles Hibbert

BANANA BOATS AND 'ROYAL SCOTS'

Frank Mason, who spent nearly forty-nine years working at Speke Junction between 1923 and 1971, recalls the atmosphere at this busy depot immediately before, and during, the Second World War:

> Just before the war up to 100 engines would congregate at weekends. Two long ash pits and a coal stage above line height were in action all through each night, particularly when banana boats were in dock.
> Oncoming engines could turn on our own triangle. The coal stage beneath the 'shed tank', containing 100,000 gallons of water, was a grim, dripping, smoky hell – especially for the shovelling coalmen: and to shunt coal wagons up its incline (between other engine movements and in bad weather) was hazardous.
> A large mess-room with brick floors, long scrubbed tables, a huge fireplace, kitchen kettle and wooden forms were our comfort. A sand furnace and great buckets to fill six sandboxes on each engine required great strength.

During the Second World War the Liverpool docks were the focus of imports both to keep domestic demand under control and to feed the war effort. As the imports of commodities such as timber, ore and bananas dried up during the war, many miles of nearby sidings became available for manufactured goods from English centres for transportation to Carlisle and Scotland, for the ship convoys to Russia. Mr Mason remembers:

We had eighteen trains per day going out to Carlisle and a larger number coming in from the south. All of these had to be shunted correctly for their Scottish destinations. Obviously, engines coming in (from the south) could also take trains onward to Scotland. This did not suit our trainmen who were really under pressure. Fireboxes were dirty, coal was at the back of the tender and repairs were required.

The inconsistent nature of the steam engine – accentuated during wartime when maintenance standards were hard to sustain – created some very hard shifts for footplatemen, as Mr Mason recollects fifty years after the event:

One engine that I was firing on the Carlisle jobs in wartime had an easily remembered number, 5678 (*De Robeck*), but was better remembered as a water cart and a bad steamer. I suspect she had a main steam pipe joint blowing in the smokebox or at the superheater pipe joints; she certainly put many firemen in a wretched condition.

Footplate crews had to contend with a range of variables – poor quality coal, the vagaries of signal checks, inclement weather, poorly steaming engines which were overdue for heavy repairs. Add to these the difficulties posed by the personalities of some of the men with whom they had to work, it was little wonder that crews thought they had won the jackpot when they had had a good day on the footplate. Frank Mason:

The longer, regular trips with your own mate, the likelihood of a sound engine, with decent coal and no delays, shunting and uncertainties – one good day turn in three weeks was a luxury.

A good day might include a suitable starting time, a good mate, the engine number correctly indicated and berthed [at the shed], a well-tooled, clean footplate, then all preparations going well. Then you'd need the train ready, a pleasant guard and ground staff; the engine responds well, weather favourable. Usually only 50 per cent of these portents were positive. If 60 per cent were negative – you'd had it, chum!

Mr Mason also highlights the difference in attitude between the men at Speke, and those at the 'A' shed – Edge Hill. The men at Edge Hill were referred to as 'Scousers' or 'Wackers', brought up in the bustle of the big city, prone to dominate and proud of their express passenger trains. But Mr Mason said they were mostly good men of principle.

Bill Walker, who spent some time at Speke Junction in 1960 as part of his Motive Power Improver's training course, obtaining first-hand experience of the depot's operations, found the staff most friendly, and alive to an emerging cultural phenomenon.

Liverpool at the beginning of 1960 was a very lively city; there were many musical groups similar to The Beatles. Many people on the railway were involved in these groups and I recall someone who was playing in a musical group and who left the railway at the time to play full-time with the group.

One incident occurred while I was at Speke, involving the banana trains which used to work from there. The bananas were loaded into heated vans and sometimes they would be ripe by the time they arrived from overseas. If so, they would be loaded into open wagons so they could be dumped. These wagons were stored in a yard at the back of Speke shed. Rather than have the bananas dumped, they would unofficially be shared out among the men in the shed.

A banana train special – from Garston Dock to Camden yard – provided a former Edge Hill driver, Charles Ebsworth, with his first main line firing turn, shortly before the Second World War. For this job he travelled from Edge Hill to Speke as a passenger on a train, where he then collected and prepared his engine for the trip to Crewe and London. On this occasion the engine, which of necessity had to be steam-heated in order to warm the vans, turned out to be 'Royal Scot' No. 6100 *Royal Scot* itself:

It was quite exciting to act as fireman on one of our top class locos, even to Crewe. About one month later the same situation occurred again, but there was no relief at Crewe, so I worked the train through to Camden yard.

War Department 'Austerities' were not a regular feature at Speke Junction – most of the engines of this type on Merseyside were based at either Aintree or, in the 1950s, at Birkenhead. However, 'Austerities' did work into Merseyside on freights from the Eastern and North Eastern Regions as had Mirfield's No. 90593 in this view at Speke shed on 27 March 1957.

J. A. Peden

For the return job, Mr Ebsworth was provided with a Warrington 'Black 5', No. 5252: 'I did well myself, worked home from Willesden coupled to the 'Sunny-South Express' (ex-Brighton) with No. 5527 *Southport*, an Edge Hill loco.'

INTO THE 1960S AT SPEKE

By the end of the 1950s Speke Junction shed had an allocation of only thirty-three locomotives, sixteen less than its allocation in 1950. Apart from a pair of 'Crab' Moguls (Nos 42849 and 42892), the bulk of the shed's allocation was made up of Stanier 8F engines, of which nine were based there, and fourteen ex-LNWR/LMS 7F 0–8–0s. Six 'Jinty' tanks were also shedded at Speke and one of them, No. 47388, had been based at the depot since at least November 1945 and would remain there until October 1962 when it was transferred away.

While Bill Walker was based at Speke he attended one of the consultation meetings to discuss crews' attitudes to the new responsibilities that had been given to the depot. Seven new jobs had been assigned to Speke as part of the dieselization railcar inter-city program. Mr Walker noted in his 1960 diary:

> The men were satisfied with them but there was some disagreement about where they would go on the links. The men wanted them split up among steam jobs so as to make two mixed links and have these following the special link in progression. All the men in the special link are railcar-trained at the moment and this would alleviate some of the training.
>
> The thing that kept creeping in was the fact that Brunswick men would be arriving at the shed at any time [in fact, this occurred in 1961] and so the trained men could go up or down according to seniority.
>
> The management side wanted a new senior link made entirely of the new jobs. The men stated that there were men in the senior link who should go forward into this new link but that they would decline because they did not want to learn anything new at their time of life.
>
> A suggestion was made that Mr Clears should see them and try to persuade them to be trained. The new jobs had four Sundays out of eight working and this might be an incentive for them to go forward to the new links.
>
> The staff side are holding a meeting this coming Sunday to get a mandate from the men on what they want. Training was the thing worrying staff and management.

Speke men travelled far and wide on goods trains, some duties necessitating men to stay over at enginemen's barracks before returning to Liverpool. Frank Mason's opinion of the barracks where Speke men would stay on lodging turns was mixed: 'The BR barracks at Carlisle and Preston were fair but many others were private lodgings and ranged from fair to poor – some were operated by widows who were poorly paid for their services.'

Following the closure of Brunswick shed in September 1961, many of that shed's engines and their rosters were transferred to Speke, including the 1652 hrs from Liverpool Central to Manchester Central non-stop, which was timed for forty minutes

Speke Junction shed on 19 May 1957, with 'Jinty' tank No. 47651 heading a very clean ex-L&YR Aspinall 3F dating from 1889, No. 52232 and another tank engine. The Stanier 8F to the left of the 'Jinty', No. 48017, found its way to Birkenhead in the mid-1960s, then Aintree, and then, for a short time, Edge Hill before withdrawal in late 1967.

J.A. Peden

start-to-stop over the 37 miles. As a result, a batch of passenger locomotives were drafted to Speke to work services between Liverpool Central and Manchester Central. These included Nos 42077, 42078, 42183, 42186, 42445, 42580, 42584, 42598 and 42612. Other engines followed in 1962.

Other new arrivals at Speke in late 1961 were an allocation of Caprotti valve-geared 'Black 5s' which generally were not greeted very well. Ken Carson, who worked as a fitter at Speke Junction from September 1961 until the shed's closure in May 1968, said these engines were generally in poor condition by the time they reached Speke: 'These locos (mechanically) were in a very bad state and most of them were withdrawn by 1963 or 1964. One of them, No. 44741, went to Crewe works for a light overhaul and was returned and put into store.'

Speke also retained some of the smallest steam engines surviving on British railways – the ex-L&YR Pug saddletanks built in the late nineteenth century. By November 1962, Speke's Pug No. 51253 was one of only four examples of this class still remaining in service. This engine was transferred from Bank Hall depot, where it had been in store, in

One of the Caprotti valve gear fitted 'Black 5s', No. 44750, allocated to Speke in the early 1960s. These engines had been transferred to Merseyside from the Bristol area and, by reports, were in poor mechanical condition when they arrived and were unpopular with Speke men. This engine arrived at Speke in November 1961 and was (at least on paper) transferred briefly to Stoke in August 1962. Returned to Speke, it was condemned by September the following year.

John Corkill

June 1962, and would spend just thirteen months at Speke – mainly shunting nearby goods yards – before being placed back in store in February 1963 and eventually withdrawn in July 1963. The other survivors of this ancient class of dock tanks comprised Nos 51218 (at Bristol) and 51232 and 51237 at Agecroft.

In November 1963 Speke received an allocation of three 'Jubilee' class 4–6–0s, a type of engine not previously based at the shed. The engines were transferred to Speke primarily to work Ford car trains. However, Ken Carson recalls these engines also being rostered on the 0758 hrs Liverpool Central–Manchester Central, along with 'Royal Scot' No. 46115 *Scots Guardsman*, which was based in Manchester. Other trains that kept the 'Jubilees' occupied included the perennial banana specials bound for most areas of the country and fast fitted freights.

Clive Boardman, who was a fireman at Speke in the 1960s, remembers Speke's 'Jubilees' regularly working evening goods services to Ford's distribution depot at Bathgate, near Glasgow. The engines also worked over the Pennines to Leeds as well as a Saturday afternoon only working to Godley, the steam-electric changeover point on the ex-Great Central Woodhead route to Sheffield:

I remember arriving at Preston one night with a northbound working, and being told to relieve a train of empty carflats from Bathgate, bound for Halewood. The motive power was a Type 2 diesel but as my driver, Billy Fisher, was not diesel trained, we were instructed to commandeer 'Jubilee' No. 45556 *Nova Scotia*, which was en route to its home depot at Crewe North and was waiting in the sidings for a path.

At best its condition could only be described as deplorable − filthy dirty and cocooned permanently in a cloud of steam. Billy described it with some accuracy as 'one of Crewe's old sores'. The train consisted of some twenty-plus carflats (more or less the chassis of a standard bogie coach with chocks and straps to keep the vehicles in place) and blowing the brake off this lengthy consist took an age.

We were turned out on the fast line from Preston and the steam gauge began to drop on the climb to Wigan. It was a dark night and, enveloped in swirling steam and fully preoccupied with events on the footplate, I had neither reason nor inclination to look out.

However, I concluded . . . from the din on the footplate that we were going fairly fast until, that is, a 'Britannia' Pacific on a parcels working appeared alongside on the slow line, its fireman shouting some garbled jibe at us across the intervening Down fast line as he passed. They overhauled us quite rapidly and soon disappeared up ahead.

From Wigan, *Nova Scotia* laboured up to Garswood, then via St Helens, Clock Face and Widnes to Halewood where we halted outside the Down slow while an arrival road was made available for us. Releasing the brake and getting this long train inside [Ford's] took another geological aeon!

During his time spent at Walton shed, Mr Boardman recalls 'Jubilees' occasionally popping up on the Long Meg–Widnes anhydrite workings − a turn that inevitably came back to Speke:

I can vividly remember relieving the return working at Amberswood, Wigan, one morning when the engine was Carlisle Kingmoor's No. 45605 *Cyprus*, immaculate and doubtless stepping in after the failure of the usual [Stanier] class '8'. The sound of the exhaust as this 800-plus ton train was lifted from Sankey station up to Widnes East Junction on the old Cheshire Lines had to be heard to be believed!

Like many enthusiasts, a lot of railwaymen regarded the 'Jubilees' as being among the most handsome of engines built by the LMS. In good condition they could be relied upon to give good performance but, despite this, many footplatemen saw them as little more than a 'Black 5'. One Speke driver, Kenny Anderson, summed up the 'Jubilees' as 'good engines, but they burn a lot of coal'. Fellow Speke driver Dick Jones said that when working an eleven-coach train to London his preference was always a 'Black 5' over a 'Jubilee'.

Clive Boardman remembers the 'tricky' start away from stopping at nearby Runcorn − the line rising on a steep gradient − when working a three-cylinder engine such as a 'Jubilee' which had stopped with its valves in the blind position:

Steam raising at Speke Junction shed on 17 June
1967 with a brace of Stanier's finest.

J.A. Peden

The odds were that a 'Black 5' would be passing Halton Junction while the more
powerful 'Jubilee' would still be messing around at Runcorn station. The ['Jubilee']
engine would stand in full forward gear with regulator open and steam oozing from
every joint and gland, but no movement. The time-honoured way out of this was to
reverse and then, as the engine moved, quickly drop the gear into forward again,
which would jolt the pistons and hopefully start the train. This was okay at Runcorn
but it could be a chancy business at other locations if there were catch points under the
train and some drivers were understandably reluctant to try it.

By 1964, work for Speke's 'Jubilees' was becoming harder to find and in May No.
45571 *South Africa* was officially withdrawn. The other two of this class, No. 45663 *Jervis*
and No. 45664 *Nelson*, were transferred to Warrington Dallam in July.
   In May 1964 the nearby shed at Widnes closed resulting in the transfer of three Ivatt 2
Moguls to Speke, Nos 46410, 46423 and 46424. These were joined by green liveried ex-
Western Region members Nos 46503, 46515, 46516 and 46518 during 1965, together
with an ex-Western Region '8F' No. 48493. Speke also received its first allocation of
Standard 9Fs that year when engine Nos 92020, 92054, 92084, 92089, 92111, 92115
and 92158 were all drafted to the shed. These were joined in 1965 by Nos 92008,
92025, 92027, 92091, 92117, 92153 and 92228.

Ken Carson recalls that, of the 1965 influx of these engines, No. 92091, which had recently been shopped from the workshops, was 'the most powerful out of the batch'. Frank Mason was highly complimentary about these heavy freight locomotives which were so much more economical on water than other engines to which he was accustomed. He remembers: 'I had some experience of a new traffic with these engines, returning empty hopper trains to Blackburn for the mineral anhydrite for treatment at Widnes.'

KEEPING THEM IN TRAFFIC – A FITTER'S TALE

Following the closure of Widnes shed in 1964, freight turns from that town came under the control of Speke Junction, including the 'Long Megs', the anhydrite traffic between Carlisle and Widnes. Ken Carson recalls the heavy toll this traffic could place on engines: 'The weight of this train – and the fact it was downhill all the way to Widnes – meant that the engines would come on shed at Speke minus engine brake blocks. This happened every trip down from Carlisle – ten brake blocks!'

Speke's Standard 9Fs also found employment on heavy freight trains from Shell's Falwood sidings (near St Michaels) and 'Dingle Jetty' to Holywell, Preston and Salford power station. The Holywell tank trains were so heavy they went double-headed with two 9Fs. Ken Carson said the Standards were also rostered to work Ford car trains to Bathgate, Scotland.

On one memorable day in 1967, No. 92138 blew a boiler seam, leaking 'fountains of water' everywhere. The locomotive was examined and found to be beyond economical repair and so, with the end of steam imminent, the engine was condemned.

Of engines visiting from other sheds that were serviced at Speke, Mr Carson rated those from Heaton Mersey as being the worst and they soon gained the title of 'wrecks'. In the main, these engines were 'badly maintained' 8Fs and Ivatt 4s. If much work was required on these locos they would be sent back light to Heaton Mersey. Towards the end of steam at Speke Junction some of the engines became a little worse for wear, according to Mr George Crossland, who was a chargehand boilermaker at the shed from 1961 to 1968: 'By the 1960s, engines were rather run down. Before this they were in good condition – as engines were prepared for scrapping, all serviceable spare parts were kept for remaining locos.'

Parts that would be cannibalized from condemned engines for use in other engines included exhaust injectors and cab gear, including jets, injectors, gauge frames and so on.

Mr Crossland said that once Crewe Works had completed its last general overhaul of a steam locomotive in February 1967, it influenced the decisions made by sheds such as Speke about whether or not to repair engines. If the fault was not repairable by the shed or Edge Hill the engine was, in most cases, condemned.

During the period 1965/66 a handful of Speke engines were despatched to workshops in England and Scotland to receive what turned out to be final general overhauls. Mr Carson remembers Nos 45386, 45388 and 48493 being sent to Crewe Works, with Nos 44732, 44950 and 45332 being despatched to Cowlairs in Scotland for a full job. Two 8Fs (Nos 48711 and 48722) also received overhauls at Darlington and were returned coupled to 3,500 gallon capacity tenders. Mr Carson:

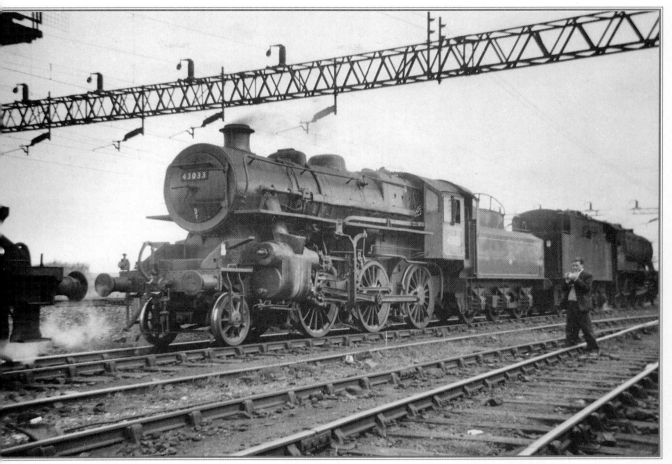

One of the Ivatt 4MTs that sometimes found their way to Speke from Heaton Mersey (Stockport) shed. Former Speke fitter Ken Carson said 'poorly maintained' engines from Heaton Mersey gained a reputation for often being 'wrecks' and, if too much work was required on them, they would be despatched home light engine. This view of Ivatt 4MT No. 43033 with an unidentified 'Austerity' was taken in 1965.

Bob Bartlett

No. 48722 had to be connected back to a 4,000 gallon tender after ten months' work carried out at Speke – the tender on this engine was a write-off due to the back foundation of the drag box being in a very rusted condition.

The tender on No. 48711 broke loose after the draw bar split open at the tender ends. The engine was repaired at Speke Junction with new draw gear and put back into traffic.

With age and declining maintenance priorities, it was not unusual by the mid-1960s for tenders on some of the Stanier 'Black 5s' to show signs of wasting due to rust and decay. When this became evident at Speke, tenders were removed from engines with poor boilers and paired with engines considered to have a longer boiler life. Mr Carson recalls engine

Speke Junction in the final years: Stanier 8F No. 48681 stands beside the mechanical coaling stage on 18 February 1967. This plant was finally installed in the mid-1950s as part of a somewhat belated modernization of the depot. Just visible on the left is the original LNWR coaling stage with traditional overhead water tank.

J.M. Tolson

Nos 45441, 45332 and 44877 being among those to have their tenders removed and replaced with those from Nos 45032, 45103 and 45137, which all had 'very bad boiler defects':

At the same time, No. 45181 had an overhaul at Cowlairs Works, No. 44725 was overhauled at Crewe Works – this loco had a steel firebox and was ex-Carlisle Kingmoor – and No. 45466, ex-Perth shed, was also overhauled at Crewe.

Speke Junction also started to become the dumping ground for locos that were beyond overhaul but good enough for spare parts. All unserviceable locos were dumped in Speke Junction 'A' section sidings.

'Black 5' No. 45370, which was ex-Cowlairs [works], arrived at Speke Junction and its tender was found to be in poor condition, so the tender was swapped on this loco with that on engine No. 44738.

Mr Carson also remembers an interesting situation that arose in 1966 when five engines which had received expensive, general overhaul at workshops around the country were stored at Aintree 'after only a month's work' at Speke. The engines involved were 'Black 5s' Nos 44950, 45386, 45388 and 45407, and Stanier 8F No. 48493. Mr Carson explained:

When Aintree closed in June 1967 the five locos were dragged back to Speke Junction in a very bad state because of missing parts.

There was a heavy row between CME management and local management about the condition of these locos and the cost involved [in their overhaul], in particular because the engines had received new boilers.

I . . . had the job of virtually rebuilding Nos 45386, 45388 and 48493 . . . completed by taking parts off other locomotives, and then they were put back into traffic.

The other two engines – Nos 44950 and 45407 – were repaired at Edge Hill, and the latter placed in store at Speke next to the old ex-LNWR coaling stage. Both engines

One of the engines at the centre of a row with management in the mid–1960s, 'Black 5' No. 45407 was given an expensive general overhaul and placed in store about a month after being outshopped. Stored at Aintree, it was incredibly cannibalized for parts, so much so that when it was shifted to Speke after Aintree's closure in June 1967 some stern questions were asked. Ken Carson recalls No. 45407 and another largely ex-works engine, No. 44950, which had been subjected to parts removal, basically having to be 'rebuilt' at Edge Hill. (Ken repaired other equally poorly cared for engines at Speke.) Both engines worked right up to the end of steam and survive today in preservation.

Charles Hibbert

Edge Hill's 'Black 5' No. 45055 raises steam at Speke Junction on 3 March 1968. This engine was withdrawn to the period 10 August 1968 – the penultimate day for steam on British Railways – having survived the closure of Edge Hill and Patricroft, to succumb at Lostock Hall (Preston).

Charles Hibbert

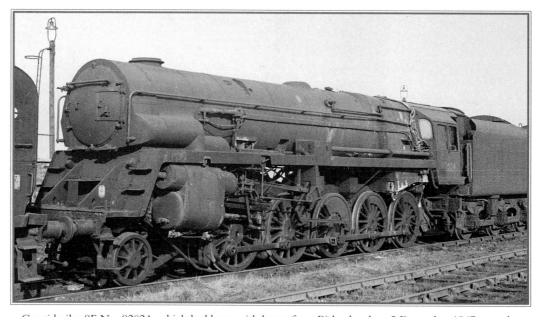

Crosti boiler 9F No. 92024, which had been withdrawn from Birkenhead on 2 December 1967, was also among the engines at Speke awaiting despatch for scrapping.

Charles Hibbert

were subsequently transferred to Lostock Hall shed in April and May 1968, respectively, and survived in traffic until 10 August 1968. Nos 45407 and 44950 were later saved for preservation.

THE FINAL YEARS

In the last four to five years of BR steam hundreds of railtours were organized by enthusiasts' clubs, whose members were keen to see last runs by surviving examples of various classes. Often these tours would bring locomotive types to unfamiliar territory – like 'West Country' Pacifics to Crewe, or a Gresley A4 to the Southern Region. On other occasions, however, the tours provided an opportunity to spruce up a local shed favourite for a brake van jaunt along lines which no longer saw passenger trains.

By March 1968 Speke Junction had become the collection point for engines from several depots that were awaiting, or on their way to, scrapping. 'Britannia' Pacific No. 70024 *Vulcan*, once the pride of some Western Regions crews, awaits its fate on 3 March. The engine had been withdrawn from Carlisle Kingmoor the previous December.

Charles Hibbert

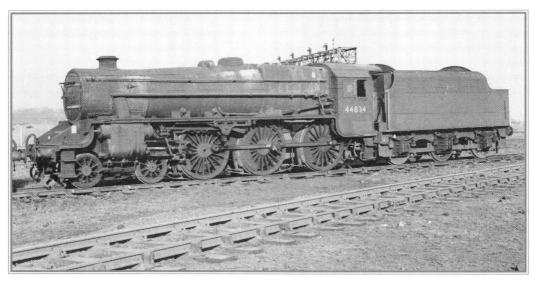

Edge Hill's 'Black 5' No. 44834 awaits its call to the scrap merchant at Speke depot on 3 March 1968. This locomotive had been withdrawn from Edge Hill on 30 December 1967.

Charles Hibbert

So it was that Speke's named 'Black 5', No. 45154 *Lanarkshire Yeomanry*, was chosen for the Railway Correspondence and Travel Society's 'South Lancashire' railtour on 24 September 1966, and was specially cleaned for the trip. Wooden nameplates were also fixed to the engine to replace the cast metal versions which had been removed several years before.

By late 1967 Speke began to be used as a collection point for condemned steam engines awaiting the final call to the scrapyard. On 12 November 1967, for example, there were no less than fifty-one engines dumped in sidings near the depot. Of these most were Standard 9Fs from the recently closed Birkenhead shed, with the remainder being redundant 'Black 5' 4–6–0s and 8F 2–8–0s.

By 19 February 1968 an even starker illustration of the pace of modernization was evident at the shed. On this day, besides the twenty-seven condemned steam locomotives at the depot, there were also thirty-three withdrawn diesel shunters awaiting transfer to Australia.

Ken Carson recalls only four engines being in steam at Speke shed during its last week of operation: Nos 45386, 45388, 48493 and 92160. The 'Black 5s' went to Lostock Hall, Preston, following the closure of Speke, and the 8F to Rose Grove. All three engines were withdrawn on the very last day of BR steam, 10 August 1968. The 9F, No. 92160, had the distinction (with No. 92167) of being the last of its class in traffic when withdrawn from Carnforth during the period ending 13 July 1968.

With the end of steam at Speke, in May 1968, there was certainly some regret at the shed's closure, and the end of an era. Mr Crossland remembers: 'Everybody I knew regretted losing steam; the majority were so familiar with it.'

8E BRUNSWICK

The Liverpool dockland shed of Brunswick was located just off Grafton Street, near Harrington Dock, and comprised a curved, five-track shed, turntable and manual coaling stage. The red brick depot, erected by the Cheshire Lines Committee in 1879, was the third engine shed to be built at Brunswick. The first, a wooden construction built for the Garston and Liverpool Railway around 1864 and probably numbering three lanes, eventually became the property of the Midland Railway and was demolished between 1889 and 1893.

A second three-lane wooden shed was erected by the CLC in 1874 and was entirely let to the Midland four years later. This shed continued to be used by Midland engines, following the opening of the CLC's 'new' brick shed in 1879 and was used by the LMS until its closure in February 1929.

A feature of the final Brunswick shed was the large flight of steps (ninety-two in all) that railwaymen or visitors would have to scale to enter or leave the shed proper. The shed was in a particularly tight location owing to its proximity to the harbour and the site was literally hewn out of the local sandstone. The spoil from the depot area formed the base for the extensive sidings built at Halewood. Because of the restricted site, a decision was taken to build a shed building with curved walls, thereby maximizing the number of engines that could be accommodated under cover. The five tracks within the shed, in pre-grouping times, were alloted 3:2 for Great Central and Midland Railway use.

Brunswick depot was accorded the code '19' by the Midland Railway. It was recoded 13E in 1949 until 22 May 1950, when it became 8E. In February 1958 Brunswick was recoded 27F, effectively coming under the control of Bank Hall, which was the 'A' shed. Brunswick retained this code until its closure on 12 September 1961.

In BR days the shed boasted a mix of ex-LMS, ex-LNER types and, in particular, ex-Great Central Railway locomotives. To assist with maintenance of its locomotives, the shed possessed a set of sheerlegs, a foundry, a blacksmith shop and a lathe for turning various locomotive parts.

Brunswick shed's role was to provide motive power for shunting at the nearby dock area, as well as passenger engines for the hourly passenger services on the Liverpool Central to Manchester Central route and goods engines for the route to Cheadle Heath near Heaton Mersey. Locomotives were also provided for freight services as far afield as Hull and Grimsby.

Halewood West and East were the sorting sidings for freight traffic from Brunswick and Gladstone docks, and for freights to the north, south and east. Departing Brunswick yard, trip engines would take freight for sorting at Halewood. Direct freight from Brunswick yard went to destinations as far away as Whitmoor, Hull, Rowsley and Guide Bridge. Engines also left Brunswick to pick up their trains at Halewood when on outward trips. Freights into Brunswick in the 1950s also included special trains container low-loader vehicles required for transporting narrow-gauge Beyer-Peacock-built Garratts bound for Africa.

Among the many passenger turns covered by Brunswick shed crews and engines were the 0435 hrs Liverpool Central pilot job, the 0505 hrs and 1050 hrs Stockport trains, and the 0545, 0615, 0630, 0712, 0730, 0735, 0758 and 0830 hrs, and then hourly, Manchester Central trains. The non-stop Manchester trains, which travelled via the Warrington viaducts – therefore missing Warrington Central – were scheduled a very tight thirty-seven minutes for the journey. Trains which stopped at Widnes North and Warrington Central were allowed an extra five minutes. In between these services were the 'locals' to Warrington Central and Gateacre.

Walton-on-the-Hill shed also covered trains from Aintree Central to Liverpool Central, with one train working in the morning peak hour and one in the evening. Engines frequently used on these trains included Stanier 4s Nos 42111 and 42112, and Midland 4F No. 44122.

Stanier and Fairburn 4MT tanks were based at Brunswick for working the Liverpool Central–Manchester Central passenger services, a task they performed with commendable ability if the recollections of former drivers are any guide. Timings of under forty minutes for the 35 miles between the two cities called for some very disciplined working. No. 42186, shown here at Brunswick on 10 October 1959, survived the closure of the shed less than two years after this photograph was taken, transferring first to Speke Junction, then Stafford and Aston sheds. It was withdrawn in 1964.

J. Oatway

Before the Second World War, and even shortly afterwards, Brunswick played host to a wide range of LNER locomotives ranging from this ex-Great Central B7 No. 5476, photographed on shed in 1938, right down to the smaller goods engines.

photo: the late G.H. Platt, courtesy Eddie Johnson Collection

Although Brunswick was closed in 1961, remains of the shed building (one side wall) were still standing more than thirty years later. Although I never had the pleasure of visiting Brunswick shed before its closure, I was familiar with the Stanier/Fairburn 4MT tanks from that depot which worked the Manchester Central route and gave Liverpool Central High Level its evocative smoky atmosphere in the late 1950s and early 1960s.

BRUNSWICK DURING AND AFTER THE WAR

One of the footplatemen who fondly recalls life at Brunswick shed in the 1950s is Stan Rimmer, who joined the staff at Edge Hill depot in 1934 and spent two years at Brunswick shed from 1953. While there, he recalls about 150 to 200 men being attached to Brunswick shed. Maintenance staff at the shed included twelve fitters with a similar number of fitter's mates, two boilermakers together with mates, three steam raisers and three men assigned to boiler washout duties.

Mr Rimmer recalls the mix of locos that were typically based at Brunswick in the early 1950s:

The engines we used most were the Stanier Class 4 2–6–4 tanks on the Manchester jobs; the Cheadle jobs were 0–8–0 goods fitted with a steam brake; Class 2 tender engines (4–4–0s), and, now and again, an ex-LNER B1.

Being in the goods links one had to study the working that the foreman would place up and having my route card from Edge Hill, I could work some jobs Brunswick men could not.

Some jobs could start from Brunswick and then branch off to the ex-LMS at Garston. Needless to say, some of the Brunswick men did not like me at the time for they should have been provided with a conductor.

George Crossland, who joined Brunswick in 1943 as an apprentice boilermaker, remembers an amusing incident during the Second World War when men at the shed had reason to curse the long flight of steps which provided access to the depot:

A troop train at Walton required a set of firebars, so we had to send them from Brunswick. The shedmaster confiscated a tram car from Dingle sheds and then every able-bodied man carried the bars up the ninety-two steps to Mill Street to load up the tram. They then proceeded through Liverpool, up Scotland Road to Walton where a traffic policeman stopped the traffic while they were unloaded. The train went out on time.

Tom Lockwood, who began his railway career in the mid-1940s at Frodingham shed (LNER) as a cleaner, spent more than four years as a fireman at Brunswick shed from February 1945, and three years there as a driver from August 1958 until the shed's closure in September 1961. During his first period at Brunswick, he recalls firing for drivers including Dick Lewis, Charlie Nicholas, Ike Kellrick and Fred Billington while working the passenger links. Other drivers remembered from the period 1945 to 1948 include Bob Askew, Bob Snape, Dick McQueen, A.B. Wright, Danny Kellrick (Ike's brother), Jack Nimmo, Jimmy Gray, Jack Jackson, Billy Dumbell and three Book brothers – Bob, Jimmy and Arthur.

During his first stint at Brunswick, Tom Lockwood lodged near the shed and was roused by a knocker-upper named Nes Peterson, assisted by a shed labourer who will remain nameless:

One week on duty at 3.55 a.m. to work the 5.05 a.m. Stockport, Nes was assisted by this shed labourer who knocked at house No. 19 instead of No. 29 (where I was lodging) and also put the time slip through the letter box.

On his arrival back at the shed the labourer informed Nes he had got no reply at No. 19 and was told of his mistake. He returned to knock me up, but before doing so he knocked up No. 19 again for the time card instead of writing out a new card. My name was mud at No. 19 and I had to walk the other way to work to avoid embarrassment!

On the eve of Nationalization – 31 December 1947 – Brunswick boasted an allocation of forty-one engines, made up of: a B9 (No. 1470); thirteen D9 4–4–0s (Nos 2302, 2303,

2304, 2306, 2308, 2309, 2315, 2318, 2319, 2321, 2324, 2332 and 2333); two D10s (No. 2653 *Sir Edward Fraser* and No. 2658 *Prince George*); five J11s (Nos 4376, 4405, 4406, 4417, 4420); two J39s (Nos 4714 and 4954); eight J10s (Nos 5126, 5127, 5136, 5144, 5149, 5163 5172, 5182); two F1 2–4–2 tanks (Nos 7099 and 7100); two J67/J69s (Nos 8547 and 8559); and six N5s (Nos 9250, 9258, 9288, 9337, 9339 and 9342).

The F1 tanks were noteworthy, being the last survivors of a class of thirty-nine engines built by Mr T. Parker for the Manchester, Sheffield and Lincolnshire Railway, dating back to 1889. This pair of engines was withdrawn from service by 1949.

Following Nationalization, and especially after 1950, the LNER influence at Brunswick would markedly decline as ex-LMS types began to be drafted to the depot.

Also by the early 1950s, a substantial part of the shed roof had fallen into poor repair, so much so in fact that there was little protection for engines or railwaymen from the elements. In 1956 the building was re-roofed, greatly improving working conditions for the shed staff. During this period the front half of the shed – which was likewise in a fairly poor condition – was demolished, enabling additional disposal pits to be provided for engines coming on shed.

A DAY ON THE FOOTPLATE FROM BRUNSWICK SHED

Working on a steam engine involved considerable preparation by footplate crews, even before an engine left the depot. There was a regime of checking, oiling and greasing numerous working parts of the engine, as well as coaxing a sometimes languid fire to raise steam. Tom Lockwood outlines the daily routine of preparation that preceded an engine's departure from the shed, for example, for a passenger working to Manchester Central, and the method of disposal that was required at the end of a turn of duty.

A crew's day began by booking on duty at the assigned time, checking the late notices and details of the turn they had been rostered to work. Tom Lockwood:

The engine number and location in the shed would be ascertained from the engine board. Next we would proceed to stores to pick up engine tools comprising: bucket containing hand brush, oil feeder and spanners, making sure there was a gauge glass spanner and various large open-ended spanners for opening and closing steam stop valves. Two lamps would also be collected, and gauge lamps for the water gauge frame – these would be filled with paraffin or rape oil for gauge lamp, and the wicks examined. A firing shovel, coal hammer, can of axlebox lubricant and a can of cylinder lubricant would also be collected.

On arrival at the engine you would make sure no other person was working on it. Then, after ensuring the tender handbrake was fully applied, the reversing screw/lever was in mid-gear and the cylinder drain cocks were open, you would test the water in the boiler by closing . . . gauge glass cocks and then open the drain cock.

Next you would make sure all the fire irons were on the tender or tank, i.e. straight dart, bent dart, and that you had a clinker shovel long enough to reach the end of the firebox. You would place a headlamp at each end of the engine, to be lit during the hours of darkness.

A view that evokes the smoky, cramped, sulphurous atmosphere that was Brunswick shed. This photograph, taken on 27 February 1955, depicts Stanier 4MT No. 42466 and Pollitt J10 No. 65182 at the coaling stage. In 1955 the Stanier tank was one of fourteen members of that class based at the harbourside shed, while six other J10s were also based there.

F.W. Shuttleworth

Then you would open the smokebox door and ensure all the ashes had been removed, then close and screw it tight to prevent any leak. You'd ensure the sandboxes had been filled.

If the engine had inside motion, the fireman would – after taking precautions to prevent the engine being moved – climb up and fill all oil wells, including big ends, eccentrics, little ends and slide bars. Some drivers, however, preferred to do this themselves.

The driver would continue to oil the axleboxes, side rods, tender axleboxes and horn cheeks, ensuring that any water that had found its way into the oil wells was removed by using a brass pump, or some drivers used a siphon pipe. Whilst doing the oiling, the driver would examine brake blocks and other working parts, as well as filling the cylinder lubricator. Before coming out from under the engine, the fireman would make sure ashpans were empy and dampers were workable.

Provided there was sufficient steam in the boiler, both water injectors would be tested by the fireman. He would then spread the fire and build it up with coal, raising the boiler pressure to the required level. He would ensure fire irons were secure on the rack and that coal was stacked safe, preventing any falling off. If the water tank required filling the engine would be moved to the water column and its tank filled.

After wiping down the faceplate and brushing up the footplate, the vacuum ejectors, sanders, carriage warmer equipment and brakes would be tested.

Using water in the bucket from the slacker pipe on the injector, hands would be washed and then the most important task – making a can of tea – was begun, the tea being placed on the warming plate.

The time allowed for engine preparation was forty-five minutes to one hour – according to the engine's grate area.

At the booked 'off shed' time, the crew would ring out and, when signalled, proceed to Liverpool Central where they were coupled to their train by the station's shunter.

The driver would ensure this had been done correctly – that is, coupling screwed tight, vacuum brake pipes coupled, also carriage warming pipes connected and cocks opened during the warming period.

Following consultation between driver and guard as to the length of train, weight and any special instructions, the driver would test the continuous brake and the fireman would open the carriage warming valve. He would then ensure that the fire was in good condition and steam pressure was near maximum, and water level was at a high level.

The journey to Manchester Central would then proceed and hopefully, barring signal checks and any other incidents, a reasonable schedule was kept. 'On approaching Manchester Central the carriage warming valve would be closed to ensure that the 40 lb/sq. inch would be lost before arrival – thus preventing the shunter being scalded when uncoupling the engine from the train,' Mr Lockwood recalls.

After turning their engine, filling the tender or tank with water and removing any built-up clinker from the fire, the crew might snatch enough time to grab a sandwich and a drink of tea before heading their train back to Liverpool Central. 'If there was sufficient time the sandwich would be toasted on a cleaned shovel, or better still bacon and eggs was cooked on the shovel before moving to the train for the return journey,' Mr Lockwood said.

Of course, at journey's end, crews did not simply deliver their engine to the depot. There were disposal duties to attend to before their day's work was complete. After reporting to the shed foreman, upon arrival on shed, the crew would position their engine over the disposal pit where the hard work would continue, as Mr Lockwood recounts:

The fireman – having run down the fire from Liverpool – would open the smokebox door and empty the ashes, then close the door tight, after noting whether any leaks existed in the smokebox. Some (ex-Great Central) D9s had smokebox ash ejectors, which were used during the journey.

The sandboxes would be filled by the fireman with dry sand and he would then proceed to clean the fire using a long clinker shovel to move good fire to one side of the firebox, and break up clinker underneath, withdrawing this with a long shovel and throwing it out on the pit side. The good fire would then be moved back to the cleaned side and the clinker from the other side thrown out.

He would then examine the brick arch (inside the firebox) and also the tubeplates for leaks, then build up the fire to stand, at the same time filling the boiler. This done, he would then proceed under the engine and rake out the ashpans.

The dampers would be closed and, in the meantime, the driver would have examined the engine for any defects. Before returning all tools, lamps and so on to the stores the crew would confirm that the handbrake was applied, the reversing lever/screw was in mid-gear, and the cylinder drain cocks were open.

The driver would book any known defects, complete the driver's ticket and both would book off duty after confirming their next turn of duty.

THE FINAL YEARS – 1954 TO 1961

Ken Carson, who joined Brunswick shed in June 1956 as an apprentice fitter, and remained there until the shed's closure in September 1961, recalls there always being a wide range of 'foreign' engines at the shed. These included ex-LNER, B1s, K2 and K3 Moguls, J37 and J39s, L1 tanks, D10 and D11s, as well as ex-Great Central and ex-LNER 01s and 04s.

Two Robinson O4 2–8–0s inside Brunswick shed on 27 February 1955, No. 63721 (of Gorton shed, Manchester) and No. 63739, which appears to have collected two tenders in its travels! Because of the tight location in which Brunswick was situated, the shed had a slight curve thus maximizing the number of engines that could be stabled.

F.W. Shuttleworth

Ex-LNER J39 engines were also regularly seen around Liverpool while Brunswick shed was operational, even though not formally based there. On this grey autumn day, 10 October 1959, No. 64738 releases a whisper of steam from its safety valves as it awaits its call to duty. The shed roof, which was virtually non-existent by 1955, has by now been repaired and reclad.

J. Oatway

In fact, it was a J39 that provided the most memorable incident during Ken's time at Brunswick. In the late 1950s, one of this class had 'taken off' apparently of its own free will, from the coaling plant and on to the turntable. The engine struck the nearby wall, rebounding back on to the turntable before dropping one pair of its tender wheels into the turntable pit!

Mr Carson also recalls, in particular, a specific Fowler 4F 0–6–0, No. 44587:

This loco was large for its class; you could not compare this loco with any other 4F on Brunswick depot. It was fitted with a high-sided 3,500 gallon tender to suit the loco. The side rods were of plain and robust steel in contrast to its sister 4Fs, which had fluted side rods. The axleboxes on this loco were fitted with removable tyres under keeps. No. 44587 was a very powerful 4F loco for passenger and freight work and was transferred to Trafford Park shed when Brunswick closed in 1961.

Railwaymen could be a superstitious bunch and many are the tales handed down about 'jinx' engines that seem to have had more than their share of misfortune. Mr Carson spoke of one Stanier '5', No. 45333, as being in this category:

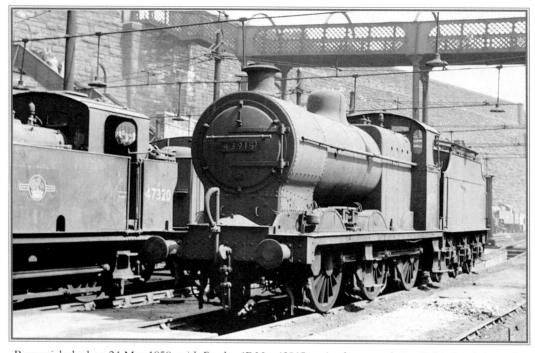

Brunswick shed on 24 May 1959, with Fowler 4F No. 43915 resting between duties. Behind and above the engine is the pedestrian access bridge to the shed and some of the ninety-two steps railwaymen had to negotiate coming on, or going off shed. 'Midland' 4Fs were not common at Brunswick until the late 1950s as the shed had ex-LNER goods types based there until then. However, by 1959 Brunswick was home to ten of these goods engines of either LMS or Midland Railway lineage.

J.A. Peden

This loco had a bad name amongst crews who worked her. It was involved in a mishap at Tanhouse level-crossing, Widnes, cutting a van in two and killing three people. Every time this loco left the depot, it seemed some mishap or damage would occur. The loco was eventually transferred to Wellington shed and Brunswick received No. 45262 in its place, and thus we had no more problems.

Two incidents of quite alarming potential – had they occurred at other locations – were recalled from 1957. In the first, Fowler 2–6–4T No. 42352 lost its left-hand side crosshead gudgin pin, resulting in its connecting rod buckling while the engine was working a local passenger train. The rod was eventually driven through its side tank, although, alarmingly, as Mr Carson points out, parts of the rod were also found at Mersey Road station. Thankfully nobody was injured. The engine was repaired at Derby Works and returned to traffic at Trafford Park (Manchester) later in the year.

The second incident, again involving a Fowler tank, this time No. 42349, resulted in the engine buckling a connecting rod through cylinder back pressure, requiring its despatch also to Derby for repairs.

Inside Brunswick shed on 24 May 1959, and ex-LMS designs predominate with one of the depot's four 'Black 5s', No. 45262, stabled alongside Fowler 4F No. 44489. With the departure of the ex-LNER J10 and J11 classes from the Liverpool shed in the late 1950s, an influx of Fowler 4Fs began to fill in their predecessor's duties.

J.A. Peden

Of course, it was not only steam engines that were causing heartache for the motive power authorities by the late 1950s. The newly introduced main line diesels were tried out on various ex-Great Central routes and one of the first intrusions of these diesels into the Liverpool area came in late 1958/early 1959, when 'Peak' class diesels made a foray onto Merseyside – only to beat a swift and embarrassing retreat. Mr Carson:

In 1958/59 the first diesel-hauled passenger train was worked between Derby and Liverpool Central and it failed a couple of times. It was put on Brunswick shed and shipped back to Derby, never to be seen again on that route.

Despite the inglorious performance of main line diesels on Merseyside, diesel multiple units began to take over many of the local services that had until then been steam powered. However, the prestige turns out of Liverpool Central in the 1950s remained the noon departure to Hook of Holland and late afternoon trains to Nottingham and Derby.

Mr Lockwood recalls Brunswick shed having up to 28 passenger turns, 20 freight turns including trip workings and 20 shunt turns – including passenger shunts – and eight shed shunt and disposal/preparation turns. The goods turns included trip work to Halewood, Wavertree and Warrington. Mr Lockwood said:

Fifty per cent of our freight work was coal from Yorkshire for shipment via Herculaneum Dock. We worked on local trip and shunting duties between Brunswick, Halewood, Warrington and Wavertree with (ex-)LNER J10s and N5 tanks.

We also had main line freight trains between Brunswick and Dewsnap sidings (Guide Bridge). The link included shed disposal and preparation turns too.

I moved into the passenger links after about six months, enjoying express work between Liverpool Central and Manchester Central, also stopping trains between Liverpool Central, Manchester, Stockport and Southport Lord Street.

Mr Lockwood recalls the engines used on these services included various classes of ex-Great Central 4–4–0s, and, when there was an engine shortage, J10s and N5s.

Mr George Crossland, who was a chargehand boilermaker at Brunswick shed from 1954 to 1961, said maintenance staff at Brunswick had an affinity for working on ex-LNER types, which still made up a good proportion of engines there in the 1950s. He regarded the British Railways' Standard designs, which began appearing at the depot in

A very smoky and evocative overview of Brunswick shed in 1957 with O4 No. 63743, J10 No. 65147 and behind it Stanier 'Crab' No. 42929. This view illustrates quite starkly the cramped nature of Brunswick shed.

J.A. Peden

A wintry scene at Brunswick shed in February 1955, with the depot's 'Jinty' tank No. 47566 in company with Gorton's K3 No. 61832.

F.W. Shuttleworth

the early 1960s, as 'no improvement' on pre-Nationalization classes and, in fact, felt they were generally disliked by Brunswick staff.

Individual locomotives of any class, however, could provide problems for crews in the days of steam, and like most footplatemen from that era, Mr Lockwood still shudders at some 'rough trips' he had with certain engines – with poor quality coal or poorly steaming locomotives caused by a variety of factors. Some ex-LNER J10s were quite reluctant steamers on occasions and so it should come as little surprise that, while he was at Chester Northgate prior to February 1945, Tom came across an 'illegal device' used by some men to make these beasts steam.

A metal rod was jammed under the blower pipe ring, across the centre of the blast pipe, which had the effect of splitting the blast, thus creating a greater vacuum in the smokebox so drawing more air through the firebox. The device was called a 'Jimmy' and quite a few drivers carried one with them. Mr Lockwood recollects:

One of the worst rostered turns I had at Brunswick as a fireman was a Saturday-only turn booking on around 6.35 a.m. and working with a D9 on a stopping train from Liverpool all stations to Stockport Tiviot Dale. Then all stations back to Warrington, all stations back to Stockport and finally all stations back to Liverpool, excepting Otterspool, St Michaels and St James.

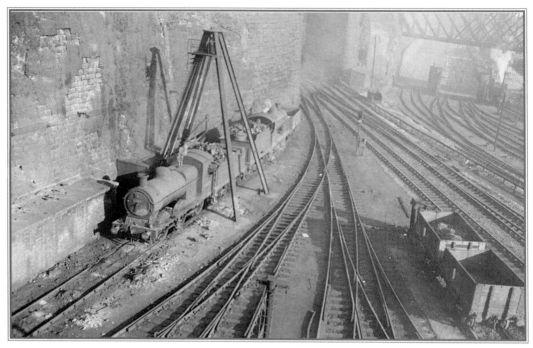

Ex-LNER J11 No. 64405 and an unidentified engine under Brunswick's sheerlegs, September 1957. The huge rock wall gives a clear indication of the volume of spoil that had to be removed from the area to establish the depot site. Immediately behind the engines is the 1,078 yard long Dingle tunnel. Away to the right are the coal sidings leading to the Herculaneum coal tips.

J.A. Peden

It necessitated working tender-first for half the turn and as the tender tops were flat with only a coal shute down to footplate, about 4 feet by 3 feet, I had to shovel coal towards this shute at available opportunities towards the end of the turn. Whilst working tender-first, it was a good thing some of the wartime blackout sheets were still fitted to engines. If my memory serves me right we stopped at around forty-five stations, arriving back at Liverpool at 1.15 p.m.

After completing this turn, then carrying my cycle up ninety-two steps and cycling 7 miles home, a visit to Anfield football ground to see Liverpool was out!

When Mr Lockwood returned to Brunswick shed in August 1958 he was immediately placed in the junior shunt and shed disposal link:

Due to loss of work at the depot I was displaced from the link being a junior driver and became a put back driver. A put back driver retained his rate of pay and was utilized to cover vacancies created by other men being on annual leave or sick. This I found very enjoyable as I covered work in the passenger links. By this time the

Stanier 2–6–4 tanks were being used on these turns, which I found were excellent engines, doing the job with ease.

Preparation and disposal duties were made much easier owing to the outside Walschaerts valve gear, axlebox mechanical lubrication and cylinder mechanical lubricators, also rocker grates, drop ashpans and self-cleaning smokeboxes.

This enabled some turns doing two return trips to Manchester and engines being prepared and disposed of by shed crews.

Mr Lockwood said that while at Brunswick as a put back driver he sometimes worked an additional afternoon turn involving working tanker trains from Brunswick yard using Standard 9Fs.

By the late 1950s – with the slow but relentless influx of 350 hp diesel shunters and the introduction of diesel multiple units on previously steam rostered turns – it became obvious to many men that Brunswick shed's days were numbered. By 1959, Brunswick shed boasted only thirty-two permanent engine allocations – all of them of ex-LMS background. The allocation included 9 Stanier/Fairburn class 4 tanks, 8 ex-LMS 4F 0–6–0s, and 4 Stanier 'Black 5s'. Mr Lockwood is of the opinion that '. . . most men accepted the closure as inevitable and those transferred to Liverpool Central seemed fairly satisfied to book on and off there, rather than booking on at Brunswick and travelling to Liverpool Central for diesel multiple unit work.'

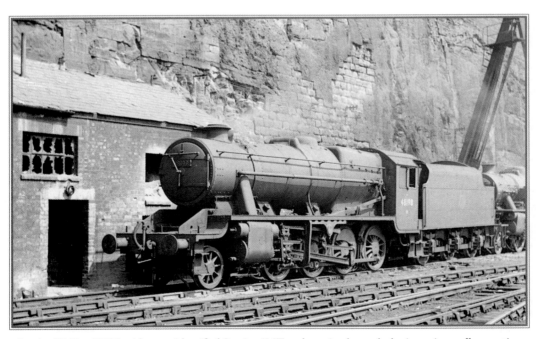

Stanier 8F No. 48198 with an unidentified Stanier 4MT tank engine beneath the imposing wall separating the shed level from Grafton Street. This view was taken on 24 May 1959.

J.A. Peden

With its proximity to Liverpool's docklands it was natural that Brunswick shed should have an allocation of small tank engines for shunting. In the late 1940s ex-LNER types predominated but all that had changed within a decade, and 'Jinty' tank No. 47325 signifies the 'Midlandizing' of the depot that occurred during the 1950s. This photograph was taken on 10 October 1959.

J. Oatway

Brunswick 'Black 5' No. 45346 stands in light steam outside the depot, also on 10 October 1959. The engine bears the 27F shedcode, which the depot assumed in February 1958 and retained until its closure in September 1961. By 1959 Brunswick had four 'Black 5s' allocated for goods or passenger duties. This contrasted with a single 'Black 5' based there in 1950.

J. Oatway

Eventually, the long expected closure of Brunswick occurred in September 1961, and Mr Carson, who was at the shed on the final day, noted the transfer of thirty engines to neighbouring depots as men and machines went on to new surroundings. The engines were as follows:

40127	40203	to Aintree	45217	47320	to Carlisle Kingmoor
			47325		to Edge Hill
42349	42596	}			
42352	43915	}	47228	47327	to Walton-on-the-
42445	44293	} to Trafford Park			Hill
42448	44489	}			
42579	44587	}	42491	44127	}
			42580	44232	}
42949		to Stockport Edgeley	42584	44396	} to Speke Junction
			42598	44494	}
45346		to Saltley	42612	47367	}
			44015		

8H BIRKENHEAD

To the visiting locospotter in the mid-1960s, Birkenhead shed presented a breathtaking sight. Lying beneath the gaze of the almost mandatory gasworks tower, the depot sometimes boasted up to seventy engines 'on shed' on a Sunday afternoon. By 1966 nearly half of these would be Standard Class 9Fs for working the Shotton steelworks trains. Sharing the engine stalls would be an unusual (by the mid-1960s) mix of Fairburn 2–6–4Ts, 'Jinty' tanks and the last English survivors of Hughes/Fowlers' 'Crab' class 2–6–0s. Ten years earlier the scene was markedly different, with ex-Great Western Railway engines sharing the tracks with a wide assortment of ex-LMS and even ex-LNWR locomotives of varying vintages.

Birkenhead locomotive shed was opened by the London & North Western and Great Western Railways in 1878 and closed to steam on 6 November 1967. The large sixteen-lane shed (eight lanes for each railway) was sited on the end of a short spur on the west side of the Birkenhead–Chester line about ¾ mile south of Birkenhead Woodside station, at the end of Mollington Street.

The GWR portion of the depot was built with a northlight pattern roof while the LNWR side had a pitched roof with a raised vent over each of its eight roads. Birkenhead shed was re-roofed in 1938. It came under the direction of the London Midland Region of British Railways in 1951. The shed had a permanent allocation of ex-GWR engines, as well as ex-LMS types until the late 1950s. In 1951 the ex-LNWR portion of the shed was cut back by 110 feet and in the mid-1950s the depot was modernized and new mechanical coaling equipment was installed.

After the end of steam the depot continued to serve as a diesel depot and later for the storage and stripping of old Merseyrail electric units. Notwithstanding this, it provided many enthusiasts with an evocative reminder of the days of steam, until it finally closed to all motive power on 25 November 1985.

During the 1950s, Birkenhead shed maintained six links with twelve crews allocated to each. Number one link covered all the top passenger trains rostered for Birkenhead engines, number two covered goods and one passenger train, number three was mixed goods and passenger, as were number four and five links. The sixth link was reserved for all shunting turns in Birkenhead's extensive dockland area.

At the time of Nationalization, Mr Jack Buckley, who was a fireman at the shed until 1958, recalls there having been approximately ten links at the newly merged LMS/GWR depot, employing about 260 staff. Of these, around 100 were drivers, with a similar number of firemen. About a dozen men were classed as fitting staff, about ten were cleaners, with a similar number of labourers and general staff. Other staff included about eight clerical staff and another eighteen staff classed as coalmen, fire droppers or oil storemen.

POSTWAR BIRKENHEAD: 'SAINTS', 'STUPID DS' AND 'AUSTERITIES'

Dennis L. Williams joined Birkenhead in June 1946 as a GWR engine cleaner, starting the same day as six other youngsters. Mr Williams recalls:

The Foreman Cleaner was Jack Draper, and he was a driver recovering from a serious operation, and had been given the job as light duties. He was a driver who had come up the hard way and he wanted us to do the same, or so we used to think. He used to issue us with cotton waste and the cleaning oil and scrapers — if scrapers were required — and allot us our tasks for the first period of the day.

The number of engines to be cleaned would vary daily, depending on how many cleaners were available (some might go out on firing fill-ins) and how many Birkenhead engines were on shed. As Mr Williams states: 'We did not clean what were known as "foreigners", or engines from other sheds.'

Mr Williams also recollects that at this time the passenger engines based at Birkenhead included ten 41XX class 2–6–2Ts (Nos 4120–4129) and a solitary 31XX prairie tank, No. 3169:

The 41XXs all had a driver of their own, or the first ten drivers in the top passenger link had a loco and two had to share. These were the engines Jack Draper concentrated on mostly, to see that they were up to his standard of cleaning, which was high.

In 1946 there were also two 'Grange' class locos, No. 6819 *Highnam Grange* and No. 6878 *Longford Grange*, stationed at Birkenhead and these were usually employed on the night freight jobs to Oxley (Wolverhampton) or Bordesley Junction, Birmingham. If you were allocated a 'Grange' to clean by yourself you were allowed eight hours to complete the job; if there were two of you, you only got four hours, and so on.

Boys will be boys . . . and as you can imagine the cleaners at Birkenhead were no different and they used to get up to all sorts of tricks, much to Jack Draper's annoyance.

He used to penalize us by booking us off duty and making us work an extra half-hour for nothing. This sort of thing didn't fit in with my plans so I made up my mind to do my cleaning alone if and when possible, and if one of the 'Granges' was on shed I used to ask Jack if I could have it on my own, to which he usually agreed.

After nearly four months of cleaning, Mr Williams was told one morning to book off, go home and get some rest, and book on again at 10 p.m. that night to fire for a driver named Oscar Bedwin on a shunting engine at Western Yard, Morpeth Dock. Mr Williams was 'over the moon' about this unexpected promotion and so excited that he got little sleep before booking on again at the shed. Later, he and Oscar walked down to Western Yard to relieve a crew that was in the middle of assembling the 0245 hrs goods to Oxley (Wolverhampton):

We climbed aboard and they got off almost without any pause in the operation . . . we carried on for an hour or more, at the same time Oscar was trying to keep an eye on me as well as the shunters.

A sister engine of 31XX prairie tank No. 3169, which was based at Birkenhead in the early 1950s, is
No. 3170, pictured here at Newport Ebbw Junction on 31 March 1957.

Industrial Railway Society, Brian Webb Collection

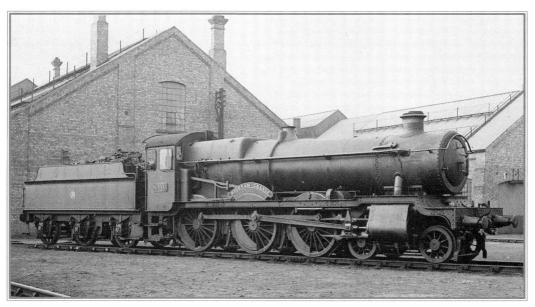

A personal favourite of Dennis Williams was 'Grange' class 4–6–0 No. 6819 *Highnam Grange*, seen here at
Stourbridge in GWR ownership on 12 March 1939. This engine went on to be based at Birkenhead in the
late 1940s and early 1950s and was usually employed on night freights to Oxley or Bordesley Junction.

A.C. Roberts, from J.A. Peden Collection

Eventually there was a break for a meal (scoff, as it was termed) and we carried on later, until it was time for the engine to go to the shed and we booked off duty.

I went feeling rather pleased with my night's effort and very tired – I did not need any rocking to sleep.

Mr Williams never returned to cleaning. The person whose place he had filled had been called up for National Service – a fate that in turn befell Mr Williams, causing a hiatus in his railway service from 6 December 1946 to January 1949.

When he returned to the railway he was told he had been made a fireman and, after going to Swindon for a medical examination and passing, he would be put in the No. 4 link, known as the Relief Link, with some weeks spare and certain jobs of their own. Mr Williams:

My first driver on the main line was Richard (Dick) Jones and . . . in order not to create too much confusion, the chaps on the railway – as in other places of mass employment – were usually numbered or given nicknames.

A general view of 6C (as it was in the 1950s) before Birkenhead came under the control of Edge Hill. In this scene are prairie tank No. 4129 – a class of engine that had its own assigned crews prior to Nationalization – one of the 'Stupid Ds' (ex-LNWR 'Super Ds'), despised so by many Birkenhead men, Stanier 3MTs Nos 40128 (nearest the camera) and 40072, and at far right Stanier 8F No. 48327.

Ken Fairey

As a driver, Dick was one of the best, he looked after his engine and mate. The first week in this main line link we had a night turn to Oswestry (about 45 miles from Birkenhead) and once there we used to go on shed and then have a meal break in the cabin before returning with another freight train to Birkenhead docks.

There were quite a few drivers at Birkenhead who had expressed their unwillingness to take me on a job like the Oswestry as I had only been out of the Army for three weeks and my main line experience was zero. But Dick was not put off.

He said that if I never went out on the main line I would never have the experience, and he told the other drivers that if I could not do it, he could, and so off shed we went and under Dick's expert tuition I learned how to fire an engine. There were more ways than one of doing it, but by watching, listening and actually firing with all sorts of drivers you eventually became good at it. Some of course became better than others – that was one of the failings of a steam engine, they usually proved to be only as good as the men on the footplate.

Mr Williams was with Dick Jones until 1951 when the two adjacent sheds at Birkenhead – ex-GWR and ex-LMS – officially came under the control of the London Midland Region of British Railways. The amalgamation resulted in the crews from both sheds being pooled, together with their engines, and caused considerable upheaval. Apart from drivers having to learn the road to places they had never visited before – and on locomotives with which very few were familiar – some men found conditions quite different to what they were accustomed to and took some time to settle in. Crews had to come to terms with different driving positions (ex-GWR men were used to right-hand drive, ex-LMS men were usually familiar only with left-hand drive) and, because ex-LMS types were made up of many constituent companies, non-standardization of cab fittings and controls caused further disharmony among staff.

Ex-GWR engines were largely standardized and a footplateman could stand on any GWR main line engine, look at the boiler back plate and, really, have a bit of difficulty in telling exactly which class of engine they were on – they were all so similar. Most footplate fittings were the same and were interchangeable, and this was not only the case on the footplate. Boilers, wheels and cylinders were also interchangeable, and on a GWR footplate there was little difficulty locating anything because they were almost identical and in the same place.

Mr Williams was weaned on ex-GWR engines and, as a result, had an affinity with them. However, as with any locomotive the important aspect was the relationship between the driver and fireman. He said:

Some drivers used to look upon you as if to say 'you're only the fireman' while others would look upon you as a mate. After all, you were supposed to be part of a team, and the engine was just a tool to do a job of work with. Sometimes the tools were good for the job and other times they might not be up to it.

Mr Williams' favourite heavy freight locomotive on the GWR road from Birkenhead was Churchward's 28XX class 2–8–0:

Most ex-GWR drivers would tell you that if you could not get one to steam it was time to pack in. They were one of the most reliable engines I have ever been on. I very seldom had any trouble with them and, as far as I was concerned, when I was firing one of my favourite jobs was the 5.50 a.m. Birkenhead to Oxley. On a summer morning, with a good mate, I was in my apple cart.

Sometimes when I was a young fireman, I got a job to Shrewsbury (58 miles) and we were allocated an old Hall class engine or a 43XX class loco.

I was sometimes a bit apprehensive about how the day was going to turn out: would the load be a heavy one, would the engine steam all right and so on? But if I was on a 28XX I was never bothered with thoughts of that nature.

One class of locomotive common at Birkenhead in the 1950s was the ex-War Department 'Austerity' 2–8–0s. Although disliked by some crews because of their somewhat rough and spartan features, the 'Austerities' did find favour with Birkenhead men. While Mr Williams describes them as 'rough and ready' beasts compared to his beloved ex-GWR thoroughbreds, they were not without merit.

We had a job from Manchester to Birkenhead over the old Manchester to Liverpool Railway as far as Earlestown, where we used to divert through Warrington then call at Ellesmere Port, then Birkenhead. The job was called the Victoria West or Vicky West . . . leaving Manchester Victoria West, calling at Ordsall Lane, about 2 miles from the start, where we picked up more freight, then we were right away Ellesmere Port next stop, all being well. It was a bit of a tight timing for a WD 2–8–0.

I remember one night I was firing for Tom Stevens, who was a gent as well as one of the finest men I ever stepped on to a loco with, and we were moving this train at a fair pace across Barton Moss. And Tom looked at me and said 'Listen to the thing, it sounds like an iron foundry gone raving mad'!

Mr Jack Buckley similarly respected the 'Austerities', which he described as 'very good freight workers':

The very first one I went on was with a driver called Joe Gardiner, who is now deceased. We took a freight train from Morpeth Dock to Wrexham. It was my first trip on the main line. Joe told me when to fire and this is how I first worked my train. It was a great thrill to run through stations. I remember thinking that everybody was looking at me.

Mr Williams recalls that the reason the 'Austerities' were tolerated at Birkenhead was that after a crew had spent a week on an ex-LNWR 'Super D' 0–8–0 or an ex-Midland 0–6–0 class 4 standard goods loco, many reckoned that an 'Austerity' 'would do very nicely thank you'.

Mr Buckley concurs with that judgment: 'The worst loco type, I think everybody would agree, was one we called a 'Stupid D'. You had no time to rest, the space in the cab to swing your shovel was limited and you would end up with sore knuckles and you had a seat about six inches square.'

Birkenhead shed also had some customs that were considered unusual by crews from other ex-LMS depots, and certainly by those unfamiliar with GWR practices and industrial conditions.

The fluctuating traffic out of the port sometimes resulted in crews being sent home with their card signed 'NFW' – no further work. If crews had finished their diagram, but not their shift, and there was no prospect of further work they were allowed to go home, and were paid for the remainder of their shift. At most sheds idle crews were kept on the premises until their shift was completed which the crews, of course, found frustrating.

Another practice that used to annoy crews not conversant with GWR regulations was one that allowed ex-GWR men to leave their engines for disposal by shed staff once they had brought their engine on shed near the end of a shift. Mr Williams remembers the antagonism this practice caused at 'foreign' depots:

> If you were an ex-GWR man it was part of your conditions of service that when you brought an engine on the shed you placed it on the ashpit and got off it. There were fire droppers to look after it: they used to empty the firebox, clean the ashpan and empty the smokebox.

Birkenhead on 21 March 1954, and one of the shed's Stanier 3MT tanks awaits its next roster in the company of ex-GWR prairie tank No. 4122. A year after this photograph was taken Birkenhead had ten of these Stanier tanks available for local passenger and empty stock working, although this particular engine had been transferred to Blackpool. Dennis Williams recalls the Stanier 3MT tanks being 'a bit of a worry for crews, as you never knew if you were going to drop a fusible plug' with them!

Ken Fairey

But when an ex-GWR man was firing for an ex-LMS man, and they took it on to a foreign shed, the shed man there would more often than not collar you and say 'dispose it'. Then sometimes all hell would break loose when you informed him that you were an ex-GWR man and then just walked away from it!

There were times, too, when a shed running staff supervisor was acutely short of men and would ring up crews (if they had a telephone) and ask a driver or fireman to come in early and cover another job. Birkenhead men – usually willing to assist, particularly when it worked out to their advantage – also had to be wary, a knock back to some supervisors was remembered by those with very long memories.

One of the frequent turns covered by Birkenhead crews in the early 1950s was a train known by the misnomer of the 'Midnight Passenger' (Chester–Shrewsbury), which by then was often a 'Hall' class working. Mr Williams, however, recalls a rare 1951 meeting with one of a fast disappearing breed – a midnight assignment with a 'Saint'.

The working required crews to book on at Birkenhead shed at 2235 hrs, and after ten minutes for reading notices, they would walk down to Birkenhead Woodside station. The crew would ride as passengers aboard the 2315 hrs semi-stopper to Chester. There they would have enough time for a quick beverage at the Coffee Tavern before working the nine-coach 'Midnight Passenger' standing at Chester's Platform 2, to Shrewsbury. Mr Williams continues:

The train would sometimes have three or four large vans called siphons, which contained baskets of pigeons, and had an engine already backed up and ready to go having been fetched off Chester shed for us.

One night as we were walking along the platform to the front of the train I could see the cylinders protruding from the engine and I said to Dick (Jones), 'It looks like we've got a 'Hall' class.'

He looked at me and said, 'No, it's too high in the frames for a 'Hall', what it might be is a 'Saint'. . . . They have always been known as a fireman's engine.'

We climbed on to the footplate and as my mate was passing the time of day with the Chester men I was looking around and getting my bearings – I had never been on a footplate this high before.

As the Chester men got off, Dick put his hand into his pocket and brought out a piece of string and asked whether I wanted to tie myself on to the footplate!

The 'Midnight Passenger', in fact, departed Chester at 0010 hrs and called at Wrexham, Ruabon, Gobowen and then Shrewsbury, where the Birkenhead men were relieved by Salop men. On this particular night Mr Jones and Mr Williams had 348 tons behind their engine, which was No. 2953 *Titley Court*.

Mr Jones showed his mate how to keep the front of the firebox covered with plenty of coal down the sides, the back corners well filled, and plenty of coal under the firebox door.

At Wrexham the men picked up mailbags from trolleys which were already lined up on the platform, and eventually they were flagged away for Ruabon. The Gobowen to

Shewsbury section was known as the fast stretch because of a fairly straight section of track between Haughton and Baschurch. Mr Williams recounts:

This is where Dick let her rip and as we were approaching Baschurch he said, 'Come over here and look at this' – and there was the speedometer which was reading around 86 mph. Before we knew it we were at Shrewsbury station, about two minutes early, and waiting for our relief to arrive.

While waiting for them, my mate spotted a chap looking at our engine and so we got off and Dick began chatting to him.

He (the stranger) had just got off the train and wanted to know how fast we had been travelling. When Dick told him it was 86 mph the stranger said, 'I would sooner you than me on that thing.'

When the stranger said he was a coal miner from South Wales, Dick turned to me and said, 'It takes all sorts!'

The return diagram for Birkenhead crews working this train in the 1950s was a train known as the 'London Goods', which had left Greenford at 2110 hrs. After arriving at Shrewsbury with the passenger train, the Birkenhead men would walk the ¼ mile to Coton Hill freight yard, where they would have a meal in the locomen's cabin, and await the arrival of the 'London Goods', usually around 0230 hrs.

After the goods had arrived (and after any wagons for Shrewsbury had been removed and any northbound wagons attached), the Birkenhead men would leave Coton Hill around 0255 hrs. They were allowed around seventy-five minutes for the 40 miles run to Chester (Saltney). Then Chester wagons were taken off and the crew would work the final leg into Birkenhead, arriving there about 0530 hrs. Mr Williams, who frequently worked this train in the early 1950s, recalls:

The 9.10 p.m. Paddington had already covered 150 miles by the time we took over at Coton Hill; the fire by then was a bit the worse for wear. One advantage of working the Down London was that no one needed rocking to sleep after that turn!

On the 'Paddy' and the 'Up Meat', Birkenhead men were often relieved by the same Salop men who, in turn, were relieved on the Down London trains. So, if a decent supply of coal had not been pulled forward for the relieving fireman on the Up train, crews could expect the same favour to be returned, later.

Mr Williams recalls Great Western men being issued with a small book of instructions which clearly stated that the crew should 'endeavour always to leave the locomotive in a condition that you would wish to find it'.

The 'London Goods' often had a 47XX class 2–8–0 at its head. These engines used to work back up to London on the 1945 hrs from Morpeth Dock, calling at Chester (Brook Lane) and Coton Hill, where the Birkenhead men used to be relieved by Salop men. They worked the train as far as Banbury; later they would work the train right through from Coton Hill, and the London train back to Shrewsbury the following night.

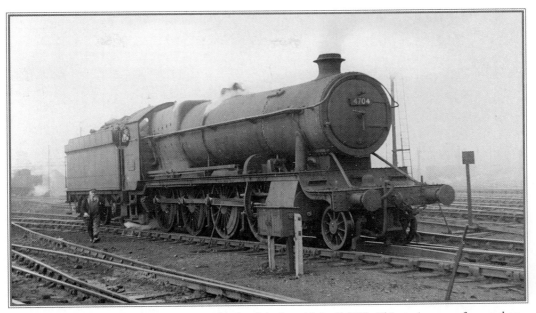

Former Birkenhead 47XX No. 4704 at Birkenhead shed on 10 April 1958. This engine was often used on the 1945 hrs 'London Goods' from Morpeth Dock (see p. 107). The 47XX engines were impressively proportioned freight locomotives that were frequently pressed into passenger duty with much success during summer peak periods.

J.A. Peden

Occasionally, Birkenhead men were given a 'Castle' class to work the 'Midnight Passenger', but this would not necessarily guarantee a good trip. Often the engine had done a trip to Wolverhampton and back before being brought back off Chester shed to work the 12.10 a.m. train. Mr Williams said:

> But I remember one night the engine for the 'Midnight' failed on the shed with a fractured superheater tube and they substituted it with a 'Castle' that had been nowhere that day. It was fresh off the shed – No. 5033 *Broughton Castle* – and she was only about three months out of Swindon works after a heavy general overhaul and was an absolute belter. You only had to show her the shovel and she steamed. It was one of the finest trips that I ever had on that job.

During Mr Williams' time at Birkenhead the shed was staffed by people from all around the country. More common names such as Williams or Jones were often duplicated, resulting in enginemen giving nicknames to one another such as 'Fat Bob', 'Abergavenny Bob' or 'The Miner's Friend' for one driver who was particularly heavy on coal.

The differences between drivers, and their relationship with their rostered firemen, were often marked and, as well as sometimes causing friction, this also led to some on-the-job education in the rights and wrongs of handling an engine. Mr Williams comments:

The Stanier 'Crabs', forty of which were built from 1933, had a strong association with Birkenhead during the 1950s and into the early 1960s. Six of the class were usually based at the shed at any one time, although by the time this view of No. 42970 was taken on 5 April 1959 the allocation had been reduced to a quartet. However, two years later nine members of the class had been drafted to the shed – three more than their historical predecessors, the Hughes-Fowler 'Crabs'. Although business-like engines in their own right, the Stanier 'Crabs' seemed neither to attract the same attention as their forerunners nor to record such spirited passenger running as epitómized by the older 'Crabs' in the final months of the Woodside–Paddington main line steam services.

Ken Fairey

When I dropped down a link at the end of summer, I went driving for a chap called Sam Foster – the first day with him I wondered what had happened . . . going off shed to work the 2.40 p.m. Birkenhead to Paddington. We were on his own engine [ex-GWR 41XX class] 4127 and it had a boiler pressure of 200 lb/sq. inch.

As we backed up at Woodside, Sam pointed at the gauge and remarked to me, 'See that . . . if I have enough steam to blow the brakes off the train I can do my job; I have no desire to hear this thing blowing its head off. All I need is enough fire in the box to generate steam and anywhere around 185 or 190 lb/sq. inch is enough.'

Heading off with the 1440 hrs and going up the bank past Green Lane, Mr Foster was dismayed by Mr Williams' suggestion that he was taking longer than necessary to get to Rock Ferry.

Foster asked Williams if he had any idea of the running time of the train from Woodside to Rock Ferry. Williams said, 'Six minutes', to which Sam Foster replied:

Exactly, and six minutes we are going to take. Oh, I know it can be done in four minutes – but then, more often than not, you need the extra two minutes standing in the station to get your steam and water back, to say nothing of the fire. And I don't want any firing in stations. No, six minutes we are allowed and six minutes is what we are going to take.

Mr Williams recounts that Sam Foster and J.B. Roberts (his earlier driver) were like 'chalk and cheese'. When he was with Sam he used less coal and less water and consequently his job was a 'pushover': 'I learnt the difference between drivers and enginemen – needless to say Sam Foster was a dyed-in-the-wool GWR man and he seldom let anybody forget it.'

Mr Williams contrasts that style of training during the days of steam with what is received by today's railwaymen. In times past it was a case of a man serving his time from, say, cleaner to fireman, fireman to passed fireman, passed fireman to driver, driver to shed boss, shed boss to footplate inspector. Then, if he was lucky, he might even aspire to district operation superintendent. Mr Williams said:

Nowadays you have area managers and assistant area managers and they have possibly attended a managerial course at Watford, or somewhere, and after eighteen months to two years they are expecting to tell you how the railway works.

Visiting Stanier 8F No. 48208 from Heaton Mersey shed moves a pair of dead locomotives around the yard at Birkenhead shed in the mid-1960s.

Roger Jermy

THE 1950S: BORDESLEY JUNCTION TURNS AND A 'NUDE LADY' IN THE CAB

Mr Jack Buckley was a fireman at Birkenhead shed until 1958, having started work at the depot in 1946 as a cleaner with the then Great Western Railway. He left the railways in 1958 amid growing rumours that the depot would soon close. He looks back at his time at Birkenhead with considerable affection, and commented: 'I have only had three jobs since I left school, and the railways was the best. It was very rare that you had a fireman or driver leave. If I could do it again I would do so willingly.'

One of Mr Buckley's favourite turns was the 0630 hrs from Birkenhead Woodside to Paddington.

We would book on at 5 a.m. and get our engine ready, for which we were allowed an hour. Then we'd leave the shed for Woodside station, work the 6.30 a.m. to Chester (and Paddington), stopping at Rock Ferry and Hooton; time allowed, thirty-one minutes.

We would run into No. 3 bay at Chester, hook off, another engine back on, and hook up and take the train on to Shrewsbury via the ex-Great Western line. We would then have our break, another train would run and we would then hook up and work the train to Woodside, stopping at Upton by Chester, Capenhurst and Rock Ferry. The coach shunt engine would then take the coaches (at Woodside) off us and we would return to the shed.

A favourite engine of Mr Buckley's was 'Grange' class 4–6–0 No. 6878 *Longford Grange*, which he remembers as 'an excellent steamer'. 'Grange' class engines were confined to goods workings from Birkenhead and were banned from Woodside station because the cylinder covers fouled the platform sides. Mr Buckley said, 'She would always steam well for me. Some didn't like her because it was extra work and you had to keep on your toes.'

Although no 'Hall' class 4–6–0s were based at Birkenhead in the 1950s they would frequently head fast freights from Shrewsbury into Birkenhead docks.

Of the ex-LMS types based at Birkenhead, Mr Buckley rated the Stanier 'Black 5' and 8F types his favourites: 'The 'Black 5' was a very good LMS engine; easy to fire and would always steam, also the class 8F freight was a good workhorse. The 'Crab' class was also a good steamer but we didn't see many at Birkenhead during my time.'

Another popular goods working was the daily weeknight vacuum fitted freight to Bordesley Junction at Birmingham. Mr Buckley recalls:

The double trip to Bordesley started at the western yard (Morpeth Dock) at 10.40 p.m. Mondays and went via Chester, Wrexham and Ruabon. We would stop at Gobowen to put off and pick up wagons and the next stop was Shrewsbury, again to put off and pick up freight. Then on to Wolverhampton, then through Snow Hill station Birmingham to Bordesley Junction where we finished with the train.

We'd then go on to Tyseley loco sheds, book off and go into the lodge for a sleep. We'd book on again at Tyseley shed, leave at 8.40 p.m. with a full load with the first stop Gobowen to put off freight and the next stop was Birkenhead where we arrived at 4 a.m.

Some of the more distant goods workings sourced from Birkenhead shed in the 1950s included meat trains to Paddington and cattle trains to Carlisle. However, two of the more unusual workings from the shed involved comparatively local trips. As Mr Buckley remembers:

We used to do a ballast train on the Mersey Railway (lines) during the night. We were not allowed on the line until after 11.30 p.m., that's when the electric third rail was supposed to be shut off. This night the signalman let us on early and you can imagine the people's faces when we went through the stations with a steam engine and about four wagons. My mate pulled up at one station and shouted, 'Last train' and then shot off!

Another unusual train Mr Buckley worked was a morning stopping train from Woodside to Liverpool Lime Street via Rock Ferry, Hotton, Helsby, Runcorn and Edge Hill. At Liverpool, Birkenhead crews would get the Mersey Railway electric service back to Birkenhead after being relieved by Edge Hill men. Then Edge Hill men would work the return train back to Birkenhead in the evening.

In the 1950s another 'local' with branch line charm that was worked by Birkenhead crews was the Rock Ferry to West Kirby auto. Mr Buckley recalls this service being worked by two pannier tanks, Nos 6404 and 6405:

We would leave the shed, go over to the carriage sidings at Green Lane and hook up to a special carriage with a draw bar enabling the driver to operate the train from the carriage.

We used to start at Rock Ferry station, pulling the coach calling at Bebington, Port Sunlight, Spital, Bromborough and Hooton. At Hooton we would go on the single line to West Kirby, changing the line staff at Heswall, Caldy and other stations.

When we arrived at West Kirby the driver would leave the loco and sit in the front of the carriage where he could operate the regulator. Most drivers would leave the lot to the fireman – the driving and the firing.

After you had been with a driver for a while he knew you and, if he had confidence in you, he would often let you have a drive. Of course, this didn't apply to all drivers. Some wouldn't let you so much as touch the regulator.

Mr Chris Magner, a railway enthusiast who spent many of his formative years on the Wirral, also recalls the Great Western heritage in this corner of near-Merseyside: 'When I was a child my grandmother used to take me every week on the Hooton–West Kirby line using 14XX class 0–4–2Ts Nos 1417 and 1457. It was a shame this line closed.'

Mr Magner, like many older enthusiasts, remembers the era when ex-GWR 47XX class 2–8–0s worked into Birkenhead, taking out fast evening freights to London. But the real thrill came when a 'Castle' was substituted for a 47XX. Between 1947 and 1951 Birkenhead had its own 47XX class engine allocated. No. 4704 was diagrammed to work the 1945 hrs. Paddington vacuum goods and would return to Birkenhead the following night with the 2110 hrs balancing turn. Mr Williams remembers the 47XX class for its

57XX pannier tank No. 5774 hurries a goods train through Bromborough on 28 May 1958.

J.A. Peden

Not **the** *Titfield Thunderbolt*, nor even the 14XX tank that had a starring role in the 1950s Ealing film classic
of the same name. Nevertheless, someone at Birkenhead shed was sufficiently smitten by the film to bestow
the legend on the smokebox door of No. 1457. This engine was one of a pair based at Birkenhead in the
early 1950s. The date, 13 March 1954.

J.A. Peden

No. 4704 again (see p. 101), this time down at Morpeth Dock preparing to take out a goods train for the south.

J.A. Peden

hazardous cab roof profile. Low at the edges, it presented a problem for any inattentive footplateman nearing 6 feet in height.

On the 1945 hrs goods to Paddington, Birkenhead crews would normally work to Coton Hill, Shrewsbury, where they were then relieved by a local crew. The Birkenhead men would then normally return home as passengers by train through Crewe and Liverpool, and the ferry to Birkenhead.

'Modified Hall' No. 6990 *Witherslack Hall* was also a regular performer on the 1945 hrs Morpeth Dock–Paddington fast freight. Mr Magner recalls that the 1945 hrs Paddington goods (known locally as 'The General') was always a thrilling sight, usually headed by an 81A (Old Oak Common) locomotive – normally either a 47XX 2–8–0 or a 'Hall' (frequently No. 6963 *Throwley Hall* or No. 6990 *Witherslack Hall*) and, on rare occasions, in charge of a 'Castle' class 4–6–0. For some reason (probably due to summer locomotive demands) 'Castles' usually appeared at Birkenhead in the autumn.

'Castles' also worked into Birkenhead each year, up to 1958, on Paddington–Woodside Grand National specials, although the final race specials in 1959 and 1960 were relegated to 'Halls'. The last known recorded appearance of a 'Castle' at Birkenhead was as late as Christmas 1964.

In the late 1950s the 1525 hrs Birkenhead to Smithfield Markets train could produce anything from a wide range of ex-GWR locomotives at its head – often a 'Hall' but sometimes a 'Castle', albeit infrequently.

From the mid-1960s, Birkenhead built up a large allocation of Standard 9F 2–10–0s, which were chiefly employed on Shotton iron ore trains. However, in the 1950s these trains were the domain of Stanier 8F engines. Mr Buckley recalls:

George Sewell, my driver, was the only driver from south shed to know the road to Shotton. We used to collect the iron ore wagons at Bidston, take them to Shotton, then sometimes we would hook up to a coke train at Shotton for Mostyn steelworks and we would run this to Dunham Hill.

Tender-first we'd run around the train and on to Mostyn via Chester, leave the coke there, go to Rhyl to turn and then run light engine back to Birkenhead.

Experience was, of course, something that could not be bought in steam days. Whether learning the road, or the firing technique on a locomotive with a different firegrate to others, or, for that matter, how to nurse a poorly steaming engine up a steep bank, such skills could only be attained with practice and learning from wiser counsel. Mr Williams recalls:

I remember one glaring incident, the salvation of which could only be put down to experience. I was firing for a driver, Bill Boyd (nicknamed 'Hopalong Cassidy', which he did). We were on the 10.40 Bordesley Junction from Birkenhead. When we booked on duty we were met by the chargeman fitter, who spun us a tale of misery about this engine. It was not one of our engines, it belonged to Tyseley. The fitter reeled off the complaints, then topped it with the fact that the engine was eighteen months overdue for the factory.

Bill told the supervisor he'd take the engine on one condition and that was if he got any papers or 'please explains' about lost time, they would all go into the firebox.

We went off the shed down to the Western Yard and picked up our train – about thirty-six wagons – with some heavily loaded vans next to the engine, which was 'Hall' class No. 6901 *Arley Hall*.

I'll never forget it because it was the first time I had ever stopped on Gresford Bank on the run up to Wrexham. We set off from the Western Yard and before we had gone 10 miles I knew that I was going to have quite an evening.

After we had got through Saltney and we were heading for Rossett, at the bottom of Gresford, I knew we would have to stop. As soon as she made a bit of steam it was time to get some water in the boiler. When you put the injector on to top up the boiler the steam just walked back. Then, as we had covered the first mile of the bank 2 miles up at 1 in 82 – we had got some 210 lb/sq. inch and I went to put the injector on.

This is where Bill showed his nous. He told me to leave the injector off and fire the engine again, which I did, then I grabbed for the injector again. Bill said leave it, to which I said, 'We're going to need water in the boiler soon.' Bill replied, 'I don't need you to tell me that.'

Eventually we got to within 10 yards of the top of the bank and when he shut the regulator the boiler water bobbed out of sight (in the gauge glass), which can be critical. Bill opened the regulator again and the water was just visible, but the regulator was not open enough to move the train, so Bill said to me, 'Put the handbrake on the tender, then make your fire up to a good one, then fill your boiler.'

We were there about eight minutes, then I asked what next?

'Now,' Bill said, 'we are going to have a royal start from here: box full, boiler full and safety valves blowing. . . . If you had had your way we would have stopped at Rossett, then when we had got to the top of the bank we would have had to stop again.'

Mr Williams recalls the wide range of men who worked at Birkenhead, originating from places as far afield as Dumfries, Carlisle, Plymouth and Swansea. The range of locomotives that made their way to Mollington Street was equally diverse – all of the ex-GWR types, with the exception of 'Kings' and smaller prairie tanks (44XX and 45XX), and, after Nationalization, a whole range of ex-pregrouping types that had been absorbed by the LMS.

On steam shunts there was a range of ex-Great Western pannier tanks 19XX, 2021, 21XX apart from 57XX, and 96XX; there were also Fowler dock tanks, a few Johnson Midland open-cab tanks, and a few of the 0–4–0 Kitson-type, built for BR. But as one Birkenhead driver recalled: 'If you went over 5 mph on one of them you would get seasick.'

With the extensive docklands near Birkenhead shed it was only natural that the depot would have a large contingent of tank engines for marshalling. During the 'Big Four' era Great Western pannier tanks would rub buffers with LMS 'Jinty' tanks. However, by the late 1950s the latter had the ascendancy. In this view, taken on 19 September 1959, 'Jinty' No. 47497 shifts another 'Jinty' and a Fowler short-wheelbase 'Dock Tank'. On shed in the background can be seen Stanier 3MT No. 40076.

H.C. Casserley

Wolverhampton-built Dean pannier tank No. 2112 awaits its next turn of duty at Birkenhead shed on 20 April 1954. These engines from the 2021 class were originally built, from 1897, as saddle tanks and later converted to pannier style. Until the mid-1950s, Birkenhead had a mix of ex-Great Western Railway tank engines to shunt the docks beside the Mersey. By May 1955, although No. 2112 had been withdrawn from service, nine other members of the class were based at Birkenhead: Nos 2040, 2069, 2072, 2082, 2092, 2101, 2107, 2134, 2160.

R.M. Casserley

Mr Magner remembers ex-North London Railway tanks being based at Birkenhead. In 1950 five of this class were allocated there, Nos 58851/54/57/61/63. The class leader, No. 58850, survives today on the Bluebell Railway, Sussex.

Mr Williams recalls only having worked twice on a Kitson Pug tank, but they were among the engines he would not miss – despite his affection for steam:

We had our share of Fowler class 3 0–6–0 shunting engines, and I have had them on passenger trains over the branch lines to West Kirby and Helsby. Usually, they performed quite well but for my money they did not compare with an ex-GWR 57XX pannier.

The engine that would give a pannier tank a run for its money on branch line work was the Ivatt class 2 2–6–2 tank. They were a bonny little engine – economical and speedy – but it was the screw reverser that let them down when it came to shunting. That is where the pannier used to shine, besides being very sure-footed.

BR-built Kitson design saddle tank No. 47009 at Birkenhead on Sunday 2 June 1957.

Duncan Gomersall

Main line passenger work out of Birkenhead during the early to mid-1950s was chiefly handled by ex-GWR prairie tanks or ex-LMS Stanier 2–6–2 tanks and Fowler or Fairburn 2–6–4 tanks. The Stanier 2–6–2 tanks worried some crews, who often wondered if they might drop a fusible plug.

For a time, too, Birkenhead also had access to some of the newly introduced BR 2–6–4 tanks which had 25 lb/sq. inch higher boiler pressure than their ex-LMS predecessors: handy for quick starts from stations or 'motoring' along on long distances, according to Mr Williams.

I remember firing for a chap named Jack Elcock. One Saturday afternoon we had to relieve a set of men and do two trips to Chester. We relieved a chap called Bill Davies and he told us this was not such a bad engine – the number on it was 80062 and it had a speedometer, which was working. As Bill put it, 'It's not such a bad old sod; it did 77 mph when we went down to Chester.' Jack Elcock just looked at me and said, 'We'll see.'

Eventually we set off for Chester calling at Rock Ferry and Hooton. . . . I was on my toes because I knew Jack Elcock would not be content with 77 mph out of this 'old sod'.

After passing Capenhurst it is all downhill to Chester so I sat down and let Jack do his bit. Just after passing Mollington signal-box Jack shut off steam and set the engine to coasting. Shortly afterwards he drew my attention to the speedometer and it was showing about 82 mph. Jack just looked at me and grinned and said Bill Davies was right, she wasn't a bad old sod.

While many drivers had a sense of humour (and some insisted that it was a prerequisite for the job), it was not, of course, confined to this particular grade. One of the most amusing incidents involved a Birkenhead fireman named Billy Bibby.

Bibby was on a coal empties train to Wrexham and on arrival found his engine had stopped alongside a wagon filled with all sorts of scrap and general rubbish. Also in the wagon was a life-size figure of a woman from a shop window display, clad only in panties and bra. Bibby didn't take long to get this semi-naked dummy onto the footplate where it was given a wash and brush up and from a reasonable distance it looked almost lifelike. Mr Williams remembers the story:

It was about 5 foot 8 inches tall and was standing with one hand on its right hip and the other held aloft. Bibby was able to clasp one of the model's hands and, with his other around its waist, move around the footplate of his Stanier 8F as if he was dancing with a semi-naked woman.

On the return journey Bibby made a point of being seen by the signalmen when passing signal-boxes. Of course, after passing the first box upon leaving Wrexham, it was a physical impossibility to pass any other box unnoticed because the telephone wires were red-hot from box to box: 'Naked woman dancing on the footplate!'

INTO THE 1960s: 'CRABS', 'JINTIES' AND 9FS

The opening of the Vauxhall motor plant at Ellesmere Port in the early 1960s, and the need to operate a daily car body train to Luton, resulted in a boost in the variety of locomotive types working into Birkenhead.

Towards the end of steam operation of this service, 'Britannia' Pacifics were drafted for this turn – for example on 28 December 1964 'Britannia' No. 70033 *Charles Dickens* headed the train and two weeks later it was the turn of No. 70046 *Anzac*. However, by the end of January 1965 this turn had surrendered to Type 2 diesel haulage.

Dockland traffic out of Birkenhead and the soap and margarine works at Port Sunlight also brought a fair variety of engine types into the district.

In the late 1950s and into the early 1960s, apart from the aforementioned ex-GWR visitors, and the usual crop of 'Black 5s' and 8Fs, it was not unknown for 'Scots', 'Patriots' and 'Jubilees' to arrive on fitted freight trains. In fact, I recorded one of the final visits of the latter class of engine to Birkenhead in June 1966 when Wakefield-based 'Jubilee' No. 45694 *Bellerophon* was observed resting outside the shed.

During the 1960s the number of ex-GWR engines visiting the Birkenhead area declined dramatically but among the types still to reach the district were 38XX 2–8–0s from Croes Newydd (Wrexham) shed and quite surprisingly, shortly after Christmas 1964, 'Castle' No. 7014 *Caerhays Castle*.

However, if there was one engine class that became synonymous with Birkenhead shed in its final years, it was the Standard 9F, which dominated the Shotton Steel trains in the mid-1960s. Eventually up to fifty-five members of this class would be based at the shed at any one time. Mr Williams recalls these engines with considerable admiration, describing them as 'incomparable' when handling freight work:

There was no other run of the mill heavy freight loco that would equal it, especially for speed and, of course, they have been known to attain 90 miles per hour on passenger trains.

We used to get them on heavy oil tank trains, but the job I think they were very good at was the Bidston Dock to John Summers (Shotwick) ore trains. These were made up of eleven 88 ton hopper wagons – sometimes overloaded – a 20 ton brake van and the 9F loco.

The combined load was sometimes in the region of 1,148 tons and no vehicles were fitted, the only brakes that could be applied whilst running were the guard's brake and the steam brake on the loco.

It was a journey of only about 13 miles but, by and large, it was uphill to the halfway point then downhill for the rest of the way. Needless to say, towards the halfway mark onwards you had to keep a very tight rein on things.

At Birkenhead crews got two weeks' training and familiarization on these jobs and were told, at the time, that they were the heaviest unfitted mineral trains in the British Isles. Once crews got the hang of things, and provided the engine was up to scratch, the 9Fs would play with the eleven hoppers. Mr Williams recalls:

One Saturday afternoon when we were diagrammed to do two trips, loads up and empties back, the boat that brought the ore to Bidston Dock was finished and there were only thirteen hoppers on the dock.

I told the guard that I was not coming back for two hoppers for the last trip, so could he hook them on now and we would take thirteen at one hit, which we did.

We hardly noticed much difference and we were on the shed with our engine about three hours earlier than we should have been. Needless to say we went home with our cards signed by the supervisor, 'NFW' – No Further Work.

Birkenhead's initial allocation of Standard 9Fs numbered just six engines (Nos 92165–7 and 92045–7), following the closure of Bidston shed on 11 February 1963. By early 1966, this allocation peaked at fifty-five engines. (Incidentally, locomotives at Bidston, just eight days before closure, comprised: 'Dock Tank' No. 47164, 'Jinties' Nos 47343, 47495, 47622 and 47628, and Standard 9Fs Nos 92046 and 92047.)

In the same month another 'Dock Tank', No. 47160, was in storage at Birkenhead shed while two British Railways built 'Kitson' tanks, Nos 47005 and 47009, also were lying idle at the depot. These locos, which were used in the dockland areas during the 1950s, were assisted in the western yard at Morpeth Dock by ex-GWR pannier tanks, assembling up to ten freight departures a day.

Birkenhead on 22 April 1951, and one of the shed's three Fowler short-wheelbase dock tanks rests partly in the shadows of the depot. Birkenhead and nearby Bidston shed made good use of these versatile locomotives in the dockland area, and, of course, Edge Hill retained one engine in the early 1960s for shed shunting duties.

H.C. Casserley

By 1966, Birkenhead's brace of 'Crab' Moguls were among the last survivors of this once numerous class (the other few examples being located around Ayr in Scotland). Because of their declining numbers, they were understandably in great demand for enthusiast specials.

Ex-LMS 'Jinty' tanks also survived at Birkenhead shed, with no less than five of them in steam at that depot on 15 March 1966. On shed that day were four 'Crabs', Nos 42727, 42765, 42812 and 42942, several of which were regulars on Birkenhead–Paddington passenger trains as far as Chester.

One of Birkenhead's 'Crabs' ventured into North Wales on Whit Monday in May 1966, when No. 42942 was used on a Birkenhead–Rhyl excursion instead of the rostered Stanier 'Black 5'. Three months later the same engine (turned out in pristine condition) was in charge of the August Bank Holiday 1006 hrs Rock Ferry–Llandudno excursion after a contrived 'failure' had eliminated the rostered 'Black 5'.

Birkenhead driver Frank Part worked the ten coach train so tightly that the ageing Horwich Mogul was recorded reaching a top speed of 66 mph, and arrived several minutes ahead of schedule. The same engine headed a 'Farewell to the Crabs' special from Liverpool Exchange to Goole in October 1966.

A month earlier it was still possible to see several 'Crabs' in steam at Birkenhead. On 17 September No. 42727 was observed running light coupled to 9F No. 92112, while

From the early 1960s Birkenhead started to collect a large number of Hughes-Fowler 'Crabs', which were utilized on a wide range of duties including passenger turns to Chester. Here, one of the shed's allocation, No. 42859, has been withdrawn (as of 31 December 1966) and is photographed in early 1967 awaiting despatch to the scrapyard. Fortunately, in this particular case it was consigned to Woodhams at Barry, South Wales, and No. 42859 lives on in preservation at Hull. Another shed mate, No. 42765, also was snatched from oblivion at Barry to be preserved.

Roger Jermy

Nos 42765 and 42942 were in steam resting on shed. The 'Crabs' final swansong came on 31 December 1966 when No. 42942 worked the 1445 hrs Birkenhead to Chester, returning with the 2108 hrs (ex Chester) section of the Paddington–Birkenhead Woodside. Mr Magner recalls that Dennis Williams had kindly swapped duties in order to drive this last 'Crab' turn on 31 December 1966.

The by now celebrated performer was withdrawn in January 1967 and then became the object of a concerted but, sadly, unsuccessful preservation appeal that attracted television coverage. It fell to an Edge Hill engine, No. 44773, on 7 January 1967, to head England's last scheduled mile-a-minute steam train, one week after the final 'Crabs' withdrawal, when it hauled a Chester–Shrewsbury express covering the 18 miles between Gobowen and Shrewsbury in seventeen and three-quarter minutes. The final 1531 hrs Chester–Shrewsbury train on 4 March 1967 was hauled by sister locomotive No. 44917.

While ex-GWR and LMS were regulars at Birkenhead shed, former ex-LNER engines were rarer, especially by the 1960s. During the early 1960s, 04 2–8–0s were recorded by some loco-spotters in the district. By 1965, these types of inter-regional incursions were rare and involved just two appearances of B1 4–6–0s, No. 61224 in February and No. 61388 in March that year.

FAST TIMES WITH BIRKENHEAD'S BEST

During 1966 the surviving Birkenhead 'Crabs' were mainly employed on goods, trip and parcel train work. The latter involved the class specifically, as the engines had to shunt a siding in Helsby which was barred to larger locomotives. During December 1966 No. 42942 was in use up to twenty hours a day on the Stanlow trip workings. Among the 'Crabs' regular rostered turns was the 1930 hrs (SX) Woodside to Chester parcels duty.

Another frequent turn for the fast declining members of the class in 1966 was the Chester–Woodside section of the Paddington–Birkenhead express, despite the availability of more modern Stanier/Fairburn 2–6–4Ts for the roster. On one occasion in 1966 Mr Magner recalls No. 42942 covering the 8 miles from Chester to Hooton (uphill for most of the distance) in twelve minutes and forty seconds, including a 20 mph slack at Ledsham Junction. At the start of this particular run, Upton was passed in three minutes fifteen seconds. Fast runs by these veterans of the old LMS were frequent during 1966, with Birkenhead men clearly determined to let the old-timers go out with a bang instead of a whimper.

At the end of March 1966 'Crab' No. 42727 was prepared for an enthusiasts' special along the North Wales coast. The train reached 64 mph at Colwyn Bay and after climbing Llandulas Bank it covered the Rhyl–Chester section inside the scheduled forty minutes. The same locomotive was in charge of the RCTS's 'St George' tour on 23 April 1966 from Hartford Junction to Nuneaton, before it proceeded to Rugby with empty coaching stock.

Also in April, Birkenhead's No. 42765 was rostered to work the 1722 hrs Manchester–Buxton passenger train. In November No. 42727 went roving even further afield, turning up at Carlisle.

With the introduction of timetable changes in April 1966 an 1800 hrs empty coaching stock train (from Woodside to Chester), which had been a duty for the Birkenhead 'Crabs', was discontinued. However, the locomotive for the 2108 hrs Chester–Woodside (1610 hrs ex Paddington) was provided by the engine which had hauled a 1445 hrs departure from Woodside.

Initially, 'Black 5' 4–6–0s were rostered for this job but towards the end of April 1966 the 'Crabs' began appearing. When No. 42727 derailed before working an 1850 hrs Woodside train, Fairburn tank No. 42086 was called to bridge the gap. The locomotive and its crew were more than a match for the job, covering the 3¾ miles from Bromborough to Rock Ferry in four minutes and fifty seconds.

The Whit Monday Woodside–Rhyl special passenger turn, referred to earlier, was initially rostered for No. 42727. When this failed, shedmate No. 42942 was brought out and delivered a stunning performance. Specially cleaned for the run by local enthusiasts, No. 42942 – hauling an eight-coach train – recorded 66 mph at Mollington and 64 mph at Talacre on the outward journey. Coming back the engine reached a peak of 70 mph at

Another class of engine declining in numbers by the mid-1960s was the Stanier/Fairburn 4MTs, and Birkenhead also had a reasonable share of the surviving members of this class. This engine, No. 42086, bridged the gap in April 1966 when 'Crab' No. 42727 was derailed before working the 1850 hrs Woodside train. It reportedly covered the 3¾ miles from Bromborough to Rock Ferry in four minutes fifty seconds. In this view, taken in early 1967, No. 42086 is dumped awaiting its fate. It was scrapped later in the year at Cohen's, Kettering.

Roger Jermy

Sandycroft. In August 1966 the same engine stood in for an enthusiasts' brake van special train after the rostered pannier tank had failed. At Mollington No. 42942 worked up to a top speed of 64 mph while hauling nine vans.

However, the most significant run by Birkenhead's 'Crabs' was reserved for No. 42942 while hauling the August Bank Holiday excursion from Rock Ferry to Llandudno. Again the engine had been cleaned to near pristine appearance. Driver Frank Part from Birkenhead shed had ten packed coaches behind his engine for this turn. Nevertheless, the train was worked up to 64 mph at Mollington, and when the train was allowed through Chester unchecked by signals, Driver Part opened up his charge, reaching a maximum of 66 mph at Holywell. The 1 in 100 climb up Llandulas Bank was achieved with speed not dropping below 40 mph.

Mr Magner recalls the driver opened up No. 42942 beyond Prestatyn with 70 mph being recorded before Holywell Junction. On the return working a previous running diesel multiple unit checked No. 42942 all the way to Ledsham Junction when the

Two of Birkenhead's unofficial engine cleaners, who spent much free time sprucing up engines during the final months of steam on the Paddington services: Chris Magner (in front of No. 42942) and Paul Boot, with back turned to camera. Invariably (at least to my eyes) it was always No. 42942 that seemed to receive the greatest attention. Beneath the tender paintwork on this engine the alert observer could discern both the legend LMS and the old 'lion and wheel' emblems. The two engines were among the last of their class to remain in traffic: No. 42765 being withdrawn to 31 December 1966 and No. 42942 to the period 28 January 1967. While a concerted preservation appeal was mounted for No. 42942, which sadly failed, No. 42765 was despatched to the scrapyard – fortunately Woodhams at Barry. Rescued from there in 1978, it was cared for by the Worth Valley Railway and is now restored to full working order.

Roger Jermy

'Crab' was again given its head. The Bromborough signalman, Dave Marks, reported that 'the night sky turned red' as No. 42942 roared past his box on the home stretch. Those aboard the train timed the ageless Mogul passing Bromborough at a mile a minute. So much for these engines being considered ungainly in their pedigree. Messrs Hughes and Fowler would have been proud!

Birkenhead's star performer was on special train duty again in September, travelling to Denbigh, and even to Goole, Yorkshire, in October. However, its efforts on the latter trip were below par, with problems of poor coal and especially wet rails. On a later, Liverpool University sponsored, trip No. 42942 was again up to the task, reaching a top of 65 mph at Ditton Junction on its way into Liverpool Central.

With the reinstatement of the 1930 hrs (SX) Woodside to Chester parcels train at Christmas 1966, No. 42942 was rostered to work this turn on at least three occasions. Then, as a tribute to the imminent end of a fine class of engine, it was turned out to work services on the Chester line on 31 December 1966.

Driver Dennis Williams of 8H managed to deliver the 1445 hrs Woodside–Chester and the 1648 hrs and 2108 hrs Chester–Woodside trains all before scheduled arrival time. The engine's performance on the 1445 hrs train was especially noteworthy. From a dead start at Rock Ferry, No. 42942 managed to cover the one mile to Bebington in just two minutes fifteen seconds, start to pass, and Hooton was reached in seven minutes forty seconds! By Mollington the train was worked up to 64 mph and Chester was finally reached in eleven minutes forty-six seconds.

'Crab' No. 42942's last day in service, 31 December 1966. Driver Dennis Williams (swathed in steam) and fireman, the late Bernard Robson, pose at Birkenhead Woodside before taking out a passenger train to Chester.

Dennis Williams Collection

On the return trip (the 1648 hrs from Chester) No. 42942 covered the 4½ miles from Hooton to Bebington in six minutes ten seconds with a mile-a-minute running from Spital to Port Sunlight. The last mile from Bebington to Rock Ferry took two minutes twenty-five seconds with a maximum speed of 44 mph.

BIRKENHEAD AT THE END

In the final days of steam on the Birkenhead–Paddington route, in March 1967, Stanier tanks Nos 42616 and 42587 also put in some stirring performances on the section to Chester which should not escape mention. No. 42616 was specially cleaned to work the 0855 hrs and 1445 hrs from Woodside and top speeds on the two trips of 64 mph and 68 mph respectively were recorded.

However, the finest performance from a tank on this route was saved for No. 42587 with Driver Layne of 8H on the 1850 hrs from Chester hauling seven coaches (235 tons). Layne managed to cover the 8.1 miles to Hooton in eleven minutes forty-four seconds despite enduring a 20 mph slack at Ledsham Junction. The highlight was 60 mph recorded over the summit at Capenhurst. The section between Bromborough and Bebington took three minutes fifty-nine seconds, with a 64 mph top speed.

The 2055 hrs from Woodside to Chester was in the hands of No. 42587, comprising eight coaches (including a sleeper) for 275 tons, and the section Bebington to

Stanier 4MT tank No. 42587 is serviced over the pits at Birkenhead shed on 18 February 1967. This engine was one of those with which Chris Magner recorded some quite spirited running in the final days of steam working on the Woodside–Chester section of the Paddington route. This engine was recorded attaining 64 mph between Bromborough and Bebington during early March 1967. The engine even survived the demise of passenger workings from Birkenhead, being transferred to the North Eastern Region and eventually Low Moor shed, whence it was withdrawn late in 1967.

J.M. Tolson

Bromborough was covered start to top in four minutes thirty-eight seconds, with a stop speed of 60 mph.

On Sunday 5 March 1967 the end of through express services between Paddington and Birkenhead Woodside was marked by eight steam specials on the Birkenhead–Chester line. Two Birkenhead 9Fs made their mark along distinguished company such as No. 7029 *Clun Castle*, with Nos 92203 and 92234 both attaining 70 mph on separate eight-coach trains.

The final two passenger steam turns on the Chester–Birkenhead route fell to 'Black 5' No. 44690 on the 1908 hrs from Chester and the 2140 hrs from Woodside. Earlier in the day No. 42587 had failed on the 1525 hrs.

Ironically, the demise of steam on the Chester–Shrewsbury route – concurrent with the curtailment of through services to Paddington from Birkenhead – also resulted in an abandonment of mile-a-minute schedules. On Monday 6 March 1967 diesels took over the Chester–Shrewsbury route and were allowed three minutes more than their steam predecessors.

Despite the withdrawal of the last 'Crabs', railway enthusiasts' demands for Birkenhead engines on railtours continued, and a Railway Correspondence and Travel Society tour of North Wales and the Wirral on 29 April 1967 saw the use of Birkenhead engines again on passenger duties.

For the farewell to steam on the Birkenhead–Paddington route, a series of special trains was run in early March involving Birkenhead engines and preserved ex-Western locomotives No. 4079 *Pendennis Castle* and No. 7029 *Clun Castle*. Here, on 5 March 1967, No. 7029 awaits the call at Birkenhead shed.

B. Taylor

Inside the stalls at Birkenhead, Standard 9F No. 92234 rests. This engine was among a select batch chosen to work final steam specials on 5 March 1967 and, as recorded by Chris Magner, distinguished itself by reaching a top speed of 70 mph with an eight-coach train. This engine, which started its life on the Western Region at Pontypool Road in South Wales, spent less than a year working out of Birkenhead – between December 1966 and November 1967.

Roger Jermy

March 1967 and Stanier 4MT tank No. 42613 rests after working one of the final Woodside–Paddington trains to Chester. This engine was withdrawn the following month. The 9F visiting from Carlisle Kingmoor shed on the adjacent track, No. 92223, had an interesting career. Outshopped new from Crewe Works in June 1958, the engine became the first 9F to be withdrawn from traffic, when it was condemned on the Western Region in February 1964. However, it was transferred to the London Midland Region where it was reinstated in June 1964. The engine spent many months dumped in a siding near Knotty Ash station. It was eventually returned to traffic and, in fact, survived to be one of the final members of its class withdrawn, for the final time, in April 1968.

Mick Pope

Standard 9F No. 92058 was used on the Crewe–Northwich–Hooton section of the trip, Stanier tanks Nos 42647 and 42616 on the Hooton–Mold–Wrexham section, and 'Black 8' No. 48697 between Wrexham and Llangollen and return. Nos 42647 and 42616 were again coupled up to work from Wrexham back to Bidston. The pair should have taken the train to New Brigton. However, because of a failure, the final leg was scrapped and No. 92058 was summoned to take rail fans from Bidston back to journey's end at Crewe.

In the final months of steam at 8H, despite the demise of the 'Crabs' and Fairburn tanks, there were still the work-stained Standard 9Fs to excite railway enthusiasts, particularly with their exploits on the Shotton ore trains. To this day Mr Williams retains the highest respect for these locomotives, which earned an esteemed reputation at the shed:

One day I had a class 9 and I put up a fair performance, close to one of the best ever, although I say it myself. When it came to diesels I never did a better time than I did with a class 9. Plenty of other chaps have put up better times than me but most of them failed to stop at Shotwick. I never once failed to stop with any of the (John) Summers' ore jobs.

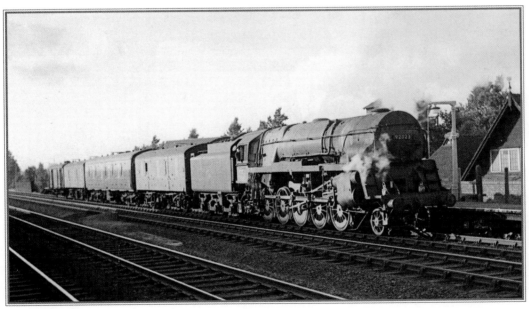

The Standard 9Fs at Birkenhead were primarily used on the Shotton Steel trains but their versatility knew no bounds. They were fleet of foot, free steamers and their working parts were easily accessible to fitting staff. In this mid-1960s view Crosti-boilered 9F No. 92023 waits at the Up platform at Port Sunlight with the evening parcels train to Chester. Note the unusual recessed tender pairing. The Crosties as built had high-sided BR1B tenders holding 7 ton of coal and with a 4,725 gallon water capacity.

Roger Jermy

The final hurrah for steam at Birkenhead shed (and also most of its Standard 9Fs) came late in 1967 when steam haulage of iron ore from Bidston Dock, Cheshire, to John Summers & Sons Ltd Steelworks at Shotton ended on 6 November.

The last steam-hauled train was made up of the customary eleven bogie hopper wagons of iron ore hauled by Standard 9F No. 92203. However, on this occasion it was driven from Bidston Dock to Shotwick sidings by Sir Richard Summers, director in charge of John Summers, and a one-time director of the former London Midland and Scottish Railway.

After the trip the driver and fireman of No. 92203 were guests at a lunch with Sir Richard and were presented with engraved ashtrays and cheques to entertain their shedmates at Birkenhead. The Standard 9Fs' duties were then taken over by Brush Type 4 diesel locomotives (Class 47).

During early 1968 there were occasional visits to Birkenhead by steam in the form of 8Fs and Standard Class 5s, although the steam shed was closed in November 1967. One of these visits occurred on 14 March 1968 when 'Black 5' No. 45305 travelled along the dock lines near Birkenhead North station to Canning Street signal-box with a small train of wagons. The engine then proceeded to Hooton on the slow line.

After steam's demise at Birkenhead Mr Williams continued to drive diesels from the depot, but by late 1985 the sad news came that Birkenhead was to close shortly. When a memo appeared in the crew notices' case offering early retirement packages for drivers aged fifty-five years and over, he decided, after forty-three years on the railways, that it was time to call it a day. In February 1986 Mr Williams retired, and bears no regrets: 'If it were possible to roll back the years to the steam days I would be back tomorrow, quite content to do it all again. There was something about steam that, if it got in your blood, you were a steam man for the rest of your life. It is still in my blood and I cannot see me changing now.'

8K BANK HALL

Bank Hall shed was located on the western side of the line between Sandhills and Kirkdale stations and always presented something of a challenge to unauthorized visitors. The main entrance at Stanley Road, Bootle, was several storeys higher than the shed yard. To gain entry the visitors (including train-spotter 'trespassers') had to negotiate several flights of stairs to reach ground level. The stairs passed administration offices.

At ground level, unauthorized visitors (as many railway enthusiasts were) faced a 100 yard sprint across the shed yard before they became hidden from the gaze of the authorities, who would normally despatch intruders with a stern warning.

I vividly remember my first visit to Bank Hall depot on a freezing afternoon in late December 1964 and waiting on Stanley Street until early evening, when the shed superintendent had gone off-shift, before stealing on shed. But my patience was rewarded. On shed that night were six 'Jubilee' class 4–6–0s in repose as well as a good variety of other interesting engines. Less than two years after that first visit Bank Hall shed would be closed – a casualty of the rapidly declining need for steam locomotives on passenger turns by the mid-1960s.

The first shed at Bank Hall, then known as Sandhills, was opened around 1850 by the Lancashire and Yorkshire Railway as its main Liverpool passenger locomotive depot. However, this shed was damaged by fire and was rebuilt in the 1860s as a large straight through eight-lane shed. Its engine stabling capacity was enlarged around 1875 when a second, eight-lane dead-end shed was built close by, on the western side of the site.

Bank Hall's 'newer' shed contained a fitters' shop and a sand-drying stove at its dead end. A third, smaller building, known as the 'Wigan Shed', which lay beside this shed and just ahead of the shed turntable, contained the wheel drop and turning machinery. A new wheel drop was installed at Sandhills depot in 1905 and in 1917 the shed's original turntable was replaced with one formerly situated at Liverpool Exchange station. In 1934 a 70 foot turntable was installed at a cost of £3,091.

Modernization in the 1930s resulted in the installation of mechanical coal and ash plants, and also the demolition of half of the 'old' shed dating from the 1860s. A redundant wheel drop capable of dealing with complete engine bogies was transferred to Bank Hall from Nottingham at a cost of £1,283 in 1938.

Sandhills also boasted its own 35 ton breakdown crane and loco tool van and, in L&YR days, prided itself on its very fast mobilization once shed staff were notified of a derailment. The 'Maggie' – as this crane was affectionately called by railwaymen – was, in its day, the most powerful on the L&YR and spent all but its last months in service (during which it was transferred to Edge Hill) based at Bank Hall.

Sandhills (renamed Bank Hall in 1920) was accorded the shed number 18 in the L&YR's coding system of thirty-two sheds. After the L&YR became part of LMS,

A quartet of Pugs on shed at Bank Hall, 13 October 1957. This view illustrates the 'new' shed at Bank Hall, built around 1875. This was an eight-lane dead-end shed that contained a fitters' shop and sand drying machine at one end. As well as this shed, and near the turntable, was a small shed known as the 'Wigan shed', which contained the machine shop. Depicted in this scene are Nos 51232, 51206 and 51229 (just inside the shed), with the fourth engine just visible to the left of the photograph.

J.A. Peden

Bank Hall was recoded 23A from 1935. In 1950 the shed was recoded 27A and from late 1963 district control was transferred to Edge Hill and Bank Hall was recoded 8K.

On the last day of the LMS – 31 December 1947 – Bank Hall had a total of forty-four engines listed as allocated. Two years later, forty-six engines from nine different classes were based at the shed. Among the engine types based there were twelve Stanier 'Black 5s', eleven ex-L&YR Pug saddle tanks (for dockland shunting), and two 'Jubilees' (*Mars* and *Dauntless*).

While the depot in LMS days maintained strong links with its L&YR heritage, by the early 1950s there were only a handful of ex-L&YR engines allocated to Bank Hall besides the Pug tanks that were long associated with this shed. Two Kitson 0–4–0ST engines were also at the shed working alongside their older L&YR brethren.

In 1955 the number of engines based at the depot had shrunk marginally to forty-two, but a wider variety, ten different classes, were now represented. Four years later forty-one engines were allocated to Bank Hall, including an extra 'Jubilee' and an unrebuilt 'Patriot' to assist with express passenger rosters.

The entrance to Bank Hall depot, with its Johnson 3F tank, No. 47230, running past Sandhills No. 2 signal-box on 3 August 1957. Although essentially a passenger locomotive depot, Bank Hall also had an allocation of small tank engines for shunting the nearby dockland area. As well as No. 47230 (which in 1955 was based at Swansea Victoria depot), Kitson and ex-L&YR Pug tanks were based here, as evidenced by the pair beneath the coaling stage.

J.A. Peden

By 1961, with the advent of dieselization of the docklands, the shed's steam power roster was reduced to thirty-two engines, with just three Pugs surviving. In May 1964 the writing was clearly on the wall, with only eighteen engines being based at the shed – half of this number made up of just two BR Standard classes. Twenty-nine months later, on 17 October 1966, Bank Hall shed was closed by British Railways.

'JUBS', PUGS AND DERBY 2S RECALLED

Bert Kelley, a former Bank Hall fireman and driver with almost thirty years' experience of working at the shed, having started there in 1939, has many recollections of shed life at the depot. Like many footplatemen, he began his railway career as an engine cleaner. In the late 1930s he says eight cleaners were assigned to the 8 a.m. shift, and four each on the 4 p.m., the 8 p.m. and the midnight shifts.

During the 1950s and 1960s the top express passenger engines available were the 'Jubilee' class 4–6–0s, including No. 45698 *Mars*, which spent most of its working life based at Bank Hall. The 'Jubilees' were employed on expresses to Carlisle and Glasgow, as well as passenger turns to destinations in Yorkshire.

During the 1950s ex-Midland Railway 4–4–0s saw out their service at places like Bank Hall. Even on the last day of the LMS, four of these engines were still based there: Nos 581, 583, 937 and Compound 1188. Mr Bill Tomlinson, who drove steam at Bank Hall from the late 1950s to 1962, remembers: 'One of my favourites was No. 40588. It used to work the 9.43 a.m. to Hellifield and Skipton. A very comfortable engine both to fire and drive, but this was an engine you had to understand.'

Mr Bert Kelley remembers the Derby 2s from the 1940s with some fondness as No. 581 (BR No. 40581) was his first firing job after being 'passed out' for main line duty. The job was an all stations 1 p.m. from Liverpool to Rochdale, via Wigan, Bolton and Bury. At the time Mr Kelley had had about thirty months' service with the railways: 'The Derby 2s were well suited for this class of work and could pull four coaches up the hills with ease. They could manage six but it was heavy going because most of our passenger work entailed climbing some pretty steep hills.'

A well-kept Pug in action: Bank Hall's spruce No. 51229 propels a small train of coal at North Docks on 2 November 1957.

J.A. Peden

A fine study of ex-LMS 2P or a Derby 2, No. 40684, at Bank Hall in October 1959. Both Bert Kelley and
Bill Tomlinson had high regard for these engines which would often work the 0943 hrs to Skipton and
Hellifield, or the 1300 hrs to Rochdale. With four carriages behind them they were in command and at a
push could take six, although they were not well suited to some of the 'Lanky's graded routes. The
2P 4–4–0s were also active on semi-fast Liverpool–Rochdale trains until the summer of 1961.

J. Oatway

Bank Hall also saw some of the Deeley Compounds, which were generally considered
unsuitable for the shed's needs, according to Mr Kelley:

The difficulty was that they were very hard to get started on a wet rail and an uphill
gradient owing to their big wheels with the three cylinders. The wheel spin would
continue long after the regulator was shut off. But they were good for, say, a run to
Blackpool with not too many stops en route.

We also had to be very careful moving them around the shed yard because the steam brake was very weak, and if you had a full boiler, once you had opened the regulator it would keep on beating long after you had shut it. Many an unwary driver was seen running his engine up and down a short length of rail, and doing frantic reverses at each end until the steam chest was finally emptied!

During the 1950s it was common for only a pair of 'Jubilees' to be based at the depot. However, by the time I first visited the shed, four 'Jubilees' (*Sierra Leone, Jutland, Mars* and *Impregnable*) were serviceable at the shed, and another two of the class (*Jellicoe* and *Basutoland*) had only recently been withdrawn from traffic and were stored pending disposal.

Bank Hall's final 'Jubilee' in service – and in fact, the last of its class in service on the London Midland Region – was No. 45627 *Sierra Leone*. The engine, photographed on shed on 12 June 1966, survived in service until the end of the summer 1966 timetable in early September. It was set aside at Bank Hall, and eventually transferred to Aintree for storage after 8K shut the following month.

Richard Picton

130

Mr Tomlinson remembers working on the Bank Hall 'Jubileees' and in particular *Mars*. I can honestly say it was a headache for the fireman. As soon as the fire started clinkering up it was hard work, believe me.

I remember driving *Mars* from Carlisle to Liverpool Exchange with the usual nine coaches on. I had a young passed cleaner with me who didn't have the experience of the main line firemen. What a trip to remember. We arrived at Exchange two hours late, lacking steam all the way. On arrival a lady came up to the footplate to say thank you and handed me a 10s note. Quite a tip in those days.

Mr Kelley, too, recalls the 'Jubilees' and 'many trips on 5698' *Mars*:

The 'Jubilees' were not really suited to our jobs as we did not often work really heavy trains above about nine coaches or go long distances without stopping, and sometimes it was like using a sledgehammer to crack a nut.

Still, during the war years we often worked troop trains with ten or eleven coaches non-stop to Carlisle and these engines with their long legs were good for those jobs.

By the early 1960s Bank Hall's brace of 'Jubilees' avoided an early appointment with the scrapyard by working the Scottish expresses, parcels trains or maybe a turn on Blackpool Illuminations' trains or a trip to Yorkshire. They put in some sterling service despite being disliked by some crews. Mr Tomlinson:

For a fireman, the 'Jubilees' were very hard work. The fireman had to keep at it all the way to Carlisle and back. We only went as far as Carlisle or Carstairs, then changed over and returned to Liverpool Exchange, stopping at Preston.

Two hours and thirty-five minutes were allowed. The Carlisle job was worth fourteen hours' pay due to the mileage allowance, which was one hour's pay for each 15 miles over 120 miles.

But while Mr Tomlinson was disparaging of the Stanier 'Jubilees' that worked out of Bank Hall, he was full of praise for some of the British Railways Standard types allocated there:

For example Standard class 4, No. 75048, a lovely engine, comfortable and easy to manage — and fast. The good thing about this engine was the rocker grate when it came to clean the fire. If the fire was becoming tired a few movements on the rocker assembly would restore the fire to tip top condition. We did this while in motion, but it was against the rules as the hot cinders used to set the countryside on fire!

In 1966 this particular engine was moved to Chester and later to Croes Newydd depot at Wrexham in North Wales where, by February 1967, in spotless condition, it was working the 'Cambrian Coast Express' from Aberystwyth. It became one of the last BR steam locomotives to remain on the books, being officially withdrawn on 10 August 1968.

The truncated 'old' shed at Bank Hall, which was reduced from an eight-lane structure to four lanes during the 1930s to accommodate the mechanical coaling stage seen on the right. This photograph, taken on 27 July 1966, shows Standard 4MT No. 75049 raising steam beside one of the 170 hp diesels that displaced the Pug tanks four years previously. No. 75049, which started its career at Accrington in October 1953, was withdrawn from service when Bank Hall closed in October 1966.

M.R. Stubbs, from the W.T. Stubbs Collection

Mr Tomlinson also remembers a Standard Class 2: '. . . No. 78041, was used at Bank Hall on the Rochdale jobs, to Southport and Preston. A nice engine to handle and very economical on coal and water. A good runner up to 80 mph.'

By the summer of 1962 Bank Hall's brace of Class 2 Moguls (Nos 78041–78044) worked a high proportion of the Liverpool–Rochdale (via Bolton and Bury) trains and, in the right hands, were capable of some quite spirited working.

Mr Tomlinson qualified as a passed fireman (able to take driving turns) in 1957. As passed firemen became knowledgeable of certain routes, a driver could sign given route cards. He recalls:

Five of the Riddles 2MT Moguls, Nos 78040–44, were allocated new to Bank Hall and quickly distinguished themselves as spirited runners. Mr Bill Tomlinson recalls these engines as being quite fleet of foot, in particular No. 78041, which would work up to 80 mph with little difficulty. The engines were frequently used on the Rochdale trains, although from 1962 they were transferred away to other depots. This engine, photographed at Bank Hall on 24 September 1961, was in store at Bolton shed by July 1967 and was withdrawn later that year.

Ken Fairey

I personally had a good route card having been at Aintree loco shed for a number of years before going to Bank Hall. My route card was for Leeds–Bradford, Manchester–Blackpool–Windermere and Carlisle, and also on the former LNER route as far as Buxton and Rowsley. Plus I could work all the local places around Liverpool.

The route card meant that you knew every signal on the route. Obviously a mistaken signal could end in disaster. As a passed fireman you would fill in for a regular driver who was off sick or any special train that was ordered.

The passed fireman who had a good route card could be called upon to work a train to whichever route he had signed for.

At Bank Hall in the late 1950s and early 1960s there were five links and two spares. The top link contained the most important rosters such as the 12.30 p.m. from Liverpool Exchange to Leeds and Bradford. The number two link was similar to the top link but had passenger turns of slightly lesser importance.

Number three link included jobs such as shunting turns at Dock Road, station pilot duties or stopping trains to destinations such as Blackpool, Rochdale, Preston and Southport.

Number four link was mainly preparation of engines for duty plus some spare work, while number five link was a variation on number four. Two spare links were usually manned by passed firemen and retained for standby work.

Normally eight drivers and eight firemen would be assigned to each link. At Bank Hall there were about fifty-six crews assigned to the links, compared to around sixty-four pairs of men working the links at Aintree.

The smallest engines allocated to Bank Hall – and indeed among the smallest assigned to any shed on BR – were the ex-L&YR 0–4–0ST Pugs. They were allocated to Bank Hall because of the shed's proximity to docklands, therefore avoiding unnecessary light-engine running from Aintree. The Pugs, usually with no more than ten wagons in tow, would inhabit Great Howard Street, Dock Road, Sandon Dock, and Wapping Dock (better known now as Albert Dock).

Dock turns with these diminutive and ancient saddle tanks were usually the preserve of drivers who had 'slowed down' somewhat and wanted a rest from the more demanding turns, according to Bill Tomlinson. Bert Kelley remembered the Pugs with a great deal of sentimentality: 'They must have been the best little workhorses ever.'

A pair worked at Dock Road, two at Sandon Dock goods yard, and two at Great Howard Street (with sidings into Tate and Lyle silcocks), the Cotton Yard and quay alongside Pall Mall. A Pug was also kept for North Docks high level. Bank Hall retained two six-wheel saddle tanks for shunting sidings between Sandhills and Bank Hall, and two 'Donkey Lizzies' (ex-L&YR) 2–4–2Ts for the North Docks low level and Bankfield sidings.

However, by 1961 the surviving Pugs were dumped out of use alongside Bank Hall shed following the introduction of 170 hp diesel shunters to the Liverpool area. In mid-1962 only six of the ex-L&YR Pug saddletanks remained in traffic throughout British Railways, and two of these (Nos 51232 and 51253) still saw limited work from Bank Hall shed. Another member of this class, No. 51206, was in store at the shed earlier in the year.

Returning to the passenger side of operations at Bank Hall, Mr Tomlinson remembers the routine that was part of working the 12.30 p.m. to Leeds and Bradford – a roster that during his time at Bank Hall was classed as a top job:

We would sign on at 12.05 p.m. and take the engine off shed and go light engine to Exchange. There we would hook on to six coaches and leave at 12.30 p.m. First stop was Manchester Victoria at 1.10 p.m., then all stations to Low Moor (Bradford).

There we would hook off and go light engine to Low Moor shed, clean the fire, coal and water the engine, turn on the 'table, have our lunch and then travel light engine down to Leeds. We would then hook on and leave Leeds at 5.10 p.m. with Manchester the next stop, arriving at Liverpool at 7.25 p.m., where we hooked off and ran light engine to Bank Hall and finish.

A regular performer on the Leeds and Bradford turn until its transfer to Southport shed in the mid-1960s was the sole Stephenson link-motioned 'Black 5', No. 44767, which survived the scrapper's torch to be preserved today in working order. Mr

'The best little workhorses ever' is the way Mr Bert Kelley remembers the ex-L&YR Pug saddletanks, and there is no denying some members of the class had a long and productive history. Here Bank Hall's No. 51253 negotiates the streets near the Pier Head on a grey winter's day, 23 January 1960. This engine and No. 51232 were still finding occasional work at Bank Hall two years later, while a third engine, No. 51206, was in store. All three survived to be transferred away from Bank Hall when dieselization of the dockland work made them redundant. Nos 51232 and 51253 were not withdrawn until 1963, after around seventy years' service on the railways.

J.A. Peden

Tomlinson has no hesitation in describing No. 44767 as 'the finest engine I've worked on, without a doubt'.

Generally, most men who worked at Bank Hall had barely a harsh word to say about the Stanier 'Black 5s'. Certainly they seemed far more suited to much of the work over the old L&YR routes that was Bank Hall's lot. As Mr Kelley commented, the 'Black 5s' could get ten coaches moving from a hill start with far les effort than was required with a 'Jubilee' and they 'could run quite fast enough for our purposes'.

Although most Bank Hall men worked passenger rosters if not assigned to local yard shunting duties, occasionally they were called upon to work a freight, often with embarrassing results, as Mr Kelley remembers:

One night I found myself driving a loose-coupled goods train from Aintree sidings to Lostock Hall, near Preston, and I did not do very well. It's all downhill from Aintree to

A profile view of Pug No. 51232. Sundays usually marked the end of the weekend on shed as the firelighters would begin slowly raising steam in the slumbering engines in preparation for the start of the working week. Here the Pug awaits its turn as, behind, a fully lined 'Black 5' begins to build up a fire.

Duncan Gomersall

Maghull, then a long haul up to Aughton Park, then down through Ormskirk and Burscough Junction. After that, it's fairly level.

I followed my usual practice of getting a move on through the Old Roan, and then shutting off to run down the hill. But the climb up to Aughton Park started, I realized, much sooner than was usual with passenger trains. Having lost the momentum, I could not get any speed up again and was chugging along at about 15 or 20 mph, with the signalmen leaning out of their cabin windows, wondering what was wrong.

I think I lost about twenty minutes and got paper to answer from the Boss. But my apology was accepted, in view of the fact that this was my first experience of driving a loose-coupled goods train.

Exchange station was the former L&YR's main terminus in the city of Liverpool. It was always a good spot to visit to see steam in use, almost right up to the end of steam. In the mid-1960s 'Jubilee' class engines would still back on to summer Glasgow expresses or Blackpool illuminations specials, despite the constant flow of electric units to and from Southport. However, by 12 March 1966 all the Bank Hall 'Jubilees' bar No. 45627 had been condemned, resulting in 'Black 5' No. 45260 of Bolton being rostered to work the 1640 hrs Exchange to Glasgow Central and Edinburgh Waverley.

J.M. Tolson

Mr Kelley rated the Liverpool–Hellifield passenger turn as the most enjoyable he worked on while at Bank Hall. For this turn the crew booked on shed at 8.35 a.m.; their engine would already be prepared for them, ready for a departure from Exchange station at around 9.10 a.m.

The roster would take them through the beautiful countryside of Whalley Viaduct, Chatburn, and Clitheroe. At Hellifield they took their loco to the engine shed, watered, cleaned the fire and then backed up onto the coaches in the siding. There would be plenty of time for the crew to have their 'scoff' (tea and sandwiches) in the comfort of a compartment on the train, with maybe even a discarded newspaper to read. Mr Kelley recalls that then there was '. . . the easy run back – downhill most of the way – and relief on arrival at Liverpool because we were just over the eight hours.'

Like other former enginemen, Mr Kelley found the Blackpool turns quite enjoyable, except for the fact that they were nearly all early morning turns, which frequently meant signing on at 4.30 a.m. The special excursions to the beachside resort in summer were rated a good day out though:

There were just two bad jobs I can remember. One of them was the 'early Rochdale' where we booked on at 4.40 a.m. to prepare the engine for a 5.50 a.m. departure from Exchange station, with all stops to Rochdale.

We had a little Lankie Tank with four or five coaches and had to rattle along to keep time, and the steep climbs into and out of Wigan, Bolton and Bury tested the fireman's stamina and skill to the utmost.

On arrival at Rochdale there was just enough time to get water, turn the engine on the little manual turntable, scrape some coal down from the back of the bunker, do a bit to the fire, fill the steam lubricator and we were off again, usually drinking our tea and scoffing our sandwiches going down the bank into Bury.

The other arduous job was a late turn, another Lankie Tank job. We were all stops from Ormskirk to Preston. We didn't stop between Liverpool and Ormskirk because the electric service took care of that. Then back from Preston to Ormskirk, then Ormskirk back to Preston and back to Liverpool stopping all holes. After a week on that job you wished you were a signalman instead!

In later years the BR Standard classes took over both of these turns and that made these two jobs a lot easier.

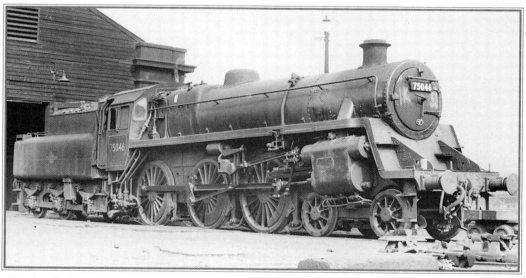

Five Standard 4MT 4–6–0s were drafted to Bank Hall in the late 1950s, with the depot's allocation of these engines peaking in 1964 when another two of the class had been transferred there. Here, on 24 September 1961, No. 75046 awaits an 'extra' working outside the 'old' shed, which dated from 1865. No. 75046 was transferred away to Chester shed in 1966, eventually finishing its days at Stoke. In fact, it was one of the final locomotives removed from that depot in January 1968.

Ken Fairey

INTO THE 1960S AT BANK HALL

Bank Hall's nameless unrebuilt 'Patriot' 4–6–0 No. 45517 (withdrawn in June 1962) was sent to Crewe South in July, where it was stored prior to removal to the workshops for scrapping. By this stage only a handful of the unrebuilt members of this class remained available for traffic throughout British Railways.

In the early 1960s the Rochdale–Liverpool Exchange 'semi-fast' was a job that would often provide running-in turns for engines freshly outshopped from Horwich Works. Consequently, it also provided turns for engines from outside the general area which had received attention at that works. On 20 February 1963, for example, rebuilt 'Patriot' No. 45522 *Prestatyn* from Newton Heath was at the head of the 1000 hrs Rochdale–Liverpool Exchange train. On 22 April it was the turn of the Eastleigh-based Standard 4 No. 76065, freshly outshopped from Horwich, to head the 1740 hrs Liverpool Exchange–Rochdale train.

'Clan' Pacifics were rare, but not uncommon, visitors to Merseyside. However, when they did make incursions into Liverpool you were more likely to find them at Bank Hall, or on the Liverpool Exchange to Carlisle route. In this view, taken on 18 July 1961, Glasgow Polmadie-based No. 72003 *Clan Fraser* heads a local passenger train through Sandhills station. The Polmadie 'Clans' (Nos 72000–4) were all withdrawn in December 1962 – most after barely ten years in traffic. Although only ten 'Clans' were constructed, originally there were plans to build a further fifteen, five of which were earmarked for the Southern Region. These five, to have been numbered 72010–14, were allocated the names *Hengist*, *Horsa*, *Canute*, *Wildfire* and *Firebrand* (respectively to the numbers above). The final ten 'Clans', which were also never constructed, were to have gone to Scotland and would have been named after clans.

John Corkill

Ex-LNER engines, too, were not uncommon on Merseyside, even excluding the resident allocation of ex-Great Central types at Brunswick shed up to its closure in 1961. Up to the winter 1963 timetable it was common for the Sunday 2250 hrs Liverpool Exchange–York train to be rostered for an ex-LNER B1. This turn was a non-stop working over the Bolton–Rochdale line, and was one of the few scheduled B1 turns in Lancashire at that time. Ex-LNER V2s were also visitors to Liverpool, from across the Pennines, until the early 1960s.

Although the Bank Hall 'Jubilees' were nearing the end of their useful lives by the mid-1960s, they were called on to perform quite rigorous turns even in their final days. For example, No. 45721 *Impregnable* worked the 1310 hrs ex Liverpool Exchange throughout to Glasgow Central on 2 July 1965. Sister loco, No. 45627 *Sierra Leone* (which would become the class's final London Midland survivor, lasting in traffic until September 1966), worked the 1400 hrs Glasgow–Manchester train on 29 August 1965.

The following May five football supporters' special trains were run from Liverpool–Glasgow on 5 May on the occasion of Liverpool Football Club's European

A pair of Pugs await their next duties at Bank Hall shed on 2 June 1957. These engines were dukes of the dockland and warehouse; in some cases the engines actually went inside the warehouses and so were fitted with blast deflectors over their chimneys for that purpose. Generally, the engines were difficult to find on shed, as the only time they would return would be at weekends for servicing.

Duncan Gomersall

Cup Winners' Final with Borussia Dortmund at Hampden Park. Merseyside-based engines used on these trains were Nos 44659, 44806, 45065, 45412, and 'Jubilee' No. 45627 *Sierra Leone*.

But five months later the closure of Bank Hall saw the virtual end of regular steam workings from Liverpool Exchange station. Yet the final rites for regular steam operation on British Railways' standard gauge lines involved occasional steam workings into Exchange station as late as 3 August 1968, when Stanier 'Black 5' No. 45318 worked the 2125 hrs from Preston. This engine ran a hot box on its tender about 2 miles from Liverpool but was able to complete its journey at reduced speed. A passenger who travelled on this train commented in the railway press of the time that while Aintree's silent coaling stage was a notable landmark on the journey, at Bank Hall hardly a trace could be seen of the former L&YR shed which had closed less than two years earlier.

As a postscript, although the site of what was once Bank Hall shed is now occupied by the Kirkdale electric multiple unit depot, some remnants of the previous depot are still evident. Mr Dave McGuire, a member of the Engine Shed Society – whose members devote their energies to recording the uses and existence of locomotive depots, both past and present – noted in the society's *Link* journal that on 29 June 1992 some traces of Bank Hall shed could still be discerned.

Mr McGuire reported to readers that:

The wall in Stanley Road shows the bricked-up door that led down to the shed, for instance. On the other side of this wall, at ground level, the outline of the power house and the stairs leading down to ground level in the shed yard can easily be seen. The shed entrance from the main line under Stanley Road is also still there but trackless.

8L AINTREE

The eight-lane locomotive depot at Aintree was a direct antithesis of Merseyside sheds such as Edge Hill or Bank Hall, which hosted Pacifics and other express passenger locomotives. Aintree was a small shed responsible mostly for the humdrum but necessary freight work over Cheshire Lines Committee and ex-L&YR routes. Its stock-in-trade was the less glamorous locomotive types, such as rusty, clanking 'Austerity' 2–8–0s, ungainly 'Crabs', often in equally unkempt external condition and, in the 1950s, pensionable ex-L&YR locomotive survivors.

However, despite being a lowly freight locomotive depot, Aintree annually had its day in the spotlight as trains from throughout England and Scotland converged on Liverpool for the Grand National steeplechase. On that day 'Duchess' or 'Britannia' Pacifics, or B1 and V2 'foreigners' from far away would line up beside 'Austerities' and 'Crabs' to be coaled and watered at Aintree, having brought in trains from around the country.

Aintree shed was opened by the L&YR in 1886. It was built by a Mr H.M. Nowell, whose tender of £16,600 for the construction of an eight-lane shed was accepted by the railway board on 13 July 1886. Most of the 11 acres needed for the depot belonged to the Cheshire Lines Committee, which eventually settled on a price of £1,200 per acre for its release.

Once the land was secured, Nowell Ltd proved to be swift builders and the shed was ready for occupation before the end of the year. Aintree engine shed was situated in the fork of the Ford to Aintree and Ford to Kirkby goods lines, immediately east of the Aintree sorting sidings. The sidings, built at a cost of £24,971, also came into operation in 1886 and at their peak covered 34½ acres with 18 miles of track.

The shed was largely unaltered until a mechanical coaling plant and ash plants, together with an improved track layout, were provided in 1936/7. At this time, Aintree's locomotive turning needs were also updated, with the installation of a 70 foot electrically operated turntable at the southern side of the shed.

By the end of the Second World War the shed's roof had deteriorated considerably and capital funds were allocated for its replacement. By October 1944 renewal of the roof with a concrete structure was well advanced; a total of £19,933 was eventually spent on this work.

Aintree was assigned the shed code number 19 by the L&YR and, until 29 September 1935, was also responsible for a small four-lane sub-shed at Ormskirk, which was located in the fork of the lines to Preston and Rainford. Also in 1935 Aintree was given the LMS shed code 23B, which the shed retained until 1950 when it was recoded 27B. In September 1963 it became 8L following a general review of London Midland Region

'Jubilee' No. 45558 *Manitoba* at Aintree shed on 12 April 1963. In my experience the 'Jubilees' were occasional rather than common visitors to Aintree shed as the depot predominantly served freight locomotives. Immediately behind *Manitoba* is one of Aintree's twenty 'Austerities' based at the depot at the time, No. 90101.

Richard Picton

shed districts. The shed was closed on 12 June 1967, but for some months afterwards was used to store condemned locomotives.

At Nationalization on 1 January 1948, there were 59 engines based at Aintree including ex-LMS 4F 0–6–0s, 13 examples of the ex-LMS version of the 7F 0–8–0, 3 members of the ex-L&YR 2P 2–4–2T class, 17 examples of the ex-L&YR 3F 0–6–0 class, and 10 ex-L&YR 0–8–0s (class '31') dating from 1912.

Until the mid-1950s ex-L&YR engines formed the larger part of locomotive types allocated to Aintree. L&YR 0–8–0s were present at the shed until 1950 and Fowler 7Fs remained there until 1959. Aintree also had a small number of passenger turns during this period that warranted a small presence of ex-LMS 4P 4–4–0s and ex-L&YR 2–4–2Ts, the solitary survivor at Aintree by the start of 1954 being No. 50648. This engine had been based at Aintree since at least 1945.

The survivors of 20 Aspinall 0–6–0 outside cylinder dock tanks were also concentrated at Aintree and Bank Hall sheds following the Second World War. By 1954, three of the four survivors (Nos 51535, 51537 and 51544) were based at Aintree. The last of this line, No. 51537, was not finally withdrawn from Aintree until 1961.

One of the ex-L&YR 2–4–2T 2P engines, No. 50648, in the back of Aintree shed on 18 April 1950. By 1960 the last three survivors of this class were confined to the Liverpool, Southport areas. No. 50721 was retained at Bank Hall for parcels duties while Nos. 50746 and 50850 were based at Southport.

H.C. Casserley

One of the former footplatemen who has strong memories of life at Aintree during the steam era is Mr Jim Blackburn, who began his working career there in 1941 as a cleaner. Mr Blackburn spoke fondly of the time when he joined the railways and the period up to the late 1940s:

> When I started we used to clean locos with stuff called 'Yak'. At the time the shed had simple coal engines known as 'Lanky Bombers', also class 6 and 7 engines, class 3s, Derby 3s and 4s and Class 4 'Crabs'.
>
> I used to love the steamers; hard work but with a good mate driving it was great. But with some of the old sods it was a long day, especially if you lodged with them at Rowsley or Wakefield. Most of the men had nicknames: Dusty Rhodes, Headlamp Harry, Mona Wimps, to mention but a few.

Another footplateman who worked at Aintree, and later Bank Hall, from 1944 to 1962, Mr Tomlinson, remembers his time there:

> My first week at Aintree in June 1944 as a cleaner was just that, cleaning the engines after service with an oil that was called 'Yak'. Why Yak I don't know. It smelt just like diesel oil. The standard of the engines was quite good, with maintenance being carried out by very efficient fitters.

Aspinall's Class 27 0–6–0s (later LMS 3Fs) were another ex-L&YR to last well into BR service. No. 52311 is shown at Aintree having just replenished her tender – although the coalman appears to have got a little carried away with the trim! The date, Sunday 2 June 1957.

Duncan Gomersall

Graduating from cleaning, Mr Tomlinson was passed out by the shed's inspector, Mr Keen, which meant he could begin firing engines:

During this time there were quite a few special troop trains up and down the country. Those most liked were Americans being brought into Liverpool. The reason why most crews liked them was because of the army rations that were given to the driver, fireman and guard by these troops – coffee, gum and other provisions which were impossible to obtain here at the time because of rationing. There were also Camel cigarettes, and nylons for the lady folk.

Other routine jobs assigned to Aintree crews during the war years and immediately after were local shunting duties and coal trippers from nearby Fazakerley yard. As well as being a major marshalling yard, Fazakerley also had a large wagon repair depot. Bill Tomlinson remembers working the wagon shops and often having up to 100 wagons attached to the shunt engine, which postwar and into early British Railways days was usually rostered for an ex-L&YR Class 27, frequently No. 12117. He remembers:

This particular engine was shunting at Dale Lane, Simmonswood, on the main line when an express from Manchester hauled by a Stanier 'Black 5', No. 5210, ran right into the engine and brake van. The driver and guard were killed instantly.

The fireman, George Davies, a passed cleaner, saw the engine coming and jumped off the footplate just one second before the impact. He was found later in a daze walking through the fields, a very fortunate young man although he lost his left hand.

Aintree had around fifty turns daily from the depot. Apart from the jobs at Fazakerley yard and local trips to the docks, the most important rosters were the coal trains to Yorkshire and Rowsley in Derbyshire. Mr Tomlinson remembers the coal train jobs and how he often had to filch a few choice cobs from the train behind his engine when coal in the tender became dangerously short:

Another ex-L&YR survivor to see service at Aintree in 1950 was the 7F 0–8–0s No. 52870, photographed near the shed on 18 April 1950. Five of the six survivors of this class by September 1950 were based at Wigan 'C' depot, the exception being No. 52857, which was at Low Moor.

H.C. Casserley

If we had a tender full of briquettes (coal substitutes) we would say we were in for a day's hard work, especially on the main line, hence the pinching of Yorkshire coal that went on.

Quite a few of the main line jobs from Aintree were to Yorkshire. Wakefield was a job where we would lodge for the return trip back to Fazakerley. Mostly it was coal trains – empty coal wagons out, full coal wagons back. The trip usually took about six to eight hours because of the amount of traffic at the time.

Trains were working twenty-four hours a day during the war. The engines usually employed on these coal trains were Stanier 'Black 5s', my favourite. Never had a bad trip with these wonderful engines.

Mr Tomlinson also recalls that Derby 4 0–6–0 No. 4481 (BR No. 44481), a regular performer on the Rowsley coal trains to and from Aintree, was 'a wonderful engine to fire or drive'.

For the Yorkshire coal trains the roster was usually a 'Black 5', a 'Crab' such as No. 42727 (which was one of the final survivors of its class at Birkenhead in 1967), or Stanier 'Black 8s', in particular No. 48008.

In the 1950s and 1960s Aintree was always well served by ex-War Department 'Austerity' 2–8–0s. Fourteen of this class were based at the depot by 1955 and a further

LMS 4F or Derby 4 No. 44241 visiting Aintree shed from Rowsley on 12 January 1958 having more than likely worked into Liverpool on a coal train from Derbyshire. Mr Tomlinson remembers sister locomotive No. 44481 being a lovely engine to fire or drive.

J.A. Peden

seven were there four years later. However, with the transfer of survivors of this numerous class to the Eastern Region from late 1964, sightings of 'Austerities' on Merseyside became something of a rarity. In 1967, for example, it was reported in the railway press that 'Austerity' No. 90625 had been seen passing through Gateacre heading towards Aintree and Walton with a freight. A noteworthy occasion, as the correspondent remarked that this was only the second sighting in two years of a member of that class in an area that was once their regular stamping ground.

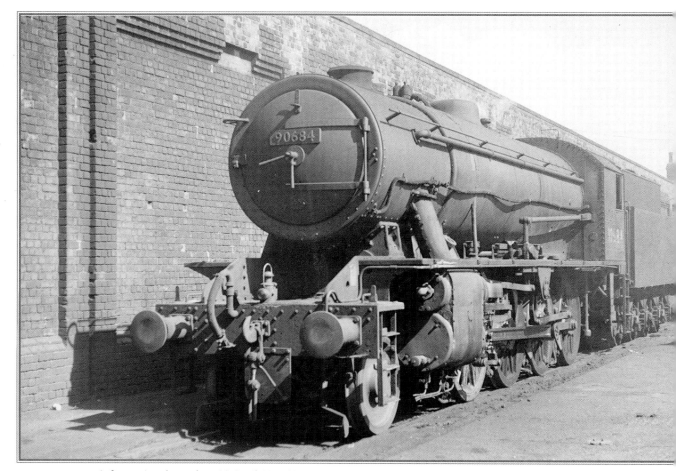

A fine spring day and on 12 April 1963 'Austerity' No. 90684 of Royston shed basks in the sunshine beside Aintree shed. Most of Aintree's allocation of these engines were either condemned or transferred away from Aintree by the start of 1965. The distinctive clank–clank–clank of the loose valve gear on these engines – combined with their usually appallingly filthy, spartan external appearances – gave them a distinct character. Within three years of this photograph being taken it would be noteworthy to sight one of these engines on Merseyside. By the end of 1967, withdrawal of the entire class of 733 locomotives was complete – even a small batch that had undergone general overhauls at Crewe in 1966 had been condemned!

Richard Picton

THE 1960S AT AINTREE

One of my first visits to Aintree in 1964 revealed a sight all shedmasters dreaded – a hapless Stanier 8F, tumbled smokebox first into the 'table pit, its tender still outside the turntable pointed skywards at a crazy angle. An attempt had been made to roll the locomotive onto the turntable, but the rail guides had not been locked into place.

Railway enthusiasts' memories of Aintree shed also recall the whippet races that were conducted informally near the shed building on Sunday mornings and, to impressionable eyes, the (by today's standards tame) 'girlie' pin-ups that wallpapered the enginemen's mess alongside the depot!

During the 1960s, locomotives working into Aintree on freight trains came from far and wide. One such working, the 1350 hrs Morris Cowley–North Mersey Class 4 freight, would often produce an unusual 'foreigner'. In early 1963, for example, this freight from the Midlands arrived into Aintree sorting sidings with BR's ultimate steam locomotive at its head, Standard 9F No. 92220 *Evening Star* (by then based at Oxford). Another stranger to reach Merseyside, on 23 February 1963, was ex-LNER B16/3 No. 61420, which took the central Lancashire line from Rochdale to Bolton to work a Hull–Aintree freight.

The elimination of 'Scots' and 'Patriots' from many passenger workings because of the influx of new diesels also resulted in these types being found increasingly on freight duties. One such engine, 'Scot' No. 46142 *The York & Lancaster Regiment*, was rostered to work the 2100 hrs Low Moor–Aintree freight on 28 May 1963.

By 1 June 1966 a visitor to Aintree shed would find, typically, less than twenty engines 'on shed'. On this day, for example, I logged in my notes the following seventeen locomotives:

Stanier 5MT:	44659, 45323
Ivatt 2MT:	46500, 46502, 46523
Fowler 3F 'Jinty':	47279, 47453, 47566
Stanier 8F:	48050, 48160, 48336, 48363, 48377, 48605, 48648, 48676
WD 'Austerity':	90360

Interestingly, although WD 'Austerities' were a rarity on Merseyside by mid-1966, the example seen at Aintree was not the sole WD observed in Liverpool that day. Classmate No. 90406 was seen trundling through Broad Green station (Lime Street–Manchester line) after our visit to Aintree.

By 20 November 1966, a typical log of locomotives at Aintree would reveal the following twenty-one engines in residence:

Stanier 5MT:	44659, 44816, 45055, 45330
Ivatt 2MT:	46419, 46439, 46500, 46502, 46523
Fowler 3F 'Jinty':	47327, 47367, 47444, 47566
Stanier 8F:	48139, 48301, 48340, 48600, 48605
Standard 4MT:	75043, 75061, 75064

A general view of Aintree shed on 2 July 1961, with the ever-present WD 'Austerities' in evidence together with an Ivatt 2MT Mogul and a Stanier 8F. The latter engines only took a foothold at Aintree once the 'Austerities' were transferred away to end their days on the Eastern and North Eastern regions.

M.S. Houlgrave, from W.T. Stubbs Collection

By January 1967, Aintree shed was also being used to store several Bank Hall engines which had been condemned after that shed's closure the previous October. Included in this category, awaiting despatch to scrap merchants, were No. 45627 *Sierra Leone* (which had been condemned the previous September), and Ivatt 2MT tanks Nos. 41244 and 41304, the latter – to my knowledge – never having steamed on Merseyside after being transferred to Bank Hall from the Western Region in August 1965. Also present was Standard 4MT No. 75049, which was condemned when Bank Hall closed.

The decline of goods traffic, and diminishing work in the nearby marshalling yards, saw the inevitable run-down of steam at Aintree shed – and in the last few months diesel shunters also began to have a greater presence at the shed. However, the depot was one

Another Aspinall Class 27, No. 52260, seen raising steam at Aintree on 22 October 1957. These workhorses had a long and colourful life, being introduced in 1889, and many examples of the class surviving into the early 1960s.

J.A. Peden

of the last to employ gainfully 'Jinty' tanks. One of the shed's examples, No. 47279, was transferred to Sutton Oak as late as November 1966. Although the engine was condemned the following month, fortunately it was sold to Woodham's at Barry and was eventually saved for preservation on the Worth Valley Railway.

Aintree depot was closed on 12 June 1967, with surplus staff and engines being transferred to Speke Junction. As recently as early 1996 the shed superstructure still survived – although badly vandalized. However, in the last week of February 1996 – twenty-nine years after it closed – Aintree shed was demolished. When Engine Shed Society members Mr Dave McGuire and Mr Bob Kneal visited the site on 5 March, they described the scene thus: 'The shed roof was a tangled heap between the remains of the walls, which had been reduced to about two feet in height.'

With the demolition of Aintree went the last poignant reminder of steam motive power depots on Merseyside.

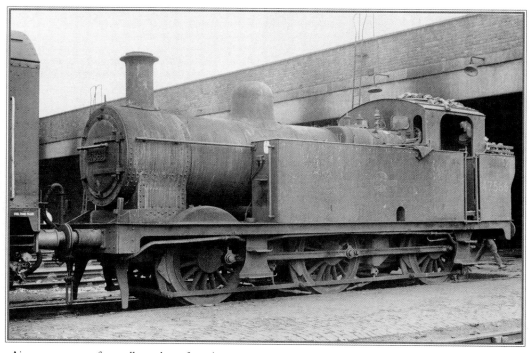

Aintree was one of a small number of north western sheds to retain an allocation of 'Jinty' tanks right up to the end of 1966 when, effectively (bar a few engines retained in the Midlands for specialist work) the class was withdrawn from traffic. No. 47566 is coaled and ready for its next job on 12 June 1966. This engine, which was transferred from Edge Hill in July 1964, was not withdrawn from traffic at Aintree until November 1966. Another Aintree 'Jinty', No. 47327, was saved from Barry Scrapyard and is now preserved in working order.

Richard Picton

GRAND NATIONAL DAYS

Aintree shed's busiest day of the year was invariably Grand National Day in late March, when dozens of trains would make their way to Liverpool from around the country, carrying punters to the world-famous steeplechase races. As a result, the heaviest and fastest express engines from both the London Midland and Eastern regions found their way to what was normally a freight engine depot.

East of Aintree Central was Walton-on-the-Hill shed, where train engines could also be serviced. For the 1962 Grand National, Walton shed provided an ex-works Midland 4F, No. 43988, as station pilot at Aintree Central. Twelve race specials arrived at Aintree on Grand National Day, 31 March 1962, over a two-hour period from 11.30 a.m. Three 'Jubilees' and three 'Royal Scots' were among the thirteen engines heading the trains. Some of the race trains were serviced at Edge Hill carriage sidings and this of course required empty stock movements. Among the engines used on these trains was 'Austerity' No. 90245.

'Black 5' No. 45147 waits at Aintree shed before being despatched to Cohen's of Kettering for scrapping on 29 May 1967. This engine had been withdrawn to the period ending 20 May. It was noted at Cohen's in September waiting to be broken up. When this photograph was taken Aintree had barely a week to go until closure.

Richard Picton

The following list was compiled by Mr Peter Fitton on 31 March 1962, and was recorded in *Steam World* magazine in March 1992.

Arrival/Depart	Train No.	Engine/Pilot★	From/To
11.24	1Z60	70031	Birmingham
(18.45)	1Z60	70031/45295★	Birmingham
12.11	1T05	45622	Luton
12.16	1Z62	45529	Watford
(17.15)		45529/45058★	Watford
12.20	1X43	45695	Newcastle
12.40	1X84	61065	Hull
(17.25)	1X84		Hull
12.43	1Z63	46126	Euston
(17.30)		46126/45196★	Euston
12.53	1T07	73142	Manchester Central
		44717	Manchester Central
			(cont.)

Arrival/Depart	Train No.	Engine/Pilot★	From/To
12.58	1Z64	46146	Euston
(18.10)		46146/45390★	Euston
13.03	1T06	44688	Kings Norton
13.11	1Z65	46159	Euston
(16.50)		46159/45052★	Euston
13.16	1X76	45680	Glasgow
13.16	1X47	76087/44868★	Cleethorpes

★ Wherever shown, pilots were provided by Edge Hill shed.

For the following Grand National, on 30 March 1963, a total of fourteen specials ran to Aintree, terminating again at either Sefton Arms or Aintree Central stations. All specials were steam hauled. Excursions from the London area brought in 'Patriot' or 'Royal Scot' engines including Nos 45530 *Sir Frank Ree*, 46125 *3rd Carabinier*, 46150 *The Life Guardsman*, 46156 *The South Wales Borderer* and 46167 *The Hertfordshire Regiment*.

One train from Coventry was hauled by 'Britannia' Pacific No. 70031 *Byron*, which had appeared the year before, while an excursion from Newcastle brought in Neville Hill

With its commercial links to the Yorkshire coalfields it was not unusual for Aintree to play host to an occasional 'foreign' based engine from the Eastern or North Eastern Regions. On shed at Aintree in April 1963 is B1 No. 61274, which was visiting from Ardsley.

Richard Picton

While 'Crabs' were frequent visitors to Aintree shed throughout the 1950s, it was late in that decade before there was a permanent allocation of these engines at the depot. Here, Agecroft 'Crab' No. 42722 rests, coaled and ready for its return home, on 29 September 1957. By September 1959 Aintree had a permanent allocation of six of these locomotives; by 1964, however, the 'Crabs' had been exchanged for five of the Stanier-built Moguls which succeeded them historically.

J.A. Peden

depot (Leeds) 'foreigner' B1 No. 61010 *Wildebeeste.* All of the London trains returned from Sefton Arms with Stanier 'Black 5s' as pilots as far as Edge Lane Junction.

In 1964, twelve specials ran to Aintree on 21 March, six of them hauled by 'Britannia' Pacifics comprising Nos 70021 *Morning Star* (from Coventry), 70047 (from Watford Junction), 70050 *Firth of Clyde* (with the Tote Investors special), and 70018 *Flying Dutchman*, 70051 *Firth of Forth*, and 70054 *Dornoch Firth,* all on trains from Euston.

On the same day there were five Down workings of trains from Aintree as a result of the race meeting, with No. 46239 *City of Chester* working No. 1Z61, No. 46245 *City of London* working the Tote Investors return train No. 1Z62, No. 46228 *Duchess of Rutland* working train No. 1Z63, No. 46251 *City of Nottingham* working train No. 1Z64, and No. 46240 *City of Coventry* working train No. 1Z65.

When the Grand National specials were at their peak, there was insufficient space to accommodate on shed all of the engines that had worked the trains to Aintree. Mr Tomlinson remembers how engines were simply serviced and coaled at Aintree depot and then went back down to the sidings near the racecourse, and backed onto their trains to await the return trip.

Standard 4MT No. 75061 parked beside Aintree shed awaits its next roster on 12 June 1966. This was one of a quartet of 4MTs that were eleventh-hour 'modern power' draftings to Walton-on-the-Hill shed in November 1963, barely three weeks before that depot was shut! The four were subsequently transferred to Aintree, with No. 75061 being withdrawn in February 1967. I recall this engine and No. 75064 (also of Aintree) being depressingly recurrent performers on the Aintree–Gateacre line with freights during the mid-1960s.

Richard Picton

Ex-LMS 7F 0–8–0 No. 49508 and 'Jubilee' No. 45706 *Express* rest beside Aintree shed on Guy Fawkes' day 1960. Fowler's development of the Bowen-Cooke LNWR G1 and G2 classes was introduced in 1929. However, the engines were not as successful and, in fact, the older engines eventually outlived Fowler's.

John Corkill

Aintree shed in March 1991 – and a very sad site indeed! Where Headlamp Harry and Dusty Rhodes once held sway, Digger, Shadey and UB40 now leave their epitaphs for the depressing 1990s.

John D'Arcy

By 1966, many of the steam specials that had made the Grand National an annual treat relished by hundreds of railway enthusiasts had been handed over to diesel haulage, or were in charge of less celebrated steam types. One 'Britannia' was recorded on Grand National Day, 26 March 1966, in the form of No. 70031 *Byron*. Also, the locomotive *3rd Carabinier* was again in charge of an Aintree-bound special but, alas, this time in the form of a 'Peak' class diesel, the 'Royal Scot' which had passed on its name to the diesel imposter having been scrapped.

8R WALTON-ON-THE-HILL

Merseyside's smallest steam motive power depot in the British Railways era was Walton-on-the-Hill. The shed, formerly operated by the Cheshire Lines Committee, was opened in May 1881 and closed on 15 December 1963.

The depot never had a large allocation of locomotives and operated chiefly on a six-day a week basis, with very little Sunday work. The shed was situated at the north end of Walton-on-the-Hill station and was responsible mainly for freight workings, with its crews and locomotives servicing the large goods depot at Huskisson yard and the marshalling yards at Walton Triangle and Halewood. The depot also provided motive power for the many coal trains to and from the Lancashire and Yorkshire coalfields.

In the pre-grouping era, Walton shed was coded 19A by the Midland Railway and was a sub-shed of Brunswick. The shed was coded 23F in 1935 under the LMS shed review and retained that designation until September 1936. Control of the depot was then transferred to the LNER, which designated the shed WAL. The LNER, and subsequently after Nationalization the Eastern Region, retained control of the depot until May 1949. It was then incorporated in the London Midland Region's register of sheds and recoded 13F. From 22 May 1950 Walton was designated 27E and came under the district control of Bank Hall shed. On 9 September 1963 Walton was recoded 8R, and in the process became the only shed on British Railways to have a suffix so far down the alphabet. However, this distinction did not last long as the depot was closed three months later.

Walton shed was built originally as a six-track dead-end building but was rebuilt as a four-track structure in 1952. At this time the opportunity was taken to reinforce the shed roof with a spray application of concrete. The smoke chutes were also renewed during the upgrading and shed lighting was improved.

The running rails along the shed road pits — which were level with the shed floor — were also raised and welded for the full length of the shed, adding an extra 3 inches of headroom for fitting staff working underneath locomotives.

The turntable at Walton shed was hand-operated and capable of turning an ex-LNER 04 2–8–0 with just a little to spare. However, some time before 1958 it failed and it was deemed uneconomical to repair; thereafter engines were turned by travelling around the Fazakerley Triangle.

Despite its size, Walton shed still retained a small fitters' workshop with a fitter and mate on duty. Running repairs were carried out by this pair following further examination of the engine by the fitter. Boiler washouts were also done during the day by the shed's boiler washer and his mate.

Staff earnings at Walton were more limited than at other, larger, depots because of the absence of Sunday work, excepting the occasional ballast working connected with permanent way specials.

A general view of Walton-on-the-Hill shed on a sunny April day in 1963, its last year. On shed are, from left to right: Nos 44134, 44177 (rear of tenders only), 48758 and 47228. The truncated shed, reduced from six covered lanes to four in the early 1950s, is clearly visible in the background.

Richard Picton

It is interesting to note that shed improvements were clearly long overdue at Walton and that staff complaints were brought to the attention of visiting Railway Executive representatives from Euston, Mr T. Neil and Mr J. Whalley, when they attended a special meeting of Walton's Local Departmental Committee at Bank Hall shed on Tuesday 11 September 1951.

On the condition of the Walton shed coaling stage it was recorded that:

The staff side [of the LDC] mentioned that this matter was first raised in 1946. Their complaints were that there had been no shelter, and that the coal stage generally is in a bad condition.

The management's representatives [Mr A.M. Todd, Mr E. Bull and Mr H. Dobson] stated that a cabin is now in the course of erection and, pending a scheme of improvements at the depot being carried out, a suggestion has been made for a windscreen to be built up at one end of the coal stage, and the engineer will be pressed to carry out this work as early as possible.

Thirteen years earlier, back in the days when a splash of London North Eastern Railway apple-green was still evident, ex-LNER B1 No. E1288 (later 61288) prepares to move off at Walton-on-the-Hill shed on 18 April 1950. The shed retained an ex-LNER influence in its mix of engines well into the 1950s, and visiting 'foreign' engines continued to reside at Walton almost right up to the shed's closure in December 1963.

H.C. Casserley

On the condition of lavatories at the depot, minutes of that meeting show that:

This matter was discussed and it was stated that the complaint, which had been of the lodgement of water, was now being removed by the attention at present being given to the floor.

Even the enginemen's messroom was clearly an unpleasant, not to say unhygienic place to be:

Enginemen's Messroom
This is a complaint of bird droppings through the louvres of roof ventilators. The matter has now been rectified.

A further meeting was held at Bank Hall depot on Thursday 6 December 1951, at which additional complaints were raised. Minutes Nos. 119 and 120 are interesting as they illustrate further difficulties staff were experiencing at Walton shed:

119. Complaint re condition of electric lighting in shed.

The staff side [Mr S.C. Greenhoulgh, Mr R. Darwen and Mr J.T. Lockwood] complained of the poor lighting, particularly with regard to the coal stage, ash pit, and between Nos. 1 and 2 roads, due to defective and unclean lights. The management side agreed to take steps to remedy the complaint, and the engineer would be contacted where necessary.

120. Condition of cycle shed – Walton depot.

The staff side complained that the cycle shed is unfit for use owing to the roof and walls requiring repairs. The management side stated that this matter was receiving attention and steps would be taken to urge the repairs forward. This complaint has already been placed before the engineer.

Closure of Walton depot had been forecast as early as 1926 but four years later it was reported in one railway periodical that more than thirty LMS engines were at the depot. Despite the modest improvements made at Walton during the early 1950s it became evident (especially in the post-Beeching Report climate) that a small depot with an allocation of around fifteen engines did not make economic sense – particularly when larger depots such as Aintree and Speke were able to take up extra work. And so, on 15 December 1963, Walton shed was closed.

Upon closure, Walton's allocation of engines was transferred to Speke Junction depot. The shed remained empty for several years and was still standing in the early 1970s. However, the relentless search for land suitable for urban development soon meant the site was levelled. The shed site is now occupied by a housing estate.

Mr Frank Mangan was employed at Walton-on-the-Hill shed for nineteen years from 1940, having joined the shed initially as a cleaner:

It was a great little shed, with a fine community spirit from Walton and the surrounding areas.

When I started, the shed was controlled by three shift running foremen, Bill Ball, Frank Johnston and Leo Palfreyman. These men were supervised by a shedmaster from Brunswick (the senior LNER depot in the city); his name was Harry Beastall. He ran both sheds and used to communicate several times a week using the tram as a means of transport.

The shed had a fitting staff supervised on days by foreman Ab Guest and on nights by foreman Arthur Ogden. We had a boilermaker by the name of Bill Coady and three steam raisers who also washed the boilers out.

We boasted a coal stage with two electrical hoists and three coalmen to fill the tubs on three shifts.

In the 1940s and into the 1950s Walton shed provided motive power for the Cheshire Lines Committee (CLC) with runs to Southport (Lord Street), Manchester Central, Godley and Wrexham in North Wales. The shed also serviced the main goods yards and sidings at Huskisson, Walton and Halewood in the greater Liverpool area, as well as Trafford Park and Heaton Mersey in Manchester, Warrington and Stockport.

Trains worked from Huskisson Dock to Newcastle, York, Dewsnap, Spink Hill, Mottram and other destinations. Most of the traffic was from shipping, coal for Clarence Dock power station, and Linacre gas works.

Lodging turns had been restricted nationally so Walton men worked to Godley, Guide Bridge and Stalybridge, where Gorton crews would relieve them; the Walton men either worked trains back to Halewood or travelled back as passengers aboard trains.

In the late 1940s most of the engines used were 'foreign-based' 04s, K2s, K3s or J39s. Spink Hill, in the Yorkshire coalfields, required trains from Walton of forty empty hopper wagons on the outward journey, returning with twenty loaded wagons of crushed coal on the inward journey to Liverpool. Mr Mangan remembers another type of goods train too:

The pride of Walton was the 'Meat Train' to York, which usually departed from Huskisson Yard at 5.25 p.m., hauling forty refrigerated containers of meat, all pipe fitted and hauled by a three-cylinder engine.

This was a train you could set your watch to. The crew had to lodge at a house in York overnight and work a train back next day after ten hours' rest.

Another lodging job was to Wrexham with a mixed goods train to supply various places on the way. To get to Wrexham we had to back our train in at Skelton Junction sidings, turn the engine on the turntable, then run around our train and shunt the guard's van to the opposite end of the train. Then right away for Wrexham.

Crews at Walton shed had a range of shunt jobs at Huskisson and Walton yards besides pick-up trains to Halewood from Walton, shunting coal and goods at West Derby, Knotty Ash, Gateacre and Halewood. There were also jobs to Southport (Lord Street) calling at Sefton, Lydiate, Altcar, Hillhouse, Woodvale, Ainsdale and Birkdale.

Mr Mangan recalls the changes brought about by the Nationalization of the railways from 1 January 1948 – a move he believed was retrograde:

When the railways were Nationalized and became British Railways we linked up with Aintree and Bank Hall and came under the jurisdiction of Bank Hall and Motive Power Superintendent, Alec Todd. This enabled staff to transfer for promotion to other depots which suited former LMS employees, who had many more years railway service than those at Walton, thus hindering the promotion from fireman to driver for many.

Mr Tom Lockwood is another ex-footplateman who spent many years at Walton. He was a fireman at the shed from 1948 to 1958, and a driver from 1962 until Walton's closure in December 1963. He began his railway career at Frodingham, LNER, in the

York B1s were quite common at Walton shed during the 1950s and early 1960s. Walton men generally found the B1s to be quite good engines, particularly with their drop grates. However, they were not so popular (as with most steam engines) when they were run down and overdue for the shops. No. 61017 *Bushbuck* awaits its balancing turn back to the North Eastern Region on 1 June 1958. The coaling stage can be seen in the background.

J.A. Peden

early 1940s and transferred to Chester Northgate shed as a fireman before making a 'mutual exchange' with another fireman to Brunswick in February 1945:

> Brunswick, Walton, Warrington, Widnes and Southport (LNER) depots were in what was known as a pocket, and came under the Loco Superintendent at Gorton (Manchester) depot. Applications for movements to depots within this pocket were accepted within the grade.
>
> Following my marriage I transferred under the above arrangement to Walton-on-the-Hill as a fireman on 11 October 1948. I remained at Walton, where I was passed for driving duties on 9 May 1949.
>
> Following Nationalization, promotion was retarded due to driving vacancies being filled by men from Aintree. I decided to apply for a driving vacancy at Brunswick, and was promoted to that position on 11 August 1958.

Mr Lockwood eventually returned to Walton shed in January 1962, via Speke, after Brunswick had closed in the previous September:

Walton was a very homely, small depot with shedmaster Mr H. Dobson and two chargemen alternating late and night turns. Following Nationalization the chargemen were promoted to Running Shift Foremen and we came under Bank Hall, becoming depot 27E, under motive power superintendent Mr A.M. Todd.

Locomotives stationed at the depot at this time comprised in the main side tanks N5 (0–6–2) for shunt duties at Walton Up and Down sidings, Huskisson Dock and Victoria yard, also 'Pom Poms' (J10 and J11s), tender engines for trip working between Walton and Huskisson, and later between Walton and Langton Dock. They were also used for pick-up goods between Walton and Southport (Lord Street) and also Walton and Halewood.

Main line goods trains, powered by Walton engines and crews, travelled far and wide, including destinations such as York, Spink Hill, Whitemoor and Macclesfield. These were usually powered by Gorton engines of ex-LNER classes, including B1, 04, K2, K3 and J39 types.

Until electrification of the Woodhead Tunnel line to Yorkshire in 1954, Walton men were usually relieved by Gorton men, either at Godley Junction, Guide Bridge or Stalybridge. Following electrification, engines were detached at those locations and used for the return workings.

Until the closure of the Southport line to passenger trains in November 1960, passenger trains were also worked by Walton men and engines from Aintree Central to Manchester Central and return, as well as summer workings to Southport.

At the end of a day's duty there was always the time-consuming task of 'disposing' of one's engine. Mr Lockwood recalls the process that was carried out upon arrival at Walton:

Engines arrived at Walton depot via Fazakerley West Junction, thence to a disposal pit where the fire was cleaned, ashpan raked out, and smokebox emptied.

From the disposal pit the engine was moved to the turntable and turned if necessary. The turntable was hand-operated, pushed around by the driver and fireman.

From there the engine was moved to the coal stage and coaled. This was by steel tubs holding about ¼ ton of coal, filled by coalmen from wagons, then hoisted by small electric jib crane with an n-shaped hanger. After releasing the catch the fireman, standing on top of the tender, tipped the coal. The operation was repeated until sufficient coal was on tender.

The fireman would then fill sandboxes with dry fire sand. The engine was then moved to a berthing road where the water tank was filled and then berthed in the shed; the driver would examine the engine and book any defects he observed.

Mr J. Davenport came from a family with a long history of involvement with Walton-on-the-Hill shed. His grandfather had been a driver there shortly after the shed opened in the late 1880s, while his father had begun working at the shed in 1900 at the age of fifteen. Mr Davenport junior was born in 1919; Walton shed was situated at the top of his street:

When I was a lad at school me and my brother often went for an engine ride with my father or uncles, when no one was looking. We used to go to Aintree often, sometimes Southport or Halewood and shunt the goods yards.

The best one, though, was the shortest – from Walton shed down to Huskisson yard. There were three long tunnels and a downhill gradient all the way. Coming back up, especially on a tank engine, was great – better than going to school!

You were black after that, yet you had only been out about one hour. I always remember the times I worked down to Huskisson. What a ride that was, just like a volcano going off.

In today's landscape of high-speed motorways and long-distance road freight haulage, it is easy to forget just how busy our railways once were, particularly on Merseyside. Mr Davenport illustrates the energetic activity that took place at the relatively small depot of Walton on a typical day during the early 1950s:

12.01 a.m. and 12.15 a.m. Mondays: Two crews book on to prepare engines for early workings later that day. Early drivers would book on between 4 a.m. and 6 a.m.

5.50 a.m.: Two light engines depart Walton shed for Huskisson yard.

6.05 a.m.: Train from Godley Junction (near Stockport) arrives at Walton, beside the shed. A driver and fireman from Walton shed relieve the incoming crew and take the train on down to Huskisson.

6.10 a.m.: Two engines travel light engine to Walton sidings. One engine would work on the Up side of the yard sorting traffic brought in from Fazakerley west end, also from Langton and Alexandra docks. The second engine works the reception siding, sorting traffic that has come in the other end of the yard.

6.30 a.m.: A Walton engine travels light to Huskisson and Victoria yard to place wagons in and out.

7 a.m.: An engine travels light off shed to work trips up and down to Huskisson until about 1.30 p.m.

7.05 a.m.: An engine runs light to Walton siding to pick up the train for Southport containing fruit jam, flowers, fish, etc.

7.15 a.m.: Three engines light from Walton shed to work, from 7.45 a.m., passenger trains from Aintree Central to Manchester.

7.45 a.m.: Engine light to Walton sidings to pick up goods containing coal and general goods for all the small stations between Walton and Halewood.

9.45 a.m.: Engine travels light to Walton, takes an oil train to Southport and shunts six small stations along the way.

4.10 p.m.: Light engine from Walton reception siding takes a train to Cressington (five stations out from Liverpool Central).

4.20 p.m.: Light engine to Walton sidings, takes stock to Halewood, then to Cressington.

4.20 p.m.: Light engine to Walton sidings – works a trip train to Allerton sidings.

4.20 p.m.: Light engine off Walton shed, shunt Walton station goods yard. Takes out all loads and empties. Occupies about ninety minutes work.

4.40 p.m.: Engine light off shed to prepare 5.25 p.m. express meat train to York.

5.25 p.m.: Engine light off shed to work 6.10 p.m. express meat train from Huskisson to Leeds and York.

5.45 p.m.: Engine light off Walton shed to work 6.05 p.m. scrap train from Huskisson to Sheffield. This train used to stop at Walton to let the following 6.10 p.m. express meat train overtake.

6.15 p.m.: Engine travels light off Walton shed to work goods from Huskisson.

7.10 p.m.: Engine travels light off Walton shed to work the 7.25 p.m. from Huskisson to Midland coalfields. (Walton men would lodge at Gorton, Manchester, for the night before returning to Liverpool the next day. Prior to the 1930s, Walton crews worked through to Colwick before lodging.)

9.15 p.m.: An LMS train to the Peak District.

9.45 p.m.: One of the pilots from Huskisson brings in a train of goods wagons and empties left over from trains which were too full or too late to pick up. This usually entailed about fifty-five wagons needing sorting at Walton for trains to originate from there.

10.07 p.m.: Book on time for 10.20 p.m. from Huskisson for train to Wrexham.

Mr Lockwood remembers some of the ex-LNER locomotive types which inhabited the shed and nearby marshalling yards.

The O4, D6, D9 and D10s which worked into Walton were rated 'very good steamers with comfortable footplates'. The engines' round firehole doors with centre swivel flap made firing easier; also, as the fireman was on the left-hand side of the engine, the shovel could be used right-handedly. The injectors and sanding gear on these classes were very reliable too. Mr Lockwood:

> The O4s were ideal for loose-coupled trains and would steam on any class of coal. One D10 'Director' I fired with driver Dick Lewis was a Manchester express which had been refurbished for an exhibition and was fitted with outside admission piston valves with loose heads – TAB valves I think they were called.
>
> The engine would coast with a train with regulator closed from Garston nearby to Liverpool. Dropping the lever down leaving the heads at the end of the steamchest would allow any back pressure in the cylinder to pass from front to back of cylinder, balancing the same.

The ex-LNER B1s Walton men worked on the York trains were good engines until they were run down. They were the first the men had come into contact with that were fitted with speedometers, electric lighting and drop grates.

With the opening of the Woodhead route to Yorkshire to electric traction in 1954 further limits were imposed on workings that were available to Walton men. Before the

B1 No. 61065 brings a freight through Walton-on-the-Hill station in the early 1960s. Opened by the Cheshire Lines Committee on 1 December 1879, this station was closed on 1 January 1918. It was adjacent to the locomotive depot.

John D'Arcy

Second World War Walton men would work through to York, Wakefield and other destinations. The war brought about restrictions on lodging turns and Walton men were relieved at either Godley or Guide Bridge. LMS Sheffield men, however, continued to work into Merseyside, leaving their engines at Walton shed and lodging at Aintree barracks.

GRAND NATIONALS, COAL STAGES AND RUNAWAYS

Walton shed became a hive of activity on Grand National Day when it provided turning and servicing facilities to the many 'foreign' engines bringing race trains to Aintree for the world famous steeplechase races. Mr Davenport remembers the period just before, and after the Second World War, when the busiest time at Walton was Grand National Day. He recalls about twenty special trains on the day, all 'engines highly polished and nearly all double-headers. They all had to be coaled, turned and back on their trains one hour before departure time from Aintree.' Sometimes there would be two or three (ex) Great Northern engines in a 'lovely green livery'.

Mr Lockwood remembers in particular the 'Green Arrows' (LNER V2s) and 'Footballers' (LNER B17) B1s as well as 6P LMS engines which worked in from Glasgow. Engines were uncoupled, travelled to Walton shed for servicing and then returned to Aintree Central, recoupled to their trains and were marshalled in departure order. Mr Lockwood said:

I recollect one train, after Nationalization, from Scunthorpe (I think) arriving with the rear streamlined observation coach used on the LNER streamlined expresses. On arrival at Aintree the whole train was drawn back around the Fazakerley Triangle with a pilot engine. The train engine was serviced at Walton then returned to Aintree so that the observation coach was in the rear again for the return journey.

Mr Thomas Prior, who served at Walton as a cleaner and then fireman from 1950 to August 1959, and as a driver from 1959 until the depot's closure in December 1963, also remembers Grand National Days:

It was a train-spotter's dream. Walton was a shed that took engines from all over the UK.

We had to prepare the engines and have them ready as quick as possible. That's where everyone would get stuck in, in respect of the time given to engines. Walton was small but very busy . . . it was used for the overspill from Bank Hall and Aintree sheds.

I saw a 'Clan' engine, (ex) Great Western, Southern engines. On Grand National Day you would have thought you were on a bigger shed, and not such a small one as Walton.

Mr Prior began his railway career, upon leaving school, as a messenger boy (and later oiler and greaser) at Huskisson goods depot, beginning in July 1946:

That's where I got my taste for the footplate; when drivers of shunting engines and main line engines would let you come on board to see how the job was done.

Walton was always a very busy place for a small shed, and was always short staffed. Many a time they would ring Aintree or Bank Hall sheds to see if they had any spare firemen.

Mr Prior said his first turn as a fireman was with Walton driver Joe Brady: 'We took a Derby 4 to Altcar to assist a goods train that had broken down. Passenger trains from Southport CLC Central were due, so we had to get a move on to clear the line.'

It was not until 8 September 1959 that Mr Prior was passed for driving engines and his first driving turn – albeit a humble turn – came on 6 October:

My first driving turn was to take light engines to Aintree shed to be coaled because the coal crane at Walton had broken down. I took three engines, Nos 63743, 44299 and 44471. The fireman's name was George Carter.

I was eventually passed to drive the English Electric 350 hp diesel shunter on 2 August 1962 – that was the only diesel Walton ever had.

Incidents at busy engine sheds were not uncommon in the days of steam and even a small depot such as Walton had its dramas. Mr Lockwood remembers an engine moving off from the ash pits' road one night, running over the turntable and knocking down adjacent buffer stops.

A few nights later, a tank engine travelled from the bottom of No. 4 shed road, past the coal stage, over the turntable, beyond the recently demolished buffer stops, and down a footpath cutting which connected Walton Hall Park to a subway under the railway main line to Huskisson yard.

As there was no access for a breakdown crane, the engine was jacked up a little at a time and a sleeper platform was built beneath the hapless locomotive until it attained the level of the table. The runaway engine was then drawn by a Stanier 8F over a bed of sleepers back on to the shed roads. 'Despite investigations by both the railway and civilian police the cause of these unattended engine movements remained a mystery,' Mr Lockwood added.

The coal stage at Walton was only used by crews with experience as it involved the fireman standing precariously on either the cab top of a tank engine or the tender top of tender engines in order to position and tip the tubs of coal.

The coal tubs (there were about ten to fifteen on the stage) were filled by the coalmen during quiet periods from wagons at the rear of the stage. These three-wheeled tubs, once filled, were pushed into position, directly beneath the radius of the 360° swinging jib. The hanger would be lowered by the coalman, using a small electric control handle. The tub would then be lifted to the required height, then pushed round using the back of the crane until positioned over the engine. Once in position, the fireman would release the catch and tip the tub on the centre fulcrum pins, then swing back and lower. The operation would be repeated until sufficient coal was on the engine.

Other ex-Walton men had similar recollections of the perils of this system. Mr Steve

'Pom Pom' J10 No. 65133 lies dumped at the side of Walton shed on 19 April 1959. In the background is
the tender of Fowler 4F No. 43993. Note the legend 'British Railways', still visible on the side of the 'Pom
Pom's' tender, and the lion-and-wheel emblem, which superseded the full lettering. Walton usually had one
or two J10 or J11 engines allocated throughout the 1950s as well as engines of that class visiting from other
sheds. However, by the early 1960s the 'Midlandization' of Walton was complete.

Peter Hanson

Raymond, who worked as a driver at the depot between 1957 and 1960, described the
coaling stage as 'primitive and very dangerous'. There were a few accidents caused
through this outdated system of coaling engines and by comparison Aintree's coaling
plant was modern and accident free.

Mr Prior vividly remembers the coaling stage: 'The coalmen worked very hard on that
coal stage, everything was done by hand.'

Mr Lockwood lists some of the common faults booked by drivers at Walton: brake
blocks requiring renewal; brakes needing adjustment; axlebox wedge bolts requiring
adjustment; horn stay bolts and big end cotter bolts needing tightening. Also, there
would be engine or tender axleboxes running warm, slide bar bolts working loose,
inoperative sanders needing attention, piston glands, valve spindles blowing, cylinder
covers blowing, and engine or tender springs breaking. Fitters would also have to deal
with faulty injectors or ejectors.

Most depots on Merseyside required footplate staff to dispose of engines after they had completed their rostered turn. Mr Lockwood says that of the six depots he worked at during his footplate career, only Speke Junction used labouring grade men – known as firedroppers – to perform disposal duties. He said:

This was one of the most arduous tasks of a fireman. At LNER depots the fireman used the long clinker paddle to throw out the clinker from the fire, but following Nationalization we were introduced to the LMS practice of lifting a few firebars out and pushing the clinker into the pit through the dampers. To perform this, depots were supplied with metal tongs about 5 feet long to grip the firebars. The emptying of the smokebox was a filthy task with some engines arriving at the depot with smokebox ash level with the top of the blast pipe!

The men who worked on the coaling stage toiled daily to replenish coal and water supplies on the engines, irrespective of the weather conditions. Tipping quarter-ton loads of coal into the tenders with an electrically operated winch and bucket was the railways' only concession to modernization. Occupational, health and safety inspectors of today would probably go pale if they saw the risks railwaymen took in bygone days to fill an engine's tender with coal. Despite the hard work, two coalmen from Walton shed can still manage a smile for Thomas Prior. On the right is John Hanna, the name of his mate is unknown.

Thomas Prior Collection

Although Walton shed did not have any J39 locomotives allocated to the depot by November 1960, those from Gorton shed frequently found their way there, as well as to Edge Hill, on occasions, for repairs. The introduction of drop grates on engines such as the J39s made fire cleaning at the end of a roster a far easier and cleaner task for footplatemen. No. 64718 has been parked in what would have been the fifth covered lane of Walton shed in the 1940s.

J.M. Tolson

Despite having slacker pipes in the pit (when working), drawing ashes out of ashpans with a long rake was a fairly dirty job. The introduction of drop grates on the J39s, K3s, B1s and a few other classes of engine made this task much easier. The ultimate luxury for footplatemen was the arrival of rocker grates, drop ashpans and self-cleaning smokeboxes on postwar engine designs.

Mr Prior preferred the improvements that made firebox and smokebox cleaning more civilized in modern locomotives at the end of a turn:

Engines like the Fairburn tanks and ex-LNER B1s had rocker bars to clean the fires and a drop ashpan and self-cleaning smokeboxes. It made your job easier when putting engines away. Then the BR standard types that were built in the 1950s seemed to demonstrate that the designers did have the footplatemen in mind, but it was a bit too late.

When he first arrived at Walton, Mr Lockwood worked in the No. 1 Goods Link, firing for a driver named Tommy Petch, whom he described as 'a fine engineman'. Petch's brother, Jimmy, was also working at the depot. Mr Lockwood remembers:

The trains were non-fitted, with the engine and guard's brake van the only means of keeping the train under control, except that at Woodley Junction on the Down train sufficient side brakes on wagons were applied by the guard to keep control until the train arrived at Brinnington Junction (Stockport) where the brakes were released.
    The York train was a fully (vacuum) fitted express freight leaving Walton at about 12.40 a.m., picking up at Halewood, making up to thirty-five to forty wagons or vans. We would get relieved at Guide Bridge, then relieve Gorton crews on the return working from York, and arrive back at Walton about 7.40 a.m.
    The other freights out of Walton were partially fitted with similar loads, bank engines were provided from Huskisson to Walton and Stockport to Woodley or Godley as necessary.

After Nationalization, a steady stream of ex-LMS engines began to replace ex-LNER types that had predominated at Walton. Ex-L&YR 'A' class 0–6–0s replaced J10 and J11 class engines, with 'Lanky' tanks taking over duties formerly handled by N5s. Mr Lockwood said:

Later, the clapped out 'A' class engines were replaced by ex-LMS 4Fs, which were a great improvement. The 4Fs were as good an engine as a 'Pom-Pom' but not as comfortable on the footplate. The 'Lanky' tanks were acceptable but lacking in comfort, again, on the footplate, compared with the J10s, J11s and N5s.

The two passenger turns worked from the depot – between Aintree Central and Manchester Central – which had been worked previously by LNER D9s, J10s or J11s were now worked by ex-Midland class 2P 4–4–0s and, occasionally, ex-LMS three-cylinder compounds. Crews found these locomotives, with their large driving wheels, unsuitable on stopping trains between Aintree and Manchester and they were soon replaced by Stanier 2–6–4Ts, which were considered 'ideal' by footplatemen at Walton.
    When Mr Lockwood returned to Walton shed in early 1962 he found little had changed at the depot, although there were a few new faces at the top. Harry Dobson had retired as shedmaster and had been replaced by Mr J. Whelan. Dobson had been easy-

A busy Sunday at Walton shed on 2 June 1957, with 'Pom Pom' J10 No. 65177 in the foreground. Some Walton men claimed that the Fowler 4Fs that replaced these engines at the shed in the late 1950s were an improvement on the 'Pom Poms', but the latter were more comfortable.

Duncan Gomersall

going, 'considerate and respected by the men', while Whelan was 'a man on the way up', who had tightened things up considerably at the shed. Mr Lockwood said:

The old oil stores had been converted into a booking hall and the stores refurbished to Bank Hall standard with gleaming oil tanks and brass taps. Previously, footplate staff walked into the old oil stores and helped themselves from 40-gallon drums on wooden stands. Now the stores issuer handed out the required amount for each engine. If this was found insufficient, a request had to be made giving the reason for the extra amount.

Thomas Prior's favourite Walton engine, Fairburn 4MT tank No. 42113, at Fazakerley West waiting to go on shed in the early 1960s.

Thomas Prior Collection

The sub-shed chargeman had been regraded to Running Shift Foreman, one position was filled by Vic Pitcher following a vacancy being advertised. The other, Jimmy Preston, was regraded from sub-shed chargeman, remaining until retirement in his early 50s.

Several new workings were handed to Walton during the 1950s, among them an ore train known as Long Meg stoppers which arrived at Walton crewed by Lostock Hall (Preston) men and, until the availability in the 1960s of Standard 9Fs, usually hauled by a Stanier 8F. Mr Lockwood:

The engine was serviced at Walton shed then worked by Walton men, moving the train from Walton sidings to ICI's sidings at Widnes Tanhouse Lane.
 A train of empty hoppers would be picked up there and worked via Glazebrook and Lowton St Mary's to Hindley Atherton Junction, via the old Great Central line. At Atherton Junction a change-over with a return loaded train was effected and worked back to Widnes ICI, then a further empty train picked up for Walton. This train was worked out in the evening by Lostock Hall men who had worked a loaded train in for the following day's work.

A further empty van train was worked by Walton men travelling out as passengers to Macclesfield Central and working the vans from Macclesfield towards Halewood, detaching at either Stockport or Warrington.

MEN FOR MUTUAL IMPROVEMENT

Mention must be made of the Mutual Improvement Classes (MIC) which were formed at Merseyside depots with the aim of assisting men to pass their fireman and driver examinations. The classes – which membership cards stated were 'available to Locomotive Men within a 30-mile radius of Liverpool' – were a voluntary concern. Such was the support for the classes, however, that at some depots accommodation was even provided for the classes to be held. The movement became so successful that an Association of Mutual Improvement Classes was formed in Liverpool. At Walton, because there was very little Sunday work, the footplate staff's messroom was used for these MIC meetings.

Apart from operational instruction on rules and regulations, staff would also receive tuition on signals and single-line working procedures, as well as lessons on all aspects of steam engine mechanics, steam generation, the economical working of locomotives and coping with locomotive defects while on a journey.

Mr Lockwood recalls that the classes proved a great help to the men who took part, with most able to pass their examinations at the first attempt:

Each secretary was usually the class instructor, with help also provided by a locomotive inspector for certain classes during each session. An instruction train visited each depot on a roster basis. It comprised a cinema coach, one containing working models of injectors, brake ejectors, sanders, lubricators, etc. and a small oil-fired boiler and a diesel-driven generator. A further coach contained sleeping accommodation for the inspector in charge.

Program guides for the Liverpool Association of MIC for the 1949/50 season and the 1957/8 season provide an illustration of the interesting nature of these classes and demonstrate the changes in syllabus which were necessary with the onset of modernization.

For example, the syllabus for 1949/50 included: on 26 September 1949, the Annual General Meeting of the association and a film entitled 'Building a Class 7X at Crewe'. On 30 January 1950, a Mr Young from Head Office at Euston was present to give a lecture on 'Modern Colour Light Signalling'. The annual class outing, scheduled for Sunday 11 September 1950, was to be a tour of the original Railway Museum at York.

By 1957/8 membership of the Liverpool Association of MIC still only cost 1s per annum, and meetings were still held on Monday evenings in the boardroom at Central Station, Liverpool, starting at 6.30 p.m. (thirty minutes later than in 1949/50), 'by kind permission of Mr C.R. Bennett Esq., Operating Supt., CLC, LMR'.

The agenda for a meeting on 18 November 1957 included a lecture on the 'Diesel Railcar' by J.G. Spencer from the Diesel Training School, Derby, and there was a follow-up

Men for Mutual Improvement: a group shot of the class secretaries when they visited Aintree shed, *c*. 1951. From left to right: Bob Constantine (Aintree), Driver Jim Farrington (Aintree), Mr Gillet (Assistant Motive Power Superintendent Bank Hall), Inspector Cudworth (inspector in charge of the train), Fireman Instructor A. Bailey (Bank Hall), Passed Fireman Ron Capstick (Walton, who left BR to join the railways in Rhodesia [now Zimbabwe]), Passed Fireman Brighouse (Walton), Driver T. McCreary (Walton), Driver Bates (Aintree), Tom Lockwood (who was a Passed Fireman at the time and Walton class secretary), Driver J. Heyes, wearing the trilby (Bank Hall secretary), Driver F. Joslyn (secretary, Aintree), Loco Inspector T.H. Hobson (Edge Hill).

Tom Lockwood Collection

lecture on 24 February 1958. Inspector W. Marsden was present to give a talk on 16 December 1957 on 'Single-line working during repair or obstruction'.

Class educational outings for the season included a visit to Messrs. Davies & Metcalfe's Injector Works at Romily on Sunday 20 October 1957, and one to Crewe Locomotive Works on Sunday 23 March 1958.

LOOKING BACK ON THE WALTON YEARS

Mr Lockwood has few regrets when looking back on his years of service with the railways, other than that he was unable to achieve all of his ambitions because of medical reasons. However, if he had his time over again, he says it is unlikely he would opt for the same occupation, for, as he notes, with today's modern power much of the challenge and a great deal of interest in the job has disappeared:

> With steam engines drivers struggled to reach journey's end, nursing the difficulties – perhaps arriving a little late. But now a loco failure means sitting and waiting for assistance.
>
> I gained satisfaction from the fact that I was able to assist fellow footplate staff in some small way to perform their duties and pass their examinations. I think they appreciated my efforts and proved this by presenting me with a lovely leather dressing case when I left for Brunswick on my promotion to driver.

Mr Steve Raymond, another ex-Walton man, similarly has fond memories of his time at that depot. Mr Raymond started at Aintree shed in 1940 and spent seventeen years working his way through the ranks to the position of spare driver. He joined Walton shed in 1957 ostensibly as a fireman, but because he was a spare driver, all his three years based at Walton were on driving turns. He remembers the area behind Walton goods sidings – Walton Hall Park – as a 'wild place to be during winter' where the wind and rain would howl and lash across, making the hardiest footplatemen wish they were back at home:

> I enjoyed my three years at Walton loco, a nice easy-going depot because of the small number of staff employed there, but the work was no less efficient. Also, the lack of admin. staff – they were stationed at Bank Hall, along with the super. Each man knew his job, working to dockets, so there was little need for supervision.

Mr Raymond said that while Walton was predominantly a freight depot it still had one of the most prestigious passenger turns out of Liverpool in the late 1950s: 'We did work the quickest train between Liverpool Central and Manchester Central. The timing was thirty-five minutes via Padgate straight line – and with a tank engine that was good going.'

Many footplatemen have recollections of incidents that they would rather forget. Sometimes by sheer application and ingenuity they would be able to rescue an awkward situation. At other times, however, crews would reap what they had sowed. Mr Raymond recalls:

> I was at Walton when this incident took place at the prison sidings at Risley; at the time I was spare driver. We were waiting to work the 5 p.m. passenger train back to the old Aintree Cheshire Lines station (Central) via Padgate and Warrington. We had a tank engine with a limited amount of coal and water and while waiting in the sidings my mate and I fell asleep.

Another general view of Walton shed, this time on 21 July 1957, with, from left to right: Nos 43843, 44151 (rear of tender), 44481 (partially hidden behind the water crane), 48472 and Stanier 3MT No. 40199.

J.A. Peden

When we came to we had about ten minutes to prepare before being due out. The fire was very low and we had to search for wood, or anything that would burn. We set off with just about 120 lb/sq. inch steam pressure. Between Warrington and Knotty Ash we stopped short of steam seven times. By this time it was dark.

Arriving at Knotty Ash distant signal we gave up the ghost – no coal, no water, so out came the fire to save the fusible plugs. Sending my mate (who will remain nameless) to the signal-box, I went back to the guard – by this time it was raining – and we had words when it was disclosed that he did not have detonators or even a lamp. The last I saw of him was as he vanished into the dark going to protect the train with God knows what – I never saw him again. He left the railway and went to live in Llandudno.

What few passengers remained were quite upset and we had to wait for assistance for quite some time. I'll never forget the remaining passengers baling out and trying to climb the grass bank, and one very irate passenger shouting at me, 'Are you the driver?'.

I said 'Yes', and he replied in a very nasty voice, 'I've **** 'em'.

When I transferred to Bank Hall in 1960 I left a good home. However, time marches on and Bank Hall itself closed in 1966.

179

Mr Raymond retired in 1988 after forty-eight years service with the railways, latterly working both diesels and electrics from Southport station. He said:

I'm happy to say I still meet my old mates for a drink and an 'All Our Yesterdays'. Yes, we do miss the steam era because you had a mate to work with, although now and then you had a narky mate – but that's to be expected, no one's perfect. There was more comradeship in those days. When steam finished we had to go on electrics and diesels and you worked alone. That's when we lost our identity and that was very sad.

Closure of Walton depot had been forecast for several years in the late 1950s and, in December 1963, the inevitable finally occurred. In the final years ex-LMS designs had replaced the ex-LNER locomotives that made up a typical shed roster immediately after the Second World War. In the final months even BR standard classes began to be drafted to the depot.

In February 1963, just ten months before closure, the following engines made up a typical log of the locomotives that would be found at Walton shed (at this stage many engines were stored pending transfer or scrapping): Nos 42054, 42540, 42617, 42793,

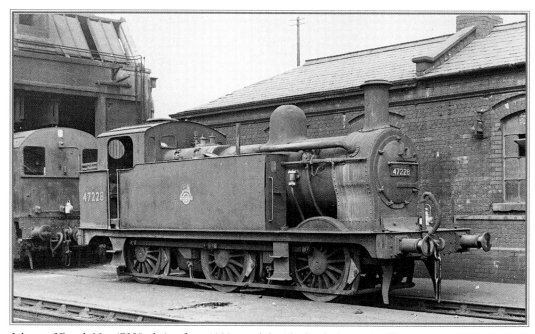

Johnson 3F tank No. 47228, dating from 1899, stands beside the shedmaster's office in 1961. This was one of a group of engines originally built with condensing apparatus (shown by the pipe going into the smokebox) for operating in the London area. It was one of three engines of this class allocated to Walton by late 1961, and the only one to be transferred to Aintree shed following Walton's closure. The locomotive was condemned in February 1964.

M.S. Stokes, from J. Reader Collection

44042, 44124, 44177, 44188, 44462, 44481, 44933, 47225, 47228, 47235, 47327, 47681, 48608, 90724.

Of the impending closure of Walton shed, Mr Prior said men at the depot were aware that it would eventually come about:

I suppose we were all hoping for an eleventh hour reprieve, or something like that.

If Dr Beeching had walked on to the shed that day in December 1963, I don't think he would have walked off – most likely he'd have been stretchered off to hospital!

It's hard to describe the feeling among the men at Walton, where they had worked, played and some had died. Homely – yes, you could say that – but there are some things inside you, you just can't explain.

I think the footplatemen from whatever shed they came from would understand, also the staff at other sheds.

Mr Prior said if he had his time over he would do it all again. In fact, despite leaving the railways in December 1963 to go and work in a factory, he tried to rejoin fifteen years later. However, that attempt failed because of the malady of the 1980s: the recession. Mr Prior summed it up eloquently:

I loved being a fireman; every day was different and every engine a challenge.

Yes, I would do it all over again, but only if it was with steam engines. Diesel and electric trains were nice clean jobs but they don't seem to have any life in them like steam engines. Some steam engines were ugly monsters, some had grace and charm and looked beautiful in their liveries. But most of all to me, they were alive and you controlled it – driver and fireman together.

Yes I would do it all again.

APPENDIX 1

SHED TRACK PLANS – SOME PERSONAL PERSPECTIVES

In the following pages I have drawn upon the knowledge of former shed staff at Liverpool's seven steam sheds to present some personal perspectives of the facilities which existed during the steam era. The diagrams are shown in the following sequence:

1. 8A Edge Hill
2. 8C Speke Junction
3. 8E Brunswick
4. 8H Birkenhead
5. 8K Bank Hall, 1953
6. Site of Bank Hall
7. 8L Aintree
8. 8R Walton-on-the Hill

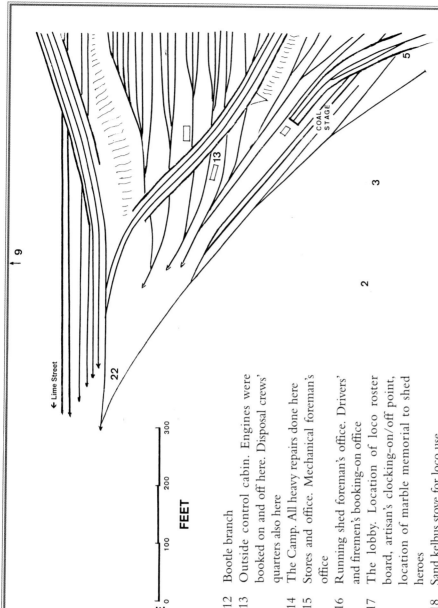

SCALE ← FEET

0 100 200 300

← Lime Street

KEY

1 Circle freight line – used also by boat train traffic to Riverside stn
2 Downhill carriage sidings (Wavertree)
3 Liverpool–London main line
4 Bridge 99 – this carried the circle line over the main line. Demolished in April 1993
5 Elevated track leading to top of coal stage. Capstan operated
6 The 1 in 27 incline which linked the main shed entrance and exit
7 The sandstone viaduct than spanned all the shed roads. Demolished in April 1991
8 The two-level girder bridge which carried the line from Edge Hill No. 4 signal-box to Olive Mount Junct.
9 Tuebrook sidings. Now used by permanent way branch for ballast train storage
10 Circle line bridge over Liverpool–Manchester main line
11 Depot water storage tank
12 Bootle branch
13 Outside control cabin. Engines were booked on and off here. Disposal crews' quarters also here
14 The Camp. All heavy repairs done here
15 Stores and office. Mechanical foreman's office
16 Running shed foreman's office. Drivers' and firemen's booking-on office
17 The lobby. Location of loco roster board, artisan's clocking-on/off point, location of marble memorial to shed heroes
18 Sand kelbus stove for loco use
19 Roads 13 to 19 – demolished in 1966
20 Fuel point – a couple of tank wagons
21 Machine shop, fully equipped for white metalling. Various lathes, coppersmith's and blacksmith's hearths, water press for removing side rod bushes, planing machine
22 Way off shed from the coaling area. The tracks connected with the Manchester line

COAL STAGE

1. 8A EDGE HILL (diagram continues below)

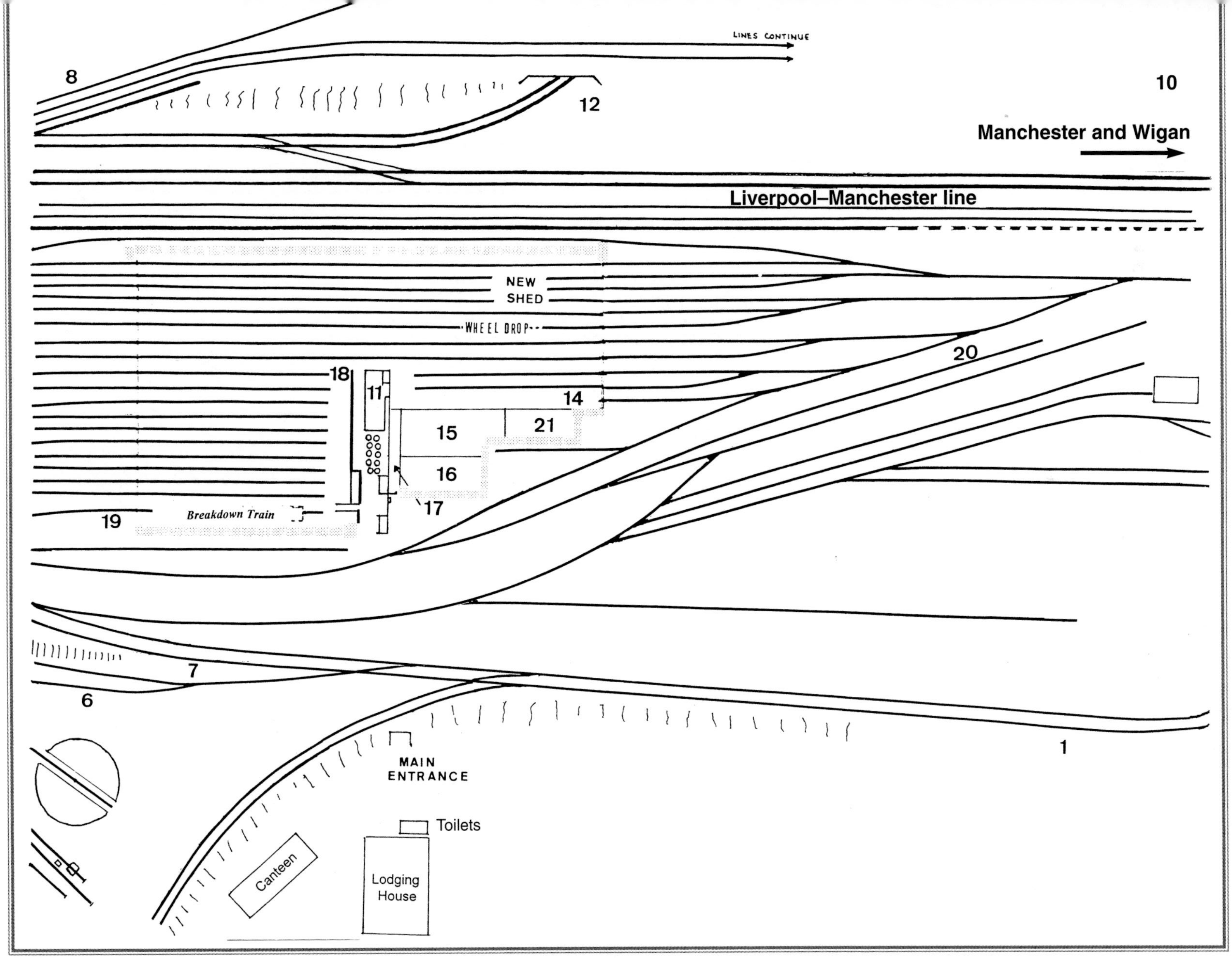

10

Manchester and Wigan

Liverpool–Manchester line

LINES CONTINUE

20

12

8

NEW SHED

WHEEL DROP

14

21

15

16

17

11

18

19

Breakdown Train

MAIN ENTRANCE

Toilets

Lodging House

Canteen

1

7

6

8A EDGE HILL (cont.)

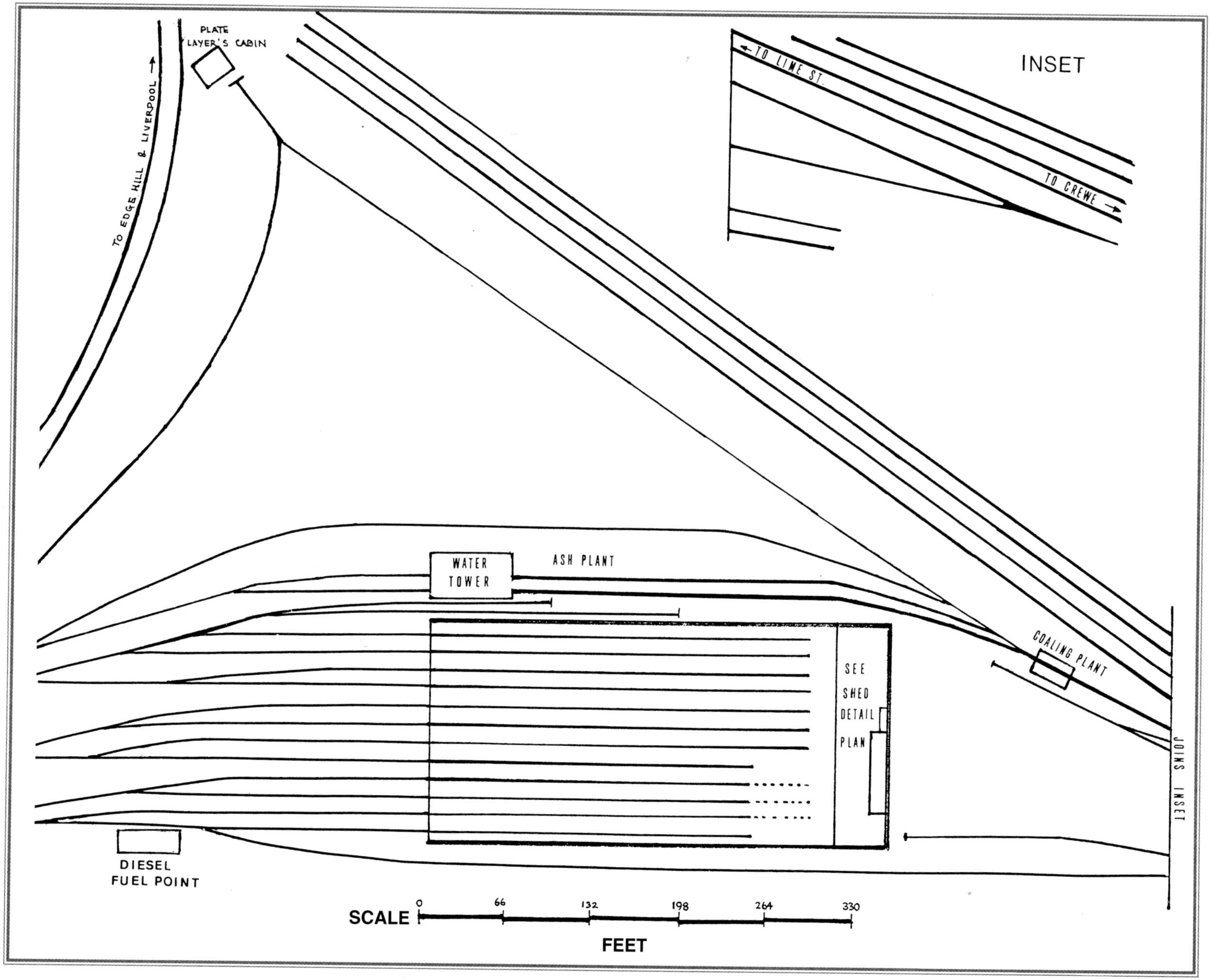

INSET

TO CREWE →

← TO LIME ST

JOINS INSET

COALING PLANT

SEE SHED DETAIL PLAN

ASH PLANT

WATER TOWER

PLATE LAYER'S CABIN

← TO EDGE HILL & LIVERPOOL

DIESEL FUEL POINT

SCALE

0   66   132   198   264   330

FEET

2. 8C SPEKE JUNCTION

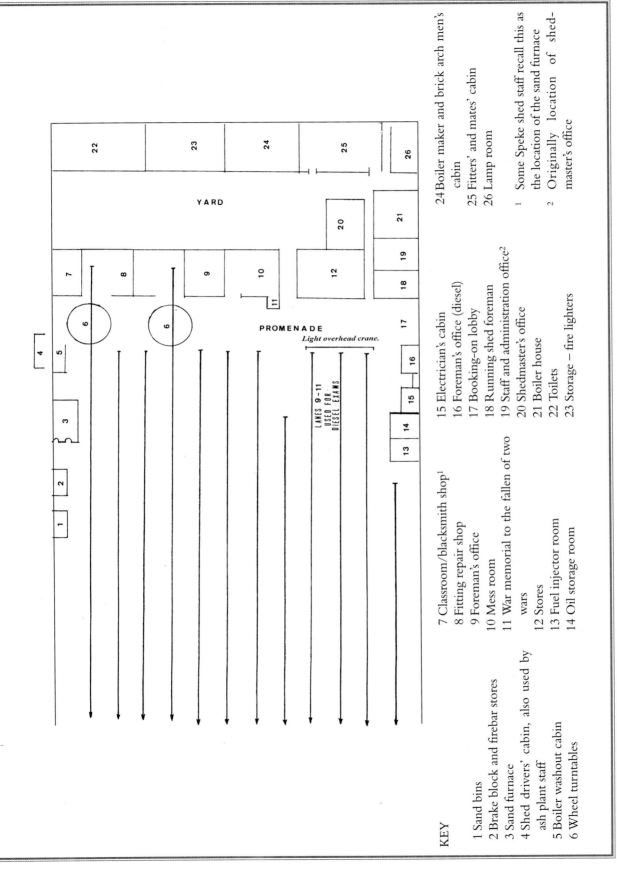

* NOT TO SCALE

KEY

1 Sand bins
2 Brake block and firebar stores
3 Sand furnace
4 Shed drivers' cabin, also used by ash plant staff
5 Boiler washout cabin
6 Wheel turntables
7 Classroom/blacksmith shop[1]
8 Fitting repair shop
9 Foreman's office
10 Mess room
11 War memorial to the fallen of two wars
12 Stores
13 Fuel injector room
14 Oil storage room
15 Electrician's cabin
16 Foreman's office (diesel)
17 Booking-on lobby
18 Running shed foreman
19 Staff and administration office[2]
20 Shedmaster's office
21 Boiler house
22 Toilets
23 Storage – fire lighters
24 Boiler maker and brick arch men's cabin
25 Fitters' and mates' cabin
26 Lamp room

1 Some Speke shed staff recall this as the location of the sand furnace
2 Originally location of shed-master's office

8C SPEKE JUNCTION, SHED DETAIL PLAN

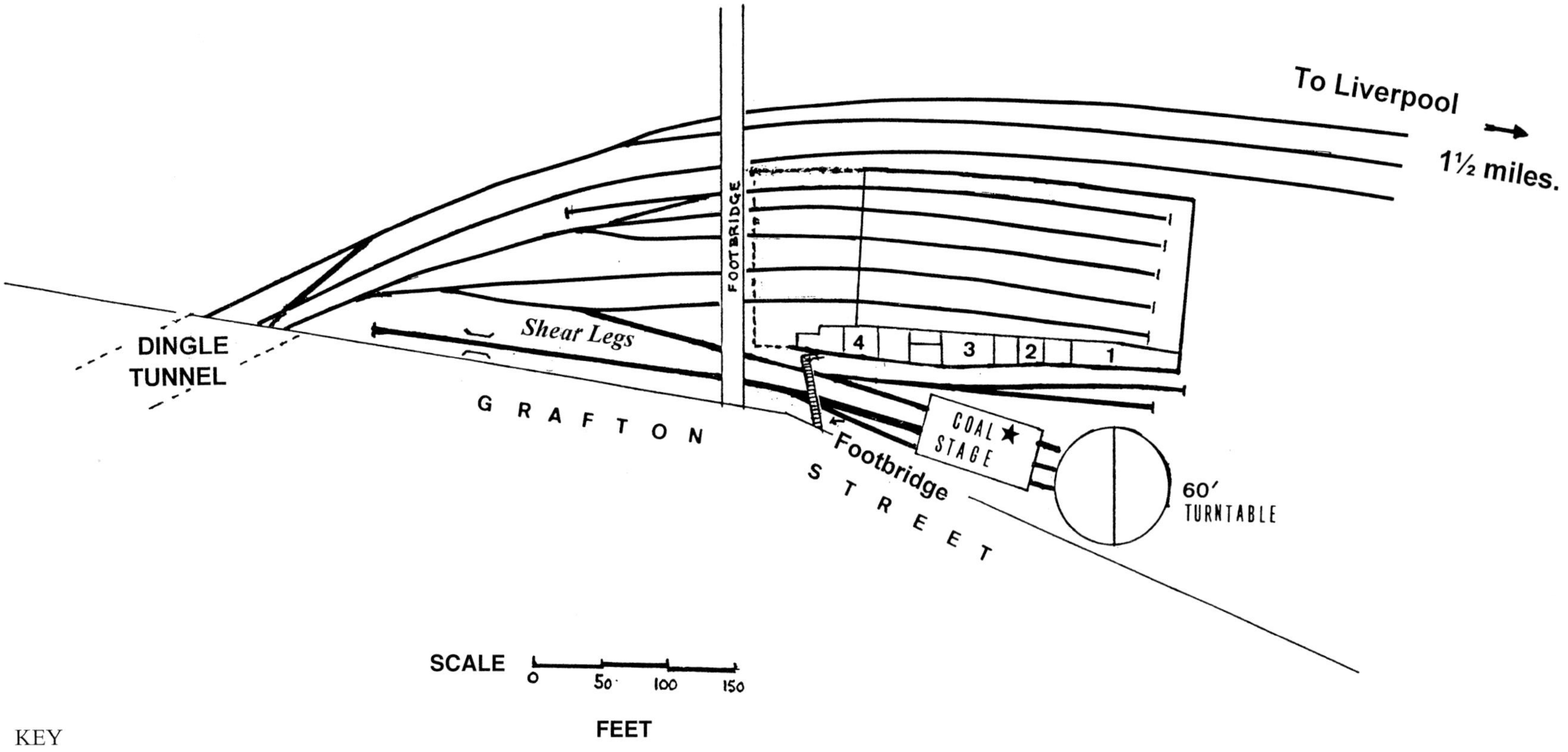

KEY

1 Rough stores
2 Washroom
3 Fitter's area
4 Stores
★ Coal stage had electric hoist and
   water tank overhead

3. 8E BRUNSWICK

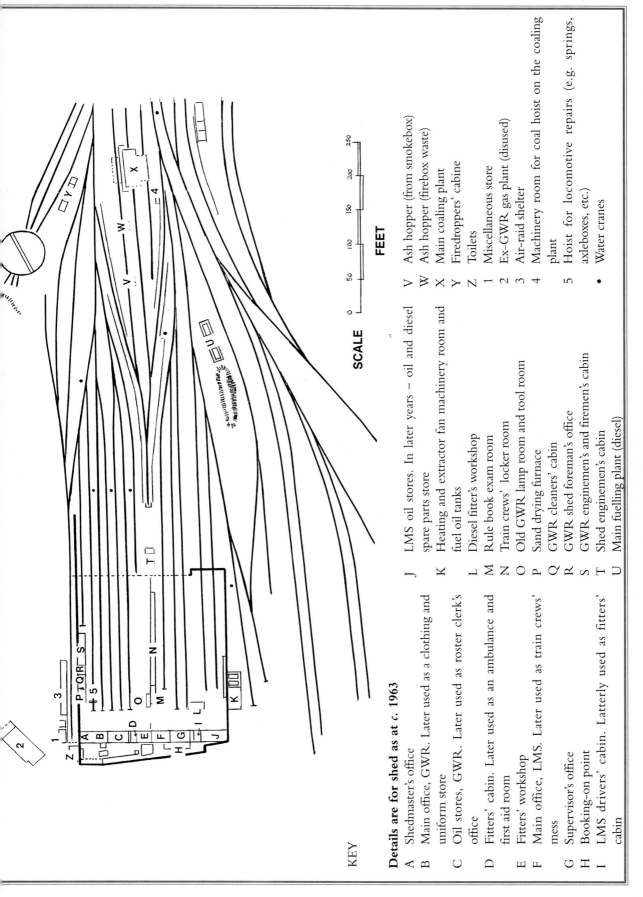

KEY

Details are for shed as at c. 1963

A Shedmaster's office
B Main office, GWR. Later used as a clothing and uniform store
C Oil stores, GWR. Later used as roster clerk's office
D Fitters' cabin. Later used as an ambulance and first aid room
E Fitters' workshop
F Main office, LMS. Later used as train crews' mess
G Supervisor's office
H Booking-on point
I LMS drivers' cabin. Latterly used as fitters' cabin

J LMS oil stores. In later years – oil and diesel spare parts store
K Heating and extractor fan machinery room and fuel oil tanks
L Diesel fitter's workshop
M Rule book exam room
N Train crews' locker room
O Old GWR lamp room and tool room
P Sand drying furnace
Q GWR cleaners' cabin
R GWR shed foreman's office
S GWR enginemen's and firemen's cabin
T Shed enginemen's cabin
U Main fuelling plant (diesel)

V Ash hopper (from smokebox)
W Ash hopper (firebox waste)
X Main coaling plant
Y Firedroppers' cabine
Z Toilets
1 Miscellaneous store
2 Ex-GWR gas plant (disused)
3 Air-raid shelter
4 Machinery room for coal hoist on the coaling plant
5 Hoist for locomotive repairs (e.g. springs, axleboxes, etc.)
• Water cranes

SCALE

0   50   100   150   200   250

FEET

4. 8H BIRKENHEAD

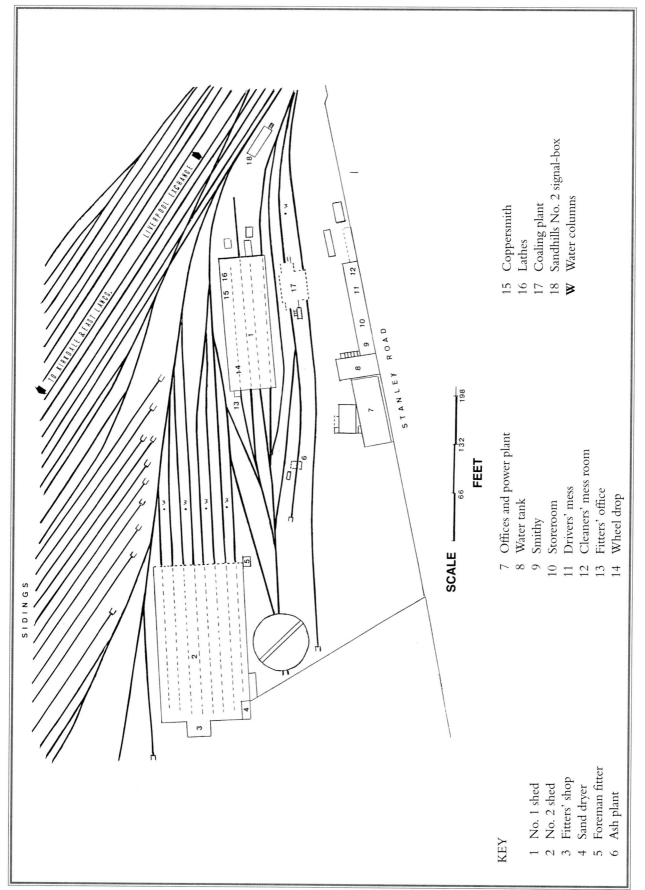

SIDINGS

LIVERPOOL EXCHANGE

TO KIRKDALE & EAST LANCS.

STANLEY ROAD

SCALE

FEET

66   132   198

KEY

1 No. 1 shed
2 No. 2 shed
3 Fitters' shop
4 Sand dryer
5 Foreman fitter
6 Ash plant

7 Offices and power plant
8 Water tank
9 Smithy
10 Storeroom
11 Drivers' mess
12 Cleaners' mess room
13 Fitters' office
14 Wheel drop

15 Coppersmith
16 Lathes
17 Coaling plant
18 Sandhills No. 2 signal-box
W Water columns

5. 8K BANK HALL

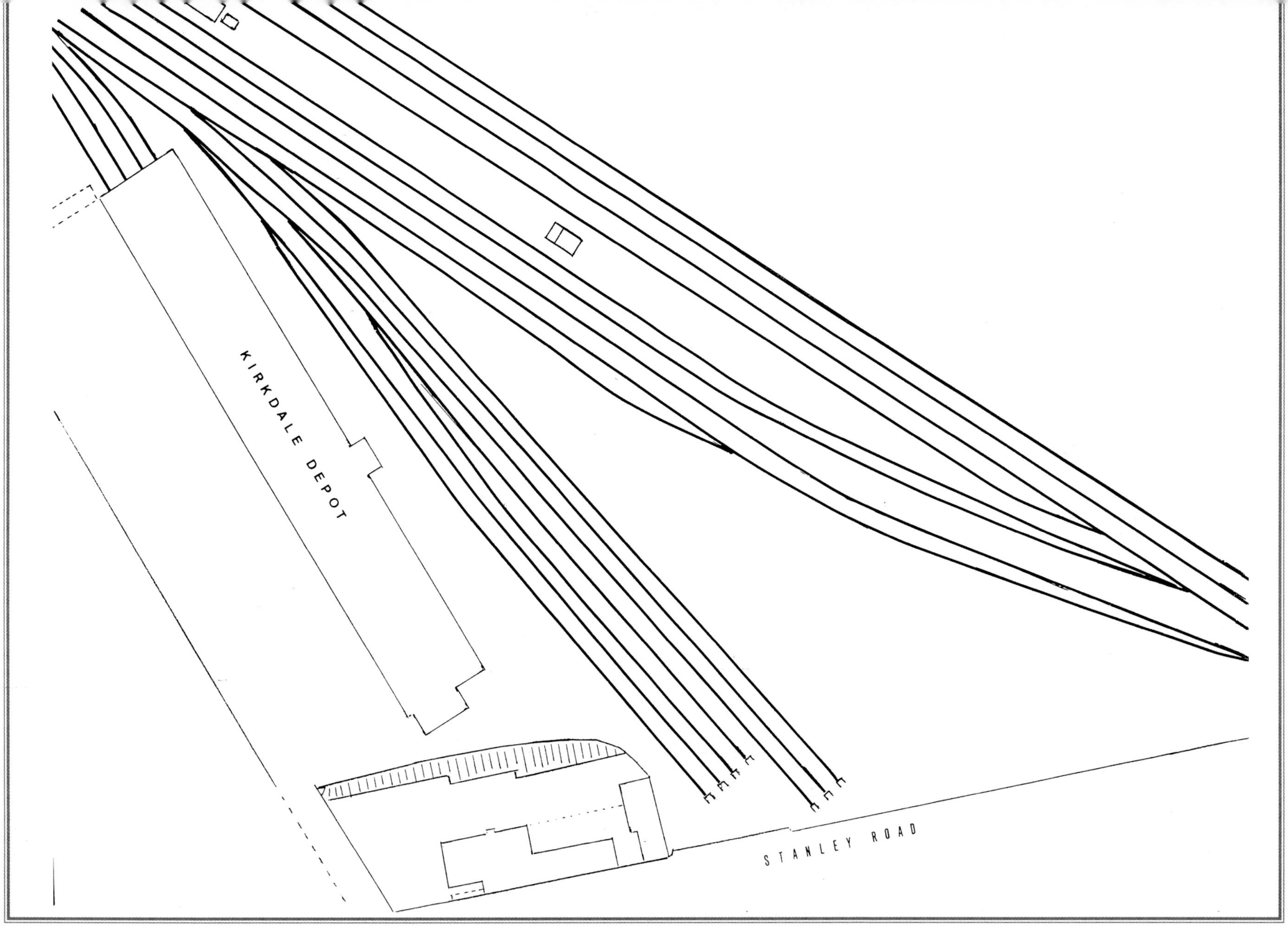

STANLEY ROAD

KIRKDALE DEPOT

6. SITE OF BANK HALL, 1987

KEY

Aintree, c. 1944–52

1. Foreman's hut (Percy Teece, Horace Bradshaw 'Razor' Billy Wright, Foreman – RSF)
2. Concrete coaling stage built 1937
3. Original coaling stage with overhead water tank. The latter was sometimes used in summer as a swimming pool by crews!
4. Outside crews' mess room
5. The point where Stanier 8F No. 48008 blew its right-hand cylinder to bits after its cylinder drain cocks had been left in the closed position. A driver later opened the regulator, unaware of the error at stabling. Engine out of traffic for around 12 months
6. Sand drier – Jackie Gallagher
7. Bill Hesketh's hut – young cleaners would sometimes, for a prank, drop detonators down the hut's chimney while a card game was in progress!
8. Engine washout line
9. Fitters
10. 'Scoff' rooms
11. Stores: Bill Manns, Fred Pitman, Peter Molly
12. Canteen – in an old carriage
13. Offices
14. Oil storage
15. Electrician's hut (Fred Howell)
16. Turntable with half-covered pit

SCALE

0   66   132

FEET

7. 8L AINTREE

SCALE

0   50   100   150

FEET

N

Original extent of shed, cut back
to 4-lane in early 1950s.

KEY

1   Walton-on-the-Hill station (closed 1 January 1918)
2   Toilets
3   Footplate staff messroom and fitters' shop
4   Shedmaster's Office
5   Coal stage and overhead water tank
6   Sand drying house
7   Turntable (damaged out of use)
8   Subway to Walton Hall Park

8. 8R WALTON-ON-THE-HILL

APPENDIX 2

LOCOMOTIVES ON MERSEYSIDE – 1961 TO 1968

The following list contains details of all locomotives officially allocated to Merseyside sheds during the final seven years of steam on British Railways. Unless otherwise stated, the first listing of an engine indicates the shed it was allocated to as at 4 November 1961.

In instances where an engine was transferred away from Merseyside, only the initial recipient shed is listed. Subsequent allocations to other depots are not recorded. However, withdrawal date of the locomotive is recorded, the indicated date being for the week ending of the listing.

Where specific engines are named, this is indicated with a note number, the legend for which is listed at the end of the table.

Engine No.	Transfers & Notes	Withdrawn
41205	to Bank Hall 31.12.60 (awaiting scrapping Central Wagon Works, Wigan, 27.3.65	21.3.64
41211	to Bank Hall 7.3.64	10.9.66
41226	to Birkenhead 16.9.61, to Bangor 7.4.62	3.10.64
41237	to Bank Hall 22.12.62	3.10.64
41244	to Bank Hall 25.7.64, to Aintree 22.10.66	3.12.66
41268	Bank Hall	11.7.64
41269	Bank Hall	29.12.62
41304	to Bank Hall 7.8.65, to Aintree 3.10.66	3.12.66
42054	to Walton-on-the-Hill 4.8.62, to Aintree 14.12.63, to Newton Heath 14.3.64	11.7.64
42075	Birkenhead 26.10.63, to Bangor 4.7.64	4.6.65
42077	to Speke 16.9.61, to Willesden 10.11.62 (awaiting scrapping Central Wagon Works, Wigan, 27.3.65)	1.7.64
42078	to Speke 16.9.61, to Southport 20.6.64, to Bank Hall 11.6.66	18.6.66
42086	to Birkenhead 15.8.64 (awaiting scrapping Cohen's, Kettering, 27.9.67)	22.4.67
42087	to Birkenhead 6.8.66	11.66
42121	Edge Hill, to Speke 1.12.62, to Stockport Edgeley 20.6.64, to Birkenhead 1/65	16.7.66
42132	to Bank Hall 11.6.66	18.6.66
42133	to Birkenhead 10.12.66 (awaiting scrapping Cohen's, Kettering, 27.9.67)	22.4.67
42155	Edge Hill, to Gorton 19.1.63	4.6.65
42156	to Birkenhead 1.5.65	26.2.66
42183	to Speke 16.9.61, to Northampton 17.2.62, to Willesden 21.4.62, to Northampton 12.5.62	8.10.66
42186	to Speke 16.9.61, to Aston 26.5.62, to Stafford 16.6.62	11.7.64
42350	to Birkenhead 25.5.63, to Chester Midland 20.7.63	
42351	to Birkenhead 30.6.62	8.9.62
42389	to Speke 23.6.62	23.3.63
42394	to Birkenhead 18.8.62, to North Eastern Region 4.1.64	18.6.66
42441	Birkenhead	25.1.64

Engine No.	Transfers & Notes	Withdrawn
42445	to Speke 16.9.61, to Lostock Hall 22.6.63	19.11.64
42455	to Speke 21.12.63	23.4.66
42459	to Birkenhead 18.6.60	23.2.65
42491	to Speke 20.4.63	5.10.63
42493	Birkenhead	16.5.64
42540	Walton-on-the-Hill	3.11.62
42542	Birkenhead, to Stoke 23.2.63	17.7.65
42548	to Birkenhead 6.8.66	
42566	to Birkenhead 25.5.63	4.6.65
42580	to Speke 16.9.61	1.12.62
42581	to Birkenhead 30.10.65	26.3.66
42583	Birkenhead, to Willesden 18.5.63	5.11.66
42584	to Speke 16.9.61 to Lostock Hall 22.6.63	5.9.64
42586	to Birkenhead 22.2.64	17.12.64
42587	to Birkenhead 12.11.66 transferred to Eastern Region 29.4.67, to Low Moor 20.5.67	10.67
42597	to Birkenhead 20.2.60	6.11.65
42598	to Speke 16.9.61	30.11.63
42599	to Edge Hill 16.9.61	6.10.62
42602	Birkenhead	26.12.64
42606	Birkenhead, to Willesden 25.5.63 then Birkenhead by 5.64	5.11.66
42608	Birkenhead	5.9.64
42612	Speke 16.9.61	25.1.64
42613	to Birkenhead 19.3.66	22.4.67
42616	to Birkenhead 12.2.66, to Eastern Region 27.5.67	7.10.67
42617	to Walton-on-the-Hill 8.9.62	30.11.63
42647	to Birkenhead 23.7.66	20.5.67
42658	Birkenhead	6.10.62
42663	to Edge Hill 8.1.66, to Carnforth 5.2.66 (at Birkenhead 9.67 with collision damage)	25.3.67
42700	to Birkenhead 6.11.65 (then stored at Hellifield pending later preservation at Keighley & Worth Valley Railway)	26.3.66
42707	to Birkenhead 20.6.64	3.10.64
42711	Aintree, to Wigan 16.6.62	7.9.63
42715	to Aintree 22.6.63, to Gorton 23.11.63	26.2.66
42721	Aintree, to Bolton 18.5.63	2.11.63
42727	Aintree, to Rose Grove 11.1.64, to Birkenhead 19.3.66	8.1.67
42730	to Aintree 15.9.62, to Wigan 23.11.63, to Birkenhead 23.5.64	17.7.65
42734	to Birkenhead 20.11.65	26.3.66
42747	to Birkenhead 31.3.62	23.3.63
42753	to Birkenhead 7.12.63 (awaiting scrapping Bird's, Long Marston, South Wales, late 1965)	11.9.65
42765	to Birkenhead 23.5.64 (saved from Barry Scrapyard 4.78, retained at Worth Valley Railway)	31.12.66
42772	to Birkenhead 18.11.61, to Buxton 18.8.62	4.6.65
42773	to Birkenhead 16.6.62	1.12.62
42777	Birkenhead	7.8.65
42782	to Birkenhead 14.9.63	3.12.66
42783	to Birkenhead 15.9.62	27.8.65
42785	to Birkenhead 31.3.62	30.11.63
42786	to Birkenhead 16.6.62	3.11.62
42797	Birkenhead	24.3.62
42804	to Birkenhead 9.1.60	29.12.62
42810	to Birkenhead 31.3.62	28.12.63

Engine No.	Transfers & Notes	Withdrawn
42812	to Birkenhead 16.10.65	18.6.66
42814	Birkenhead	11.9.65
42815	to Edge Hill 20.10.62	3.10.64
42827	to Birkenhead 20.6.64	11.9.65
42828	to Birkenhead 4.9.65	6.11.65
42831	to Birkenhead 30.10.65	1.1.66
42833	to Edge Hill 22.12.62	29.12.62
42845	Aintree, to Gorton 23.11.63	5.9.64
42848	to Edge Hill 20.10.62, to Stockport Edgeley 6.3.65	7.3.65
42851	to Edge Hill 1.12.62	11.7.64
42852	to Birkenhead 16.6.62	13.7.63
42853	to Birkenhead 18.11.61	13.7.63
42854	to Birkenhead 16.6.62	30.11.63
42856	to Birkenhead 7.12.63 (awaiting scrapping Ward's, Beighton, Sheffield, 3.4.65)	17.12.64
42858	to Birkenhead 14.9.63 (awaiting scrapping Central Wagon Works, Wigan, 27.3.65)	16.5.64
42859	to Birkenhead 16.6.62 (saved from Barry Scrapyard 12.86, retained at Hull)	31.12.66
42870	to Birkenhead 16.6.62	23.3.63
42878	Aintree, to Gorton 23.11.63, to Birkenhead 4.9.65	10.65
42885	to Birkenhead 16.6.62	28.12.63
42886	to Edge Hill 20.10.62, to Lower Darwen 20.3.65 (awaiting scrapping Ward's, Beighton, Sheffield, 7.65)	24.4.65
42892	to Birkenhead 10.11.62, to Lower Darwen 20.3.65	4.6.65
42894	to Birkenhead 15.8.64	26.12.64
42900	to Birkenhead 20.6.64	9.10.65
42920	to Edge Hill 24.11.62	26.12.64
42923	to Edge Hill 26.11.60, to Birkenhead 5.5.62	25.1.64
42924	to Edge Hill 24.11.62	26.2.66
42925	Edge Hill 24.11.62 (awaiting scrapping Ward's, Beighton, Sheffield, 3.4.65)	17.12.64
42933	to Birkenhead 26.1.63	18.5.63
42934	to Birkenhead 12.1.63	19.11.64
42935	to Birkenhead 16.6.62	26.1.63
42936	to Birkenhead 26.11.60	17.7.65
42937	to Birkenhead 22.6.63	4.6.65
42939	to Birkenhead 16.6.62	14.7.62
42942	to Birkenhead 19.3.66	28.1.67
42943	to Birkenhead 13.10.62	16.5.64
42944	to Birkenhead 13.10.62	18.5.63
42946	to Birkenhead 10.9.60, to Nuneaton 16.6.62	4.12.65
42950	Birkenhead, to Nuneaton 16.6.62, to Birkenhead 5.10.63, to Nuneaton 26.10.63	6.11.65
42951	to Birkenhead 5.10.63, to Nuneaton 26.10.63	26.3.66
42952	to Birkenhead 22.6.63, to Mold Junction 27.9.63, to Aintree 23.11.63 (awaiting scrapping Central Wagon Works, Wigan, 27.3.65)	3.10.64
42953	to Aintree 16.11.63, to Springs Branch 25.7.64	29.1.66
42956	to Aintree 9.11.63, to Springs Branch 25.7.64	3.10.64
42958	to Birkenhead 10.6.61, to Nuneaton 16.6.62	4.12.65
42960	to Aintree 23.11.63, to Springs Branch 25.7.64, to Gorton 15.5.65	29.1.66
42961	to Aintree 23.11.63, to Springs Branch 25.7.64, to Gorton 15.5.65	11.9.65
42964	to Birkenhead 5.10.63, to Nuneaton 26.10.63	4.12.65
42968	to Birkenhead 10.6.61, to Nuneaton 16.6.62 (saved from Barry Scrapyard 12.73, restored to working order at Severn Valley Railway)	31.12.66
42969	Birkenhead, to Nuneaton 16.6.62	26.12.64

Engine No.	Transfers & Notes	Withdrawn
42970	Birkenhead, to Nuneaton 16.6.62, to Birkenhead 5.10.63, to Nuneaton 26.10.63	19.11.64
42971	Birkenhead, to Nuneaton 16.6.62	26.12.64
42973	to Birkenhead 6.2.60, to Nuneaton 16.6.62	30.11.63
42978	to Birkenhead 5.10.63, to Nuneaton 26.10.63	21.5.66
42981	to Birkenhead 18.6.60, to Nuneaton 16.6.62	21.5.66
43988	to Walton 19.12.59, to Leicester Midland 28.7.62	19.11.64
44023	Walton, to Derby 13.10.62	26.12.64
44038	Walton, to Saltley 13.10.62	
44040	Walton, to Saltley 13.10.62	17.12.64
44118	to Walton 15.9.62, to Wellingborough 22.9.62 (scrapped Draper's, Hull, late 1965)	4.6.65
44126	to Birkenhead 29.6.63, to Stoke 24.8.63	7.9.63
44177	to Walton 15.9.62, to Gorton 4.1.64	17.12.64
44188	Walton, to Gorton 4.1.64	4.12.65
44192	to Walton 22.6.63, to Lower Darwen 4.1.64	24.4.65
44208	to Birkenhead 29.6.63, to Stoke 14.9.63	5.10.63
44218	Walton, to Burton 3.2.62 (and eventually Westhouses)	26.3.66
44308	to Birkenhead 29.6.63, to Stoke 14.9.63	5.10.63
44309	to Birkenhead 29.6.63, to Stoke 20.7.63	10.8.63
44395	to Birkenhead 29.6.63, to Stoke 14.9.63, to Springs Branch 9.11.63	30.11.63
44462	Walton, to Burton 20.1.62, to Walton 27.1.62, to Lower Darwen 4.1.64	4.12.65
44481	Walton, to Newton Heath 21.12.63	17.12.64
44593	to Birkenhead 29.6.63, to Stoke 14.9.63, to Crewe Works 9.11.63	26.12.64
44605	Walton, to Saltley 13.10.62	3.10.64
44659	to Aintree 30.4.66	17.7.67
44666	to Edge Hill 20.8.66	
44676	to Aintree 18.5.63, to Newton Heath 22.6.63	11.7.64
44678	to Speke 21.8.65, to Springs Branch 22.1.66	2.12.67
44679	to Speke 21.8.65, to Springs Branch 22.1.66	7.10.67
44682	to Edge Hill 8.10.60, to Lancaster Green Ayre 19.5.62	2.12.67
44688	to Edge Hill 24.7.65	10.9.66
44692	to Aintree 17.3.62, to Carlisle Kingmoor 18.5.63	21.5.66
44711	to Edge Hill 9.12.67	18.5.68
44717	to Edge Hill 31.7.65	9.9.67
44725	to Speke 14.3.64	4.11.67
44729	to Aintree 17.3.62, to Carlisle Kingmoor 18.5.63	8.10.66
44730	to Birkenhead 21.1.67	2.12.67
44732	to Speke 19.9.64, to Springs Branch 28.5.66	5.7.67
44737	to Bank Hall 14.5.66, to Springs Branch 11.66	28.1.67
44738	to Speke 9.11.63	11.7.64
44739	to Speke 9.11.63	23.2.65
44741	to Speke 23.9.61	27.3.65
44742	to Speke 23.9.61, to Bank Hall 6.1.62, to Southport 17.3.62	16.5.64
44743	Bank Hall, to Southport 17.3.62	29.1.66
44744	Bank Hall, to Southport 17.3.62	30.11.63
44745	Bank Hall, to Southport 17.3.62	19.11.64
44749	to Speke 11.11.61	5.9.64
44750	to Speke 11.11.61, to Stoke 4.8.62, to Speke (again) 18.8.62	7.9.63
44751	to Speke 18.11.61	19.11.64
44754	to Speke 18.11.61	16.5.64
44758	to Edge Hill 10.9.60, to Lancaster Green Ayre 23.6.62	10.8.68
44767	Bank Hall, to Southport 17.3.62 (preserved as 4767 *Stephenson*)	30.12.67

Engine No.	Transfers & Notes	Withdrawn
44768	Edge Hill	17.6.67
44769	Edge Hill	17.7.65
44772	Edge Hill	4.11.67
44773	Edge Hill	30.12.67
44774	to Edge Hill 20.8.66	9.9.67
44777	to Edge Hill 18.3.67, to Patricroft 11.5.68	13.7.68
44780	to Birkenhead 18.3.67, to Springs Branch 19.8.67, to Newton Heath 9.12.67	13.7.68
44806	to Speke 13.3.65, to Lostock Hall 20.4.68 (preserved at Manchester)	10.8.68
44809	to Bank Hall 18.6.66, to Aintree 22.10.66, to Warrington Dallam 17.6.67	10.8.68
44816	to Bank Hall 20.6.64, to Lostock Hall 27.6.64, to Bank Hall (again) 30.4.66, to Aintree 22.10.66, to Warrington 17.6.67, to Lostock Hall (again) 7.10.67	10.8.68
44827	to Speke 19.5.62, to Edge Hill 20.6.64	17.7.65
44834	to Edge Hill 25.3.67	30.12.67
44837	to Edge Hill 10.7.65	9.9.67
44838	to Edge Hill 14.5.60	23.3.68
44840	to Birkenhead 12.8.67	2.12.67
44855	to Edge Hill 24.9.60, to Trafford Park 11.5.63	18.5.68
44858	to Aintree 12.11.66, to Carlisle Kingmoor 17.6.67	30.12.67
44859	to Birkenhead 12.8.67	2.12.67
44863	to Edge Hill 10.7.65	20.5.67
44864	to Speke 8.10.60, to Edge Hill 13.7.63	18.5.68
44876	to Birkenhead 12.8.67	2.12.67
44877	to Speke 6.3.65, to Carnforth 11.5.68	10.8.68
44887	to Aintree 17.3.62, to Carlisle Kingmoor 18.5.63	30.12.67
44897	to Birkenhead 18.3.67, to Carnforth 12.8.67	10.8.68
44906	Edge Hill	23.3.68
44907	Edge Hill	4.11.67
44910	to Aintree 21.8.65, to Newton Heath 6.1.68	13.7.68
44926	to Edge Hill 23.4.66	20.4.68
44928	Bank Hall, to Agecroft 13.1.62	17.6.67
44933	to Edge Hill 23.4.66	4.11.67
44935	to Bank Hall 25.1.64, to Warrington Dallam 10.4.65	5.11.66
44950	to Speke 19.9.64, to Lostock Hall 20.4.68	10.8.68
44958	Aintree, to Lostock Hall 3.7.65	25.3.67
44963	to Birkenhead 31.12.66, to Carnforth 12.8.67	10.8.68
44964	to Edge Hill 11.5.63	4.11.67
45005	Edge Hill	27.1.68
45015	to Edge Hill 18.11.61	7.10.67
45031	to Speke 18.3.67	5.7.67
45032	to Speke 4.3.61	22.2.64
45034	to Speke 9.9.61	24.2.68
45039	Edge Hill	9.9.67
45041	Edge Hill, to Bank Hall 19.10.63, to Warrington Dallam 11.66	30.12.67
45043	to Speke 10.12.66	2.12.67
45055	to Bank Hall 18.6.66, to Aintree 22.10.66, to Warrington Dallam 13.5.67, to Edge Hill 7.10.67, to Patricroft 11.5.68, to Lostock Hall 13.7.68	10.8.68
45056	to Speke 18.3.67	9.9.67
45057	to Speke 5.10.63	12.8.67
45059	to Speke 6.3.65	15.7.67
45061	to Aintree 17.3.62, to Carlisle Kingmoor 18.5.63	2.12.67
45068	to Aintree 25.1.64, to Warrington Dallam 3.7.65	1.1.66

Engine No.	Transfers & Notes	Withdrawn
45069	to Edge Hill 9.12.61, to Holyhead 23.6.62, to Speke 15.9.62, to Trafford Park 16.2.63, to Edge Hill 6.7.63	15.7.67
45071	Speke	12.8.67
45073	to Speke 9.9.61, to Springs Branch 21.7.62	10.8.68
45091	to Edge Hill 19.11.60, to Llandudno Junction 2.3.63	10.9.66
45094	Edge Hill	
45103	to Speke 5.10.63, to Edge Hill 11.1.64	19.11.64
45104	to Aintree 11.1.64, to Newton Heath 27.6.64, to Bolton 10.4.65	13.7.68
45109	to Bank Hall 12.10.63, to Warrington Dallam 11.66	22.4.67
45112	to Aintree 18.5.63, to Carlisle Kingmoor 23.11.63	5.11.66
45118	to Aintree 18.5.63, to Newton Heath 22.6.63	8.10.66
45120	to Aintree 18.5.63, to Carlisle Kingmoor 23.11.63	15.7.67
45129	to Bank Hall 19.10.63	8.10.66
45131	Edge Hill, to Holyhead 23.6.62, to Speke 13.10.62	20.4.68
45133	to Edge Hill 7.10.67	24.2.68
45137	Speke	31.12.66
45139	to Edge Hill 28.7.62, to Stoke 4.8.62, to Edge Hill 18.8.62, to Trafford Park 23.2.63	
45140	to Speke 10.9.60, to Springs Branch 21.7.62	8.10.66
45147	to Aintree 24.7.65 (awaiting scrapping Cohen's, Kettering, 27.9.67)	20.5.67
45148	to Edge Hill 3.3.62, to Carlisle Kingmoor 10.11.62	1.1.66
45154[1]	to Aintree 11.1.64, to Newton Heath 20.6.64, to Speke 6.3.65	3.12.66
45156[2]	to Edge Hill 22.6.63, to Patricroft 11.5.68, to Rose Grove 13.7.68	10.8.68
45181	Edge Hill, to Holyhead 23.6.62, to Speke 13.10.62, to Springs Branch 22.6.63, to Carnforth 13.7.63, to Speke 14.9.64, to Patricroft 11.5.68	15.6.68
45188	to Edge Hill 23.10.60, to Holyhead 23.6.62, to Edge Hill 17.8.63, to Speke 19.10.63	12.8.67
45196	to Edge Hill 9.7.60, to Lancaster Green Ayre 16.3.63	30.12.67
45197	to Speke 2.5.64, to Lostock Hall 4.7.64	28.1.67
45201	to Speke 21.3.64	18.5.68
45210	Bank Hall, to Aintree 17.3.62, to Carlisle Kingmoor 11.5.63	23.4.66
45212	to Speke 6.3.65, to Carnforth 26.6.65 (preserved at Oxenhope)	10.8.68
45223	to Speke 5.2.66	31.12.66
45228	to Aintree 17.3.62, to Carlisle Kingmoor 18.5.63	25.3.67
45229	to Aintree 25.1.64	11.9.65
45231	to Speke 1.4.67, to Carnforth 11.5.68	10.8.68
45232	to Birkenhead 31.12.66	2.12.67
45242	Edge Hill	17.6.67
45244	to Edge Hill 13.7.63	10.8.63
45249	Edge Hill	31.12.66
45254	to Edge Hill 6.1.62, to Carlisle Kingmoor 10.11.62	18.5.68
45261	to Edge Hill 8.2.64, to Stockport Edgeley 13.11.65	4.11.67
45282	to Edge Hill 9.12.67	18.5.68
45284	Edge Hill	18.5.68
45287	to Edge Hill 18.3.67, to Patricroft 11.5.68, to Rose Grove 13.7.68	10.8.68
45292	to Birkenhead 12.8.67 (one of last three steam locos to work out of Stoke MPD)	2.12.67
45295	to Edge Hill 10.3.62, to Carlisle Upperby 23.6.62 (despite withdrawal date, recorded as working last steam train from Workington at 1835 hrs on 7.1.68)	30.12.67
45296	to Edge Hill 9.12.67	24.2.68
45299	to Birkenhead 12.8.67	2.12.67
45305	to Speke 9.12.67, to Lostock Hall 11.5.68 (preserved)	10.8.68
45312	to Speke 9.1.60, to Springs Branch 22.6.63, to Edge Hill 6.7.63, to Warrington Dallam 12.2.66	13.7.68

Engine No.	Transfers & Notes	Withdrawn
45316	to Edge Hill 10.3.62, to Carlisle Upperby 23.6.62	23.3.68
45323	to Aintree 14.12.63, to Warrington Dallam 3.7.65	7.10.67
45327	Edge Hill, to Llandudno Junc. 2.3.63	23.2.65
45329	to Speke 24.9.60, to Holyhead 23.6.62, to Speke 15.9.62, to Springs Branch 22.6.63, to Carnforth 13.7.63, to Speke 14.9.63	3.12.66
45330	to Aintree 11.5.63, to Warrington Dallam 13.5.67	10.8.68
45332	to Speke 15.9.62	3.12.66
45338	to Edge Hill 8.2.64, to Speke 13.2.65	5.11.66
45340	Edge Hill, to Carnforth 23.6.62	22.4.67
45370	to Speke 15.10.60	13.8.66
45375	to Speke 19.8.61, to Springs Branch 22.6.63, to Southport 6.7.63, to Edge Hill 7.10.67	27.1.68
45376	Edge Hill	20.4.68
45386	to Speke 8.7.61, to Lostock Hall 11.5.68	10.8.68
45388	to Speke 5.10.63, to Lostock Hall 11.5.68	10.8.68
45390	Edge Hill, to Carnforth 23.6.62	10.8.68
45395	to Edge Hill 9.12.67	23.3.68
45398	to Edge Hill 9.4.60, to Carnforth 23.6.62	9.10.65
45399	Edge Hill, to Carnforth 23.6.62	
45401	Edge Hill (first 'Black 5' withdrawn following collision at Warrington)	2.12.61
45404	to Speke 19.11.60, to Trafford Park 22.6.63	20.5.67
45406	to Speke 21.1.67	15.7.67
45407	to Speke 13.3.65, to Lostock Hall 11.5.68 (preserved at Crewe)	10.8.68
45412	to Edge Hill 14.5.60, to Bangor 23.6.62, to Speke 13.10.62	12.8.67
45413	Edge Hill, to Bangor 23.6.62, to Speke 13.10.62, to Springs Branch 22.6.63	3.10.64
45414	to Edge Hill 8.2.64 (withdrawn following collision at Platt Bridge, near Wigan. Cut up on the spot at Central Wagon Works 3.65 after weighbridge collapsed beneath engine)	27.2.65
45417	to Speke 2.5.64	12.8.67
45421	Edge Hill, to Barrow 23.6.62, to Carlisle Kingmoor 10.11.62	24.2.68
45426	to Edge Hill 20.8.66	23.3.68
45436	to Birkenhead 21.1.67, to Lostock Hall 19.8.67	20.4.68
45440	to Edge Hill 14.5.60	7.10.67
45441	to Speke 13.10.62	
45451	to Aintree 7.12.63, to Newton Heath 27.6.64	3.12.66
45466	to Speke 14.3.64, to Edge Hill 20.6.64, to Speke 13.2.65	
45513	Edge Hill	6.10.62
45517	Bank Hall	16.6.62
45518[3]	Edge Hill, to Lancaster Green Ayre 10.2.62	3.11.62
45520[4]	to Edge Hill 31.12.60	19.5.62
45524[5]	to Edge Hill 10.6.61	6.10.62
45531[6]	Edge Hill, to Springs Branch 19.10.63 then Carlisle Kingmoor	6.11.65
45533[7]	Edge Hill	6.10.62
45535[8]	Edge Hill, to Carlisle Kingmoor 3.11.62	2.11.63
45543[9]	to Edge Hill 31.12.60, to Lancaster Green Ayre 5.5.62, to Carnforth 2.6.62	1.12.62
45547	to Edge Hill 10.6.61	6.10.62
45551	to Edge Hill 10.6.61	16.6.62
45557[10]	to Birkenhead 29.12.62, to Crewe North 19.1.63, then Warrington Dallam	23.2.65
45571[11]	to Speke 16.11.63	16.5.64
45578[12]	Edge Hill, to Aston 6.1.62 then Newton Heath	5.64
45599[13]	to Bank Hall 5.64	9.11.64
45627[14]	to Bank Hall 3.3.62 (last London Midland Region 'Jubilee' in traffic)	8.10.66
45633[15]	to Warrington Dallam 20.7.63 (but stored at Edge Hill from mid-1964 until withdrawal)	6.11.65

Engine No.	Transfers & Notes	Withdrawn
45657[16]	to Bank Hall 21.7.62, to Patricroft 9.5.64 (awaiting scrapping at Central Wagon Works, Wigan, 27.3.65)	3.10.64
45663[17]	to Speke 16.11.63, to Warrington Dallam 18.7.64 (awaiting scrapping Ward's, Beighton, Sheffield, 3.4.65)	10.64
45664[18]	to Speke 16.11.63, to Warrington Dallam 18.7.64, to NER 3.4.65, then Leeds Holbeck	28.5.65
45684[19]	Bank Hall	1.1.66
45697[20]	to Bank Hall 22.6.63, to NER 29.2.64	9.9.67
45698[21]	Bank Hall	6.11.65
45713[22]	to Bank Hall 21.7.62	3.11.62
45715[23]	to Bank Hall 21.7.62	29.12.62
45717[24]	Bank Hall	2.11.63
45719[25]	Bank Hall	23.3.63
45721[26]	Bank Hall	9.10.65
46110[27]	Edge Hill, to Longsight 16.12.61, to Edge Hill 30.12.61, to Springs Branch 29.6.63, to Carlisle Kingmoor 6.7.63	22.2.64
46116[28]	Edge Hill, to Carlisle Kingmoor 3.11.62	7.9.63
46119[29]	Edge Hill	30.11.63
46124[30]	Edge Hill, to Carlisle Kingmoor 3.11.62	29.12.62
46134[31]	Edge Hill, to Carlisle Upperby 26.5.62	1.12.62
46208[32]	Edge Hill	3.11.62
46229[33]	to Edge Hill 11.4.61 (preserved at York)	22.2.64
46233[34]	to Edge Hill 17.9.60 (preserved)	22.2.64
46241[35]	to Edge Hill 11.4.61 (mileage at withdrawal given as more than 1.5 million miles)	5.9.64
46243[36]	to Edge Hill 11.4.61 (awaiting scrapping Central Wagon Works, Wigan, 27.3.65)	3.10.64
46402	to Bank Hall 3.7.65, to Buxton 11.65	15.7.67
46404	to Aintree 23.5.64, to Buxton 13.11.65	4.6.65
46405	Aintree, to Bury 15.9.62, to Bank Hall 22.5.65, to Northwich 5.3.66	18.6.66
46410	to Speke 18.4.64	26.3.66
46412	Aintree, to Bury 15.9.62	13.8.66
46414	to Bank Hall 15.5.65, to Northwich 5.3.66	18.6.66
46419	to Aintree 8.1.66	10.9.66
46423	to Speke 18.4.64	23.2.65
46424	to Speke 18.4.64, to Workington 10.7.65	31.12.66
46439	Aintree, to Bury 15.9.62, to Aintree 19.6.65	25.3.67
46444	to Bank Hall 23.5.64	17.7.65
46484	to Bank Hall 3.7.65, to Buxton 13.11.65	15.7.67
46496	to Bank Hall 23.5.64	23.4.66
46497	to Bank Hall 23.5.64	24.4.65
46500	to Aintree 23.5.64	
46502	to Aintree 23.5.64	
46503	to Speke 11.65, to Northwich 19.11.66	20.5.67
46515	to Speke 6.2.65, to Springs Branch 28.5.66	20.5.67
46516	to Speke 6.2.65, to Northwich 19.11.66	20.5.67
46518	to Speke 6.2.65	26.3.66
46523	to Aintree 19.6.65	20.5.67
47001	Bank Hall, to Agecroft 25.5.63, to Staveley Barrow Hill 22.5.63	12.66
47002	Bank Hall, to Lostock Hall 16.12.61	5.9.64
47005	Birkenhead, to Staveley Barrow Hill 22.5.63	12.66
47009	Birkenhead, to Agecroft 22.6.63	5.9.64
47160	Birkenhead, to Bidston 15.12.62, to Birkenhead 9.12.63	2.11.63
47164	Birkenhead, to Bidston 15.12.62 to Birkenhead 9.2.63, to Horwich Works 9.11.63	5.9.64

Engine No.	Transfers & Notes	Withdrawn
47166	Edge Hill	18.5.63
47225	Walton	13.7.63
47228	Walton, to Aintree 14.12.63	22.2.64
47230	Bank Hall, to Newton Heath 24.8.63, to Edge Hill 19.10.63, to Carlisle Kingmoor 18.4.64	17.12.64
47235	Walton	3.11.62
47259	Aintree	24.3.62
47272	to Birkenhead 15.8.64	18.6.66
47285	Edge Hill	11.9.65
47279	to Aintree 4.12.65, to Sutton Oak 19.11.66 (saved from Barry Scrapyard 8.79, restored to traffic 12.87 at Worth Valley Railway)	31.12.66
47289	Edge Hill, to Aintree 4.7.64, to Sutton Oak 19.11.66 (transferred to Westhouses 31.12.66, and in traffic 7.67; one of last four 'Jinties' in traffic)	7.10.67
47305	Aintree, to Barrow 4.4.64	27.2.65
47306	Bank Hall, to Gorton 9.11.63	26.12.64
47314	Speke, to Springs Branch 21.7.62	3.12.66
47324	Birkenhead (saved from Barry Scrapyard 2.78, retained at Avon Valley Railway)	31.12.66
47327	Aintree, to Bank Hall 13.1.62, then Walton, to Aintree 14.12.63 (saved from Barry Scrapyard 7.70, retained at Midland Railway)	31.12.66
47336	Edge Hill, to Lostock Hall 5.64	18.6.66
47343	to Birkenhead 2.2.63	5.9.64
47349	to Edge Hill 7.9.63	5.9.64
47353	Edge Hill	24.2.62
47357	Edge Hill (saved from Barry Scrapyard 7.70, in traffic 6.73 Midland Railway)	31.12.66
47367	to Aintree 3.7.65	31.12.66
47372	to Birkenhead 10.10.59	5.9.64
47383	to Speke 17.6.61, to Rose Grove 22.6.63 (reinstated to traffic 1.67, withdrawn again 7.10.67. Preserved at Bewdley)	31.12.66
47388	Speke, to Bolton 22.6.63	31.12.66
47404	Aintree	24.2.62
47406	to Bank Hall 6.4.63, to Gorton 7.9.63, to Edge Hill 1.65 (saved from Barry Scrapyard 6.83, retained at Peak Railway)	31.12.66
47412	Edge Hill	5.10.63
47415	to Edge Hill 22.8.64	23.4.66
47416	Edge Hill	16.7.66
47423	to Birkenhead 15.8.64	17.7.65
47425	Aintree	19.5.62
47444	to Aintree 7.5.66	3.12.66
47447	to Birkenhead 5.9.64	31.12.66
47451	Speke, to Stafford 27.10.62	9.10.65
47453	to Aintree 19.6.65	23.4.66
47461	to Birkenhead 15.8.64, to Derby 5.9.64	3.10.64
47478	to Birkenhead 24.2.62, to Wolverton Works 17.3.62, to Nuneaton 7.7.62	16.5.64
47480	Bank Hall, to Aintree 10.3.62, to Newton Heath 21.3.64	9.10.65
47485	to Edge Hill 2.11.63	23.2.65
47487	Edge Hill	11.9.65
47488	Edge Hill	
47493	Speke, to Springs Branch 21.7.62, to Edge Hill 4.9.65 (saved from Barry Scrapyard 11.72, in traffic at Cranmore 1.76)	31.12.66
47495	to Birkenhead 2.2.63	9.10.65
47497	Birkenhead	6.10.62

Engine No.	Transfers & Notes	Withdrawn
47507	Birkenhead, to Rhyl 28.4.62	10.9.66
47512	to Aintree 6.5.61	4.6.65
47519	Edge Hill	9.10.65
47533	to Birkenhead 13.6.64	3.12.66
47550	Bank Hall, to Horwich Works 13.1.62	21.3.64
47565	Birkenhead	23.4.66
47566	Edge Hill, to Aintree 4.7.64	5.11.66
47583	Bank Hall	23.3.63
47594	to Edge Hill 25.3.61	11.7.64
47612	Speke, to Workington 10.11.62	31.12.66
47622	to Birkenhead 2.2.63, to Crewe South 16.11.63	11.7.64
47627	Speke, then Birkenhead by 5.64	23.4.66
47628	to Birkenhead 2.2.63, to Uttoxeter 6.4.63	5.9.64
47647	to Speke 27.2.60, to Carlisle Kingmoor 6.4.63	4.6.65
47655	to Aintree 9.4.60	4.12.65
47656	Edge Hill, to Widnes 7.9.63	1.1.66
47659	to Birkenhead 8.4.61, to Wolverton Works 24.2.62, to Birkenhead 17.3.62	3.12.66
47674	Birkenhead, to Bidston 19.5.62, to Birkenhead 2.2.63	31.12.66
47681	Walton, to Aintree 14.12.63, to Agecroft 1.5.65	27.8.65
48010	to Speke 12.3.66, to Newton Heath 23.4.66	27.1.68
48012	to Edge Hill 3.6.67	20.4.68
48017	to Birkenhead 13.2.65, to Aintree 17.4.65, to Edge Hill 17.6.67	4.11.67
48026	to Edge Hill 25.4.64, to Speke 19.9.64, to Newton Heath 4.6.66	13.7.68
48029	to Edge Hill 20.7.63, to Lancaster Green Ayre 7.9.63, to Edge Hill 6.3.65, to Speke 19.6.65	
48033	to Birkenhead 14.3.64, to Sutton Oak 17.4.65	13.7.68
48045	to Speke 7.7.62, to Widnes 16.3.63, to Edge Hill 12.11.66	18.5.68
48046	to Speke 7.7.62, to Nottingham 28.3.64	27.1.68
48050	to Aintree 3.4.65	26.3.66
48056	to Edge Hill 3.9.66	18.5.68
48060	to Speke 10.12.66	20.4.68
48062	to Birkenhead 6.2.65, to Lower Darwen 22.5.65	10.8.68
48078	Edge Hill	11.9.65
48085	to Birkenhead 5.10.63, to Saltley 30.11.63	12.8.67
48094	to Birkenhead 29.9.62, to Mold Junction 20.7.63	9.10.65
48108	to Aintree 3.4.65, to Buxton 14.5.66	9.9.67
48119	to Edge Hill 12.11.66	2.12.67
48124	to Edge Hill 12.11.66	18.5.68
48129	to Speke 18.4.64, to Edge Hill 6.3.65	26.3.66
48131	to Birkenhead 1.12.62, to Mold Junction 20.7.63	17.6.67
48139	to Aintree 3.4.65	3.12.66
48151	to Edge Hill 25.4.64, to Northwich 12.3.66 (saved from Barry Scrapyard 11.75; steamed at Butterley 6.87. Preserved in main line order)	27.1.68
48152	Edge Hill	25.3.67
48153	to Speke 9.12.67	23.3.68
48154	to Birkenhead 8.12.62, to Nuneaton 9.3.63	12.8.67
48163	to Speke 19.6.65	17.6.67
48176	to Edge Hill 25.4.64, to Lancaster Green Ayre 25.7.64	12.8.67
48178	to Edge Hill 6.8.66	3.12.66
48188	to Edge Hill 5.5.62 (involved in the Chapel-le-Frith accident, 1957)	21.5.66
48189	to Edge Hill 25.4.64, to Speke 6.3.65	27.8.65

Engine No.	Transfers & Notes	Withdrawn
48199	to Edge Hill 25.4.64, to Fleetwood 3.10.64, to Heaton Mersey 19.2.66	
48200	to Edge Hill 25.4.64, to Newton Heath 13.8.66	27.1.68
48203	to Speke 12.3.66	23.4.66
48204	to Speke 17.9.66	9.9.67
48206	to Aintree 12.3.66, to Sutton Oak 23.4.66, to Springs Branch 24.4.67, to Speke 9.12.67	18.5.68
48218	to Speke 14.3.64, to Rose Grove 19.6.65	7.10.67
48249	Edge Hill	31.12.66
48250	to Speke 22.4.61	23.4.66
48251	to Speke 24.7.65, to Sutton Oak 28.8.65	5.11.66
48253	to Speke 4.3.67, to Lostock Hall 6.1.68	10.8.68
48257	to Birkenhead 7.1.61, to Rose Grove 19.6.65	10.8.68
48258	to Birkenhead 22.9.62, to Westhouses 28.3.64, to Edge Hill 17.9.66	9.9.67
48260	Birkenhead, to Rose Grove 12.6.65	4.12.65
48262	to Birkenhead 10.6.61, to Lower Darwen 22.5.65	4.12.65
48268	to Aintree 3.4.65, to Edge Hill 17.6.67	4.11.67
48279	to Aintree 4.3.67, to Sutton Oak 17.6.67	4.11.67
48280	Edge Hill	21.5.66
48290	to Birkenhead 1.12.62, to Aintree 17.4.65, to Sutton Oak 26.6.65	27.8.65
48293	to Edge Hill 24.7.65, to Lostock Hall 11.5.68.	13.7.68
48294	to Speke 10.6.61, to Edge Hill 7.10.67, to Lostock Hall 11.5.68	10.8.68
48296	to Speke 18.4.64, to Edge Hill 6.3.65, to Speke 19.6.65	8.10.66
48297	to Speke 6.5.61, to Warrington Dallam 22.2.64, to Speke 19.9.64	27.8.65
48301	to Aintree 10.7.65	25.3.67
48305	to Speke 18.9.65 (saved from Barry Scrapyard 11.85, retained at Great Central Railway)	27.1.68
48308	to Speke 18.4.64, to Edge Hill 6.3.65	20.4.68
48312	to Birkenhead 22.9.62 (awaiting scrapping Darlington 29.7.65)	27.2.65
48315	to Aintree 10.12.66, to Heaton Mersey 17.6.67	12.8.67
48318	Edge Hill, to Carlisle Kingmoor 29.6.63	5.11.66
48323	to Edge Hill 14.5.60, to Birkenhead 13.2.65, to Rose Grove 22.5.65	13.7.68
48326	to Birkenhead 29.9.62, to Sutton Oak 17.4.65	17.7.66
48335	to Speke 12.3.66, to Stockport Edgeley 23.4.66	20.4.68
48340	to Birkenhead 13.2.65, to Aintree 17.4.65	10.8.68
48348	to Birkenhead 16.2.63, to Rose Grove 12.6.65	10.8.68
48362	to Edge Hill 9.12.67 (awaiting scrapping Ward's, Beighton, Sheffield, 11.3.68)	30.12.67
48363	to Aintree 24.7.65, to Northwich 13.5.67	2.12.67
48371	to Edge Hill 6.8.66	4.11.67
48373	to Birkenhead 29.9.62, to Rose Grove 22.5.65	13.7.68
48374	to Speke 18.9.65, to Edge Hill 23.9.67, to Patricroft 11.5.68	15.6.68
48395	to Edge Hill 4.3.67	9.9.67
48408	to Speke 10.7.65, to Reddish 24.7.65	2.12.67
48412	to Aintree 23.7.66, to Speke 20.8.66	31.12.66
48421	to Aintree 3.4.65, to Northwich 29.4.67	24.2.68
48422	to Birkenhead 1.12.62, to Aintree 17.4.65, to Sutton Oak 26.6.65	26.3.66
48423	Speke, the Birkenhead, to Rose Grove 19.2.66	10.8.68
48425	to Edge Hill 23.6.62, to Speke 7.9.63, to Edge Hill 11.1.64, to Speke 6.3.65, to Bolton 12.3.66	4.11.67
48433	Edge Hill	20.4.68
48435	to Birkenhead 6.4.63, to Rose Grove 12.6.65	20.5.67
48441	Birkenhead, to Lower Darwen 12.6.65	20.4.68
48446	to Birkenhead 8.12.62	27.8.65
48447	to Birkenhead 13.2.65, to Rose Grove 19.6.65	29.1.66

Engine No.	Transfers & Notes	Withdrawn
48448	Birkenhead, to Rose Grove 22.5.65	10.8.68
48450	to Edge Hill 19.8.67	7.10.67
48451	to Aintree 3.4.65, to Rose Grove 26.6.65	18.5.68
48455	Birkenhead	17.12.64
48457	Edge Hill, to Speke 6.3.65	8.10.66
48467	to Edge Hill 25.6.66, to Patricroft 11.5.68	15.6.68
48469	to Speke 7.9.63, to Bury 19.10.63	30.12.67
48476	to Birkenhead 10.6.61, to Speke 6.3.65, to Lostock Hall 6.1.68	10.8.68
48479	to Speke 25.3.61, to Willesden 23.6.62	26.2.66
48493	to Speke 10.7.65, to Reddish 24.7.65, to Speke again by 11.66, to Northwich 3.2.68, to Speke 9.3.68, to Rose Grove 11.5.68	10.8.68
48500	to Aintree 3.4.65	1.1.66
48506	Speke, to Northampton 5.10.63	7.10.67
48509	Edge Hill, to Warrington Dallam 5.5.62, to Edge Hill 22.9.62, to Lancaster Green Ayre 7.9.63, to Speke by 11.66	20.5.67
48512	Edge Hill (involved in a runaway 3.65)	8.10.66
48513	Edge Hill	25.3.67
48520	to Speke 17.6.61	8.10.66
48522	Speke, to Bescot 23.6.62	9.9.67
48528	to Edge Hill 25.6.66	12.8.67
48529	to Edge Hill 4.3.67, to Newton Heath 11.5.68	13.7.68
48535	Speke, to Trafford Park 25.12.65	12.8.67
48536	to Speke 26.9.64, to Newton Heath 2.4.66, to Edge Hill 6.8.66 (awaiting scrapping Cohen's, Kettering, 10.6.67)	28.1.67
48554	to Birkenhead 22.9.62, to Bletchley 17.8.63	13.8.66
48558	to Aintree 3.4.65, to Rose Grove 26.6.65	9.10.65
48600	to Aintree 12.11.66 (one of several featured in the 1950s movie 'Train of Events', at Hull MPD 9.4.67, awaiting scrapping Draper's, Hull)	3.12.66
48604	to Edge Hill 10.12.66	20.5.67
48605	to Aintree 17.4.65	13.8.66
48614	to Edge Hill 9.12.67	18.5.68
48629	to Birkenhead 12.10.63, to Saltley 30.11.63	
48646	to Birkenhead 5.10.63, to Saltley 30.11.63	15.6.68
48648	to Birkenhead 11.11.61, to Llandudno Junction 14.9.63, to Aintree 17.4.65, to Speke 20.8.66	12.8.67
48650	to Aintree 12.3.66, to Northwich 13.5.67	9.9.67
48665	to Edge Hill 4.3.67, to Newton Heath 11.5.68	10.8.68
48676	to Aintree 3.4.65, to Sutton Oak 17.6.67	4.11.67
48682	to Speke 26.9.64	9.10.65
48684	Speke, then Birkenhead, to Lower Darwen 12.6.65	18.5.68
48687	to Edge Hill 21.1.67, to Newton Heath 11.5.68	15.6.68
48691	Birkenhead, to Rose Grove 22.5.65	26.3.66
48692	Speke, to Edge Hill 23.9.67, to Bolton 11.5.68	13.7.68
48697	to Birkenhead 23.9.61, to Mold Junction 19.6.65	30.12.67
48702	to Edge Hill 1.9.62, to Speke 7.9.63, to Heaton Mersey 14.12.63	18.5.68
48704	to Aintree 17.4.65	11.9.65
48709	to Speke 18.4.64	15.7.67
48711	to Speke 10.6.61	28.1.67
48714	Speke, to Widnes 16.3.63	4.11.67
48715	to Aintree 3.4.65, to Springs Branch 26.6.65, to Edge Hill 9.12.67, to Rose Grove 11.5.68	10.8.68

Engine No.	Transfers & Notes	Withdrawn
48716	to Birkenhead 13.2.65, to Lostock Hall 22.5.65	11.9.65
48722	to Speke 30.4.60, to Sutton Oak 21.5.66, to Northwich 20.5.67, to Edge Hill 9.3.68	18.5.68
48742	Edge Hill	9.9.67
48743	to Edge Hill 22.10.66	25.3.67
48746	to Edge Hill 5.5.62, to Newton Heath 11.5.68	15.6.68
48747	Speke, to Bescot 23.6.62	10.9.66
48752	to Edge Hill 9.12.67, to Rose Grove 11.5.68	10.8.68
48774	(withdrawn 29.12.62, reinstated 30.11.63, to Speke 30.5.64, left Workington MPD 15.11.65 for scrap to Bird's, Long Marston, South Wales)	27.8.65
48927	to Edge Hill 30.1.60	2.12.61
49037	to Edge Hill 12.11.60	29.12.62
49114	to Edge Hill 18.11.61	1.12.62
49130	Edge Hill 3.6.61	1.12.62
49142	to Edge Hill 17.6.61, to Bescot 20.10.62	29.12.62
49144	to Edge Hill 30.1.60	1.12.62
49155	to Edge Hill 20.8.60	16.6.62
49173	Edge Hill, to Bescot 20.10.62	5.9.64
49216	to Edge Hill 27.10.62	1.12.62
49224	Edge Hill	1.12.62
49293	to Edge Hill 5.5.62	1.12.62
49352	Edge Hill	6.10.62
49375	Edge Hill (this engine still in store at Edge Hill late 1964)	29.12.62
49377	to Edge Hill 5.5.62	3.11.62
49394	Edge Hill	3.11.62
49404	Edge Hill	19.5.62
49415	to Edge Hill 28.1.61	1.12.62
49416	Edge Hill	8.9.62
49432	to Edge Hill 28.1.61	1.12.62
49434	Edge Hill	3.11.62
49437	Edge Hill	8.9.62
49448	to Edge Hill 17.9.60, to Crewe South 22.12.62	13.7.63
51206	Bank Hall, to Agecroft 26.5.62	6.10.62
51232	Bank Hall, to Agecroft 25.8.62	13.7.63
51253	Bank Hall, to Speke 9.6.62	13.7.63
52311	Aintree	24.3.62
75015	to Aintree 14.12.63, to Springs Branch 25.4.64	30.12.67
75020	to Aintree 11.3.67, to Carnforth 6.67	10.8.68
75026	to Bank Hall 6.2.65, to Aintree 22.10.66, to Skipton 19.11.66	30.12.67
75027	to Bank Hall 6.2.65, to Aintree 22.10.66, to Skipton 12.11.66 (the last steam banking engine at Oxenholme 4.5.68. Preserved at the Bluebell Railway)	10.8.66
75032	to Bank Hall 20.7.63, to Stoke 5.2.66	24.2.68
75033	to Bank Hall 20.7.63, to Chester 30.4.66	30.12.67
75043	to Walton 23.11.63, to Aintree 14.12.63, to Carnforth 17.6.67	30.12.67
75045	Bank Hall, to Nuneaton 25.5.63	23.4.66
75046	Bank Hall, to Chester 30.4.66 (removed from Stoke MPD on 12.1.68 for scrap)	12.8.67
75047	Bank Hall, to Stoke 5.2.66 (removed from Stoke MPD on 12.1.68 for scrap)	12.8.67
75048	Bank Hall, to Chester 30.4.66	10.8.68
75049	Bank Hall	8.10.66
75050	to Bank Hall 25.5.63, to Stoke 5.2.66	3.12.66
75060	to Walton 23.11.63, to Aintree 14.12.63, to Edge Hill 26.6.65, to Heaton Mersey	

Engine No.	Transfers & Notes	Withdrawn
	2.4.66 (awaiting scrapping Hughes Bolckow Ltd, Tyneside, 23.9.67)	22.4.67
75061	to Walton 23.11.63, to Aintree 14.12.63	2.67
75064	to Walton 23.11.64, to Aintree 14.12.63	20.5.67
78002	to Bank Hall 14.9.63	
78022	to Aintree 11.5.63, to Lostock Hall 28.12.63 (saved from Barry Scrapyard 6.75, retained at Keighley & Worth Valley Railway)	8.10.66
78023	to Aintree 18.5.63, to Nottingham 23.5.64	12.67
78027	to Bank Hall 11.5.63, to Wigan 'C' 29.6.63	9.10.65
78041	Bank Hall, to Lostock Hall 20.4.64	9.67
78042	Bank Hall, to Nottingham 23.5.64	9.10.65
78043	Bank Hall, to Aintree 15.9.62, to Willesden 25.5.63	9.10.65
78044	Bank Hall, to Aintree 15.9.62, to Lostock Hall 28.12.63, to Aintree 11.4.64, to Toton 3.4.65 (in store at Bolton 7.67)	9.67
78055	to Aintree 21.3.64, to Nottingham 23.5.64	9.67
78060	to Aintree 15.9.62, to Willesden 25.5.63	8.10.66
90101	Aintree	16.5.64
90107	Aintree	30.11.63
90123	to Aintree 4.7.64, to Lower Darwen 25.7.64 (scrapped Draper's, Hull, late 1965)	27.3.65
90125	to Aintree 19.1.63, to Springs Branch 13.7.63	17.7.65
90141	to Aintree 19.1.63	22.2.64
90157	to Birkenhead 16.6.62, to Widnes 15.9.62 (awaiting cutting up Central Wagon Works, Wigan, 27.3.65)	11.7.64
90164	Aintree, to Rose Grove 15.9.62	17.4.65
90192	Birkenhead, to Widnes 15.9.62	18.5.63
90204	Aintree, to Lower Darwen 3.4.65	2.7.65
90216	Aintree	5.9.64
90219	Aintree, to Rose Grove 15.9.62	16.5.64
90227	to Birkenhead 28.4.62, to Warrington Dallam 22.9.62	10.65
90242	to Aintree 14.12.63, to Eastern Region 12.9.64	2.10.65
90245	to Aintree 12.12.59 (awaiting scrapping Central Wagon Works, Wigan, 27.3.65)	16.5.64
90248	to Aintree 3.10.64	13.11.65
90267	to Aintree 3.10.64	27.3.65
90271	to Aintree 4.7.64, to Lower Darwen 25.7.64	24.7.65
90278	Aintree	29.12.62
90282	Aintree, to Eastern Region 12.9.64	23.2.65
90283	Aintree, to Springs Branch 25.7.64	7.10.65
90289	to Aintree 4.7.64, to Lower Darwen 25.7.64	17.12.64
90316	to Aintree 18.1.64, to Bolton 15.2.64	
90327	Aintree, to Rose Grove 15.9.62	23.2.65
90343	Aintree	28.12.63
90346	to Aintree 13.6.64	13.11.65
90369	Birkenhead, to Warrington Dallam 15.9.62	26.3.66
90381	Aintree, to Frodingham 5.5.65	13.11.65
90392	Birkenhead, to Warrington Dallam 15.9.62	26.12.64
90399	to Aintree 11.7.64, to Springs Branch 25.7.64 (awaiting scrapping Ward's, Beighton, Sheffield, 7.65)	27.3.65
90413	to Aintree 14.12.63, to Eastern Region 12.9.64	26.2.66
90416	Aintree (awaiting scrapping Central Wagon Works, Wigan, 27.3.65)	16.5.64
90474	to Aintree 25.4.64, to Eastern Region 12.9.64	24.7.65
90486	to Aintree 3.10.64	24.4.65

Engine No.	Transfers & Notes	Withdrawn
90516	to Aintree 19.9.64	27.11.65
90520	to Aintree 11.7.64, to Newton Heath 29.8.64	27.2.65
90527	Aintree	18.5.63
90533	to Aintree 13.2.65, to Retford 5.5.65	26.2.66
90535	Aintree, to Springs Branch 13.7.63	19.11.64
90552	Aintree	16.5.64
90561	to Aintree 11.7.64, to Springs Branch 25.7.64 (awaiting scrapping Ward's, Beighton, Sheffield, 7.65)	27.3.65
90563	Aintree 25.4.64	27.8.65
90566	to Birkenhead 11.11.61, to Warrington Dallam 15.9.62	11.7.64
90576	to Aintree 9.4.60, to Rose Grove 4.8.62	23.3.63
90584	to Aintree 29.2.64	5.9.64
90599	to Aintree 20.2.60	5.9.64
90606	to Birkenhead 18.6.60, to Sutton Oak 15.9.62	26.2.66
90632	to Aintree 23.2.65	4.6.65
90641	to Aintree 3.10.64	27.8.65
90643	Aintree	22.2.64
90687	Aintree, to Springs Branch 25.7.64, to Aintree 22.8.64, to Eastern Region 12.9.64	1.1.66
90689	to Aintree 3.10.64	26.2.66
90702	to Aintree 19.10.63, to Sutton Oak 25.7.64	11.8.65
90706	to Aintree 30.5.64	26.2.66
90712	Aintree (awaiting scrapping Central Wagon Works, Wigan, 27.3.65)	5.9.64
90718	to Aintree 19.9.64	12.3.66
90724	Aintree, to Rose Grove 15.9.62, to Aintree 23.2.65	2.7.65
92002	to Birkenhead 10.12.66	2.12.67
92008	to Speke by 11.66, to Warrington Dallam 12.8.67	7.10.67
92011	to Birkenhead 7.8.65	2.12.67
92014	to Birkenhead 22.5.65	4.11.67
92020	to Speke 26.9.64, to Birkenhead 23.2.65	4.11.67
92021	to Birkenhead 24.7.65	2.12.67
92022	to Speke 5.2.66	2.12.67
92023	to Birkenhead 10.7.65	2.12.67
92024	to Birkenhead 24.7.65	2.12.67
92025	Speke 11.66	2.12.67
92026	to Birkenhead 22.5.65 (at Whifflet, Scotland awaiting transfer to G.H. Campbell's Scrapyard 4.68)	2.12.67
92027	Speke 11.66	12.8.67
92028	to Birkenhead 30.11.63, to Saltley 18.4.64	5.11.66
92029	to Birkenhead 30.11.63, to Saltley 18.4.64, to Birkenhead 10.12.66	2.12.67
92032	to Birkenhead 24.7.65	22.4.67
92045	to Birkenhead 9.12.63	7.10.67
92046	to Birkenhead 9.12.63	4.11.67
92047	to Birkenhead 9.12.63	2.12.67
92048	to Birkenhead 15.5.65	7.10.67
92049	to Birkenhead 19.12.66	2.12.67
92050	to Speke 5.2.66, to Warrington Dallam 12.8.67	7.10.67
92054	to Speke 13.6.64	18.5.68
92055	to Speke 7.10.67	30.12.67
92058	to Speke 17.6.67, to Carlisle Kingmoor 12.8.67	4.11.67
92059	to Birkenhead 15.5.65	8.10.66
92069	to Birkenhead 22.5.65, to Speke 11.11.67	18.5.68

Engine No.	Transfers & Notes	Withdrawn
92070	to Birkenhead 15.5.65	2.12.67
92073	to Birkenhead 17.9.66	2.12.67
92079	Birkenhead	2.12.67
92082	to Birkenhead 30.11.63	2.12.67
92083	to Birkenhead 22.5.65	2.67
92084	to Speke 26.9.64, to Birkenhead 23.2.65 (at Whifflet, Scotland, awaiting transfer to G.H. Campbell's Scrapyard 4.68)	2.12.67
92085	at Birkenhead by 11.66	31.12.66
92086	to Birkenhead 19.6.65	2.12.67
92088	to Birkenhead 24.7.65, to Carnforth 11.11.67	18.5.68
92089	to Speke 26.9.64, to Birkenhead 23.2.65	2.67
92090	to Birkenhead 22.5.65 (awaiting scrapping Cohen's, Kettering, 27.9.67)	20.5.67
92091	to Birkenhead 31.7.65, to Speke 21.8.65, to Carnforth 11.5.68	15.6.68
92092	to Birkenhead 22.5.65	5.11.66
92094	to Birkenhead 22.5.65, to Speke 11.11.67	18.5.68
92100	to Birkenhead 10.4.65	20.5.67
92101	to Birkenhead 10.4.65	4.11.67
92102	to Birkenhead 10.4.65	2.12.67
92103	to Birkenhead 10.4.65	17.6.67
92104	to Birkenhead 15.5.65	2.67
92106	to Birkenhead 10.4.65	12.8.67
92107	at Birkenhead by 11.66	2.67
92108	to Birkenhead 10.4.65	2.12.67
92109	to Birkenhead 10.4.65	2.12.67
92111	to Speke 26.9.64, to Birkenhead 23.2.65	4.11.67
92112	to Birkenhead 10.4.65 (at Whifflet, Scotland, awaiting transfer to G.H. Campbell's Scrapyard 4.68)	2.12.67
92113	to Birkenhead 31.7.65	7.10.67
92115	to Speke 13.6.64	26.2.66
92117	to Speke by 11.66	30.12.67
92119	to Speke 17.6.67, to Carlisle Kingmoor 12.8.67 (awaiting scrapping Lockerbie, Scotland, with severed rods 11.67)	7.10.67
92120	to Birkenhead 10.4.65	15.7.67
92121	to Birkenhead 10.4.65	12.8.67
92122	to Birkenhead 10.4.65	2.12.67
92123	to Birkenhead	4.11.67
92127	to Birkenhead 23.2.65	9.9.67
92131	to Birkenhead 15.5.65	7.10.67
92133	to Birkenhead 10.4.65	12.8.67
92134	to Birkenhead 10.4.65 (saved from Barry Scrapyard 12.80, retained at Brightlingsea)	31.12.66
92138	to Speke 20.8.66	15.7.67
92139	to Speke 10.12.66, to Carlisle Kingmoor 12.8.67 (awaiting scrapping at Lockerbie, Scotland, with severed rods 11.67)	9.9.67
92151	to Birkenhead 12.11.66	22.4.67
92152	to Birkenhead 12.11.66	2.12.67
92153	to Speke 26.6.65	27.1.68
92154	to Birkenhead 24.7.65, then Speke by 11.66	12.8.67
92155	to Speke 20.8.66	3.12.66
92157	to Birkenhead 18.4.64	9.9.67
92158	to Speke 13.6.64	13.8.66
92159	to Birkenhead 22.5.65	12.8.67

92160	to Birkenhead 19.2.66, to Speke 11.11.67, to Carnforth 11.5.68	13.7.68
92162	to Birkenhead 22.5.65	2.12.67
92163	to Birkenhead 19.6.65	2.12.67
92165	(to Bidston 23.6.62), to Birkenhead 9.2.63, to Speke 11.11.67	23.3.68
92166	(to Bidston 23.6.62), to Birkenhead 9.2.63	2.12.67
92167	to Birkenhead 9.2.63, to Carnforth 11.11.67 (together with 92160, was last of its class in service. At 5.68 was running in traffic as a 2–8–2 with last pair of driving wheels uncoupled from rest)	13.7.68
92203	to Birkenhead 17.9.66 (at Crewe South MPD 30.12.67 awaiting transfer to Longmoor Military Railway. Left Crewe South for Cricklewood under own steam 6.4.68. Preserved at Cranmore)	2.12.67
92204	to Speke 20.8.66	30.12.67
92218	to Speke 11.3.67, to Carlisle Kingmoor 12.8.67, to Speke 6.1.68	18.5.68
92227	to Speke 11.3.67	4.11.67
92228	at Speke by 11.66	28.1.67
92233	to Speke 6.1.68	24.2.68
92234	to Birkenhead 10.12.66	2.12.67
92249	to Speke 6.1.68	18.5.68

1 *Lanarkshire Yeomanry*	10 *South Australia*	19 *Jutland*	28 *Irish Guardsman*
2 *Ayrshire Yeomanry*	11 *South Africa*	20 *Achilles*	29 *Lancashire Fusilier*
3 *Bradshaw*	12 *United Provinces*	21 *Mars*	30 *London Scottish*
4 *Llandudno*	13 *Basutoland*	22 *Renown*	31 *The Cheshire Regiment*
5 *Blackpool*	14 *Sierra Leone*	23 *Invincible*	32 *Princess Helena Victoria*
6 *Sir Frederick Harrison*	15 *Aden*	24 *Dauntless*	33 *Duchess of Hamilton*
7 *Lord Rathmore*	16 *Tyrwhitt*	25 *Glorious*	34 *Duchess of Sutherland*
8 *Sir Herbert Walker KCB*	17 *Jervis*	26 *Impregnable*	35 *City of Edinburgh*
9 *Home Guard*	18 *Nelson*	27 *Grenadier Guardsman*	36 *City of Lancaster*

The site of what was once the huge depot at Edge Hill, April 1991. The building just right of centre, distant, is on the site of the old Grid Iron sidings. Just to the right of that two-storey building is the brick entrance to the Bootle branch. The houses in the right foreground are on Taunton Street, the back yard of the first house facing what was once the shed's 'coal hole'. The electricity post (just visible on the extreme left of the picture) is for the main Lime Street-Crewe line. The right foreground was formerly occupied by the shed and yard; the left foreground by Edge Hill's coaling stage.

John Corkill

APPENDIX 3

MOTIVE POWER COMPARISONS – 1950 TO 1966

The following charts provide a comparison of the motive power strengths of Merseyside engine sheds during the period 1950 to 1966.

For the purposes of simplicity, the shed code prefix of 8 has been used for all Merseyside depots, irrespective of their specific prefix during the period covered in this book, 1948–68. The depots and their corresponding codes that have been adopted for this survey are as follows:

8A Edge Hill

8C Speke Junction

8E Brunswick

8H Birkenhead

8K Bank Hall

8L Aintree

8R Walton-on-the-Hill

1950

Loco class	8A	8C	8E	8H	8K	8L	8R
			Number of engines based at depots				
14XX				1			
'1901'				3			
'2021'				9			
47XX				1			
43XX				4			
57XX				6			
51XX				10			
'Grange'				6			
Fowler 3	3						
Stanier 3			1	9			
MR 2P			7		4		1
LMS 4P			6		2		2
Johnson 1F				3			
2–6–4T 4M	9						
'Crab' 5MT		2					
Stanier/5MT		6	1	6			
Fowler 4F						2	
'Black 5'	22				12		
'Patriot'	5						
'Jubilee'	9				2		
'R/Scot'	13						
'Princess'	4						
Ivatt 2MT					5		1

Loco class	Number of engines based at depots						
	8A	8C	8E	8H	8K	8L	8R
Kitson 0F					2		
Fowler 2F				3			
'Jinty' 3F	13	6		9			
0–8–4T 7F	3						
Stanier 8F	5	10		9		5	
0–8–0 6F/7F	17	18				27	
L&YR 2P						2	
0–4–0 'Pug'					11		
L&YR 2F	2	1		2	4	5	
L&YR 1F					4	1	
L&YR 3F	4	5		5		12	4
0–6–0T 2F				4			
LNWR 2F	3						
J10			9				1
J11			6				
J67/69			1				2
N5			6				4
2–8–0 'WD'				2			
Totals	112	48	37	92	46	54	15

1955

Loco class	Number of engines based at depots						
	8A	8C	8E	8H	8K	8L	8R
14XX				2			
'850'				3			
'2021'				9			
43XX				5			
51XX				10			
57XX				4			
'Grange'				4			
Stanier 3			2	9			
MR 2P					2		
LMS 4P	3				1		
Ivatt 2						2	
MR 1F				2			
2–6–4T 4MT	9		14				3
'Crab' 5MT		3					
Stanier 5MT		1	1	6			
Fowler 4F			3				4
'Black 5'	27		3		12		
'Patriot'	13						
'Jubilee'	6				2		
'R/Scot'	10						
'Princess'	5						
'Duchess'	1						
Ivatt 2MT						2	
Kitson 0F 4 2							

MOTIVE POWER COMPARISONS – 1950 TO 1966

Loco class	Number of engines based at depots						
	8A	8C	8E	8H	8K	8L	8R
Fowler 3F	15	7	4	5			
Stanier 8F	4	13		12			
0–8–0 6F/7F	19	12				13	
'Pug' 0F					10		
L&YR 2F	3	1			4	4	1
L&YR 1F					2	3	
L&YR 3F	1	4		1		10	
J10			7				2
J67/69			2				
N5			2				4
BR 2MT					5		
2–6–2T 2MT					2		
2–8–0 'WD'						14	
Totals	116	41	38	76	42	48	14

1959

Loco class	Number of engines based at depots						
	8A	8C	8E	8H	8K	8L	8R
Stanier 3			2	5			
MR 2P					2		
Ivatt 2				1	2		
2–6–4T 4MT	8		9	4			2
Fowler 4MT			2				
'Crab' 5MT		2		5		6	
Stanier 5MT				4			
MR 4F			2				
Fowler 4F			8				11
'Black 5'	24		4	1	7		
'Patriot'	13				1		
'Jubilee'	11				3		
'R/Scot'	10						
'Princess'	7						
Ivatt 2MT						3	
Kitson 0F				2	2		
Fowler 2F				2			
MR 3F					1	1	3
'Jinty' 3F	15	6	5	10	4	2	2
Stanier 8F	11	8		8			
LNW/LMS 7F	23	14				3	
L&YR 2P					1		
'Pug' 0F					8		
L&YR 2F	1						
L&YR 1F					1	1	
L&YR 3F		2				5	
J10							1
N5							3
BR 5MT				2			

213

Loco class	Number of engines based at depots						
	8A	8C	8E	8H	8K	8L	8R
BR 4MT					5		
BR 2MT					4		
2–6–4T 4MT				3			
2–6–2T				2			
2–8–0 'WD'				4		21	
Totals	123	32	32	53	41	42	22

1961

Loco class	Number of engines based at depots						
	8A	8C	8E	8H	8K	8L	8R
Ivatt 2				1	3		
2–6–4T 4MT	3	9		9			1
'Crab' 5MT				6		6	
Stanier 5MT				9			
Fowler 4F							9
'Black 5'	35	15			6		
'Patriot'	10				1		
'Jubilee'	1				3		
'R/Scot'	5						
'Princess'	1						
'Duchess'	4						
MR 3F					1	1	3
Ivatt 2MT						3	
Kitson 0F				2	2		
MR 2F	1			2			
'Jinty' 3F	12	8		7	4	5	1
Stanier 8F	11	15		9			
LNW/LMS 7F	18						
'Pug' 0F					3		
L&YR 3F						1	
BR 4MT					5		
BR 2MT					4		
2–8–0 'WD'				4		20	
Totals	101	47	Nil	49	32	36	14

1964

Loco class	Number of engines based at depots						
	8A	8C	8E	8H	8K	8L	8R
Ivatt 2					3		
2–6–4T 4MT		2		7			
'Crab' 5MT	7			11			
Stanier 5MT						5	
'Black 5	26	25			4	8	
'Jubilee'		2			2		
'Duchess'	2						
Ivatt 2MT		3					
'Jinty' 3F	10			7		4	
Stanier 8F	18	12		19			
BR 4MT					7	4	
BR 2MT					2	3	
2–8–0 'WD'						14	
BR 9F				10			
Totals	63	44	Nil	54	18	38	Nil

1966

Loco class	Number of engines based at depots						
	8A	8C	8E	8H	8K	8L	8R
Ivatt 2						2	
2–6–4T 4MT				6			
'Crab' 5MT				5			
'Black 5'	29	23				7	
Ivatt 2MT		2				4	
'Jinty' 3F	3			5		5	
Stanier 8F	15	14				9	
BR 4MT						5	
BR 9F		14		56			
Totals	47	53	Nil	72	Nil	32	Nil

FURTHER READING

Of necessity, this book examines Merseyside steam depots – in general terms – only during the period 1948 to 1968. For readers who wish to know more about the depots since their inception, or indeed more about locomotive depots in general, the following list for further reading is included.

Beavor, E.S. *Steam Motive Power Depots*, Ian Allan, London, 1983
Bolger, P. *An Illustrated History of the Cheshire Lines Committee*, Heyday Publishing, 1984
——. *BR Steam Motive Power Depots*, Ian Allan Ltd, Addlestone, 1983
Griffiths, R.P., *The Cheshire Lines Railway*, The Oakwood Press, Oxford, 1947
Hawkins, C., Hooper, J. and Reeve, G. *British Railways Engine Sheds – London Midland Matters*, Irwell Press, Pinner, 1989
Hawkins, C. and Reeve, G. *LMS Engine Sheds: Their History and Development, Volume 3, The Lancashire & Yorkshire Railway*, Wild Swan Publications Ltd, Didcot
Hooper, J. *LMS Sheds in Camera*, Oxford Publishing Company, Yeovil, 1983
Lyons, E. *A Historical Survey of Great Western Engine Sheds*, 1947
Lyons, E. and Mountford, E. *Great Western Engine Sheds 1837–1947*, Oxford Publishing Company, Yeovil
Mason, E. *The Lancashire & Yorkshire Railway in the Twentieth Century*, Ian Allan Ltd, Addlestone, 1975
Mason, F. *Life Adventure in Steam – A Merseyside Driver Remembers*, Countyvise, Birkenhead, 1992
'Locomotive Sheds Part 1: London & North Western Railway, "Perseus"', *Stephenson Locomotive Society Journal*, June 1959

Various volumes of particular railway journals were consulted in this book, including *Railway World, Railway Magazine, Trains Illustrated, Steam Railway, Steam World* and numerous issues of the Engine Shed Society's magazine *Link*.

INDEX